T0152456

PUT COLLEGE TO WORK

How to Use College to the Fullest to Discover Your Strengths and Find a Job You Love Before You Graduate

Kat Clowes, M.B.A.

Quill
Driver
Books

Fresno, California

PUT COLLEGE TO WORK

How to Use College to the Fullest to Discover Your Strengths
and Find a Job You Love Before You Graduate

copyright © 2015 by Kat Clowes, M.B.A.
Cover image: Pressmaster/Shutterstock.

All rights reserved.

Published by Quill Driver Books,
an imprint of Linden Publishing
2006 South Mary, Fresno, California 93721
559-233-6633 / 800-345-4447
QuillDriverBooks.com

Quill Driver Books and Colophon are trademarks
of Linden Publishing, Inc.

ISBN 978-1-61035-253-6

Printed in the United States
First Printing

Library of Congress Cataloging-in-Publication Data on file

To my parents, who supported me.

To my daughter Millie, who changed my life.

*To Foster and Frances Brinkley, my grandparents,
who showed me that the impossible is possible.*

*And to Jarred, who gave me the confidence
and support to follow my dreams.*

Contents

PART 3 - SUCCEED *AFTER* COLLEGE

PART 4 - HAVING A PARTICULAR SET OF SKILLS

RESOURCES

Foreword

Navigating college is no easy task. It's not always clear that
what you do in college will lead to a career, and it's easy to get
frustrated. I know this firsthand, having taken a few wrong turns
in college. Fortunately, I got some solid advice from Kat Clowes,
the author of this book.

When I was younger, I knew I wanted to work in the video game
industry. I enjoyed playing video games, and I'd even managed
to make a little money playing in video game tournaments in
high school. But how could I turn that into a career? Should I
be a coder? That just wasn't me. I wanted to enter the business
side of the industry, so my first choice for a major in college was
economics. I found out very quickly the skills necessary for an
economics major—statistics, formulas, and quantitative analysis—
just weren't me, either.

I talked to Kat about this several times over the course of my
first few months of college, and eventually she advised me to
switch my major to political science and get more involved in
extracurricular activities. That seemed weird—what does political
science have to do with video games? And weren't extracurriculars
just a distraction from classwork? Kat answered that political
science was a better match for my natural skills, and that
extracurriculars gave important practical experience that would
pay off later.

Switching my major was the best decision I made in college.
Political science took skills that came much easier to me,
like research, public speaking, and writing. I was able to
comfortably complete my classes and have the time and energy
for extracurricular clubs and activities that enriched my college

experience. Doing activities such as the Model United Nations, the debate team, and an internship at a local laboratory increased my confidence and taught me a lot about preparation and time management that helped me tremendously in college.

I even had the time to hang out at video game conventions, where I met some great people and started building connections that led to my current job with Turtle Entertainment, Inc., the world's best gaming promoter. (Apparently, I was networking, but I didn't know it at the time. I thought I was having fun.)

I'm not necessarily working in the realm of my major, but the experience that I built up going the extra mile in college is paying major dividends today. Kat's advice to get more involved outside of classes didn't quite make sense at the time, but her forward thinking paid off for me in more ways than one.

Put College to Work is the end result of the many years that Kat has spent helping students heading to college find the right mix of using the skills they already have and stretching to develop new skills. I hope that, like me, you'll find Kat's advice will help you use college as a foundation for moving forward. I am excited that you will have a chance to share in her experience and advice in order to enrich your life.

Eric Brinkley
Product Manager,
Turtle Entertainment, Inc.
ESL Gaming

First and Foremost

Do you throw up a little in your mouth at the thought of finishing your senior year of college and stepping out into the "real world"? Are you having nightmares about being chased through postapocalyptic job fairs by the undead, two-headed statistics that news outlets toss around like grayscale confetti: "This just in! Only 40 percent of Millennials have full-time employment! Thirty-six percent will move back in with their parents! What about the rest? Yep, it's cat-food under a bridge for you!"

Well my friends, I'm here to tell you that you're not going to become a cat-food eating troll. Instead, you're going to learn how to use all of the resources available to you so that you can carve a new path that lets you make the most of college while you're there—and when you leave. It doesn't matter if you're a senior or a freshman in college, or even if you're still in high school.

The information in this book will give you a head start and keep you running in front of the pack. The book is designed so that you can read straight through or skip to the parts you need the most right now. To make things even easier on you, I've broken everything up into parts. In the first section, "Put Yourself to Work," you'll learn how to be your own advocate so that you can get the education and make the contacts that will take you in the direction you want to go—not the direction someone else thinks you should be headed.

Section Two will show you how to succeed *in* college. You'll get tips on figuring out which courses to take, how to build productive relationships with your professors, and how to use some little-recognized resources that can prove to be invaluable.

By the time you finish Section Three, you will no longer be worrying about cat-food prices because you will be ready to go out and find a job—a real job where you can enjoy yourself AND earn a living wage! This is the section where you learn how to put college to work—to employ the career center and leverage informational interviews and internships so you are in a good job or a good grad school by the time you walk off the stage with your diploma in hand.

Section Four contains the nuts-and-bolts chapters. This is where you will find the details to help you acquire and practice all the skills you need to take the steps I describe in this book. This is the section you can flip to if you're a senior panicking about tomorrow's campus job fair or internship interview. Here's where you will find the practical tips about networking and writing a résumé.

But that's not all! In the Resources section, I've provided a four-year timeline checklist that can help you see what you need to do when to make your college years as productive as possible. There are also questionnaires and other exercises to get you started and keep you moving along this path toward success.

Like I said, this book can help if all you want is some practical information about a specific subject, like internships or job fairs. But if you read it all, you'll get a cohesive strategy for creating an education you'll cherish and finding a career you'll love. I've included a few personal stories along the way and some tidbits from professionals currently in the working world.

In the next section, I'm also offering you a little timeline of my life; I haven't always had the answer. But through my own struggles, I know exactly what you're going through and I know how to help. Hopefully, you can use what I have learned to help you avoid some of the mistakes I've made. I want you to:

> Take action.
> Use what you have.
> Act courageously in a scary world.

Put. College. To. Work.

Look Who's Talking: Chronology of the Clueless

1982

Determined to keep everyone on their toes and despite my mother's insistence that I would be born in *late* April, I arrived in this world three weeks early. Some have said that rushing into things is an Aries trait. But I'm pretty sure that my newborn self was simply determined not to be a *Taurus*.

1986

I make my stage debut singing "Like a Virgin" for my very religious great-grandmother, causing my mom to get an earful about what she's letting me listen to. Madonna, lace tutu skirts, and fingerless gloves still occupy soft warm places in my heart.

1987

Tomorrow I'm supposed to start kindergarten—but I'm so excited that I make myself sick and spend the night projectile vomiting. So my first day of school was on the second day of school; I had Mrs. Patterson; I wore a blue, frilly dress; and I somehow kept from puking that whole day.

1989

Another student, Dane (who was dreamy and smart), and I are moved up from my second-grade class and into the third grade for reading and spelling hour. I blame the jump for my less-than-fluid knowledge of things like the color wheel and my left from right but credit it with a vibrant and not inconsequential vocabulary.

1990

I have to decide between taking dance classes or horseback riding lessons. I choose horses. Thus begins my equestrian career. Giddyup!

1991

My aunt bet me $100 that I couldn't memorize the four-page poem *The Highwayman* for the language festival. But I do. Also, I win the festival. The next year I bested myself with the *to be or not to be* soliloquy; every student in the auditorium is bored to tears, but the teachers pay attention. I become addicted to overachieving.

1992

After watching equestrian competitions all summer, I decide that I'm going to be an Olympian. I spend the entire summer at the barn and earn a chance to try out for a local trainer who was an alternate on the '84 Olympic equestrian team. I'm walking on clouds when she makes me her youngest student. But I can't afford the new lessons, so she accepts me as a working student. No more walking on clouds; it's horse manure from here on out.

1993

Bullies. Failed student council bid. I join the cheerleading squad, but I smell like horses . . . so it doesn't work out.

1994

We move. New school, massive school. I'm placed in all the wrong classes and spend the first five months of my junior high years fighting to be in the "smart" classes. I join the band and orchestra, finding my people. Competitions for horseback riding fill my weekends; my friends aren't quite sure what I'm doing until I make the local paper.

1996

I begin training in earnest in an attempt to qualify for the Junior Olympics. I compete all over the state and in national competitions. My mornings consist of waking up at 3 a.m., doing my homework until 5 a.m., going to the barn to ride, and coming home in time to shower and go to school. After school it's back to the barn for lessons, prepping for competition, and taking care of the horses as per my working student agreement.

1998

One week before my Junior Olympics qualifying competition, my boyfriend and I get into a massive car accident. I suffer brain trauma; I lose my equilibrium and my equestrian career along with my short-term memory. I spend the better part of four months of the school year at home, recovering, and learning how to go from a photographic memory to . . . something else. Another type of memorization. My teachers generously come to my house and try with difficulty to keep me current. On a lighter note, this is my first exposure to MTV and pop culture as I spend my hours watching movies and television. My horse is put to pasture in the hopes that I might be able to regain my ability to ride.

1999

I return to school to find my world is different and I don't relate to my friends or classmates anymore. Depression kicks in, coupled with teenage angst. But something else soon occurred to me. After watching school administrators make changes as they saw fit to help me, I realized that the *System,* with a capital "S," is flexible. So I decide to present a case to my principal to allow me to graduate high school a year early. She agrees but with the stipulation that I go to community college first. I graduate that summer.

2000

Freshman year of community college, I overload my semester in a fit of optimism. My introduction to theater class, an instant favorite in my day of math and pre-vet science classes, becomes my refuge. I start making friends and end up spending most of my time in the theater building.

2001

I begin applying to colleges based primarily on whether I've seen their name on a sweatshirt and like their colors. I attend a college fair for an opportunity to meet the admissions officer from Yale (nice sweater—yale blue), my *first* first-choice school. When I tell him I would be a transfer student, he laughs at me (in the face). I'm rejected from my *second* first-choice school (thanks, calculus, for the only C in my academic career—79.5), the University of Pennsylvania (just a subtle big P—red and blue), but I'm accepted to my *third* first-choice school (Go Broncos!), Santa Clara University (nice hoodie—red and white). Fortunately, I never had to send off my application to my one second-choice, fallback, safety school, Clemson (looks like a frat tattoo—orange & purple); I don't know if you have seen my complexion but orange and purple? (shudder). Anyway, good news; much to my surprise, I'm homecoming queen at my junior college. Shocking for a nerd like me (I hope it wasn't meant as some kind of joke—though if it was, the joke is on them 'cause I didn't get it).

I arrive on campus two weeks before the planes hit the Twin Towers in New York, and school is delayed a week while students try to navigate the ban on air travel to get back to school. I can't mention this sad event without saying that a Santa Clara student was on United Flight 93, heading back to the West Coast to start the quarter.

2002

I shoot my first full-length feature on video—an adaptation of *Agamemnon,* a Greek tragedy. I decide that I'm either going into cinematography or will be a history teacher, one of the two. Investigating my school's offerings and running low on cash, I enroll in the graduate education program and start taking graduate classes while finishing up senior year.

2003

Graduation, yeah! I decide two days before graduation that I'm going to abandon my idea of being a teacher (and my master's degree) to move to Los Angeles with my best friend to be a STAR (what could go wrong?). I also go to a concert the day before graduation, end up massively sunburned, and oversleep on graduation morning, nearly missing it entirely. Not the best hair day of my life, let me tell you.

Moving to L.A., my best friend and I find an apartment and jobs by networking with Santa Clara alums who had been seniors when we were juniors. I land a job as a receptionist at a talent agency and work my way up to talent agent assistant. I lived *The Devil Wears Prada;* I kid you not.

2004

After leaving the talent world and pursing a few internships and positions in the entertainment industry, I decide it's not for me. I move home, get a job as a waitress, and try to figure out what to do with my life. A friend of a friend recommends me to be hired at our local costume shop, and I start working full-time again. Networking with people I used to know from the theater at my junior college, I start costuming community theater shows.

2004–2008

I establish myself as the go-to costume person in my area, start branching out to other counties, and join organizations that make me known in the historical costuming world (yes, that means I made gowns for the Renaissance Faire). And, to bring things into somewhat of a circle, I become the head costumer at my former junior college.

2009

In the costuming world the hours are long, the money is small, and advancement is slow. Pretty soon I'm again looking to try something new and journey out. I make a New Year's resolution to spend an entire year learning about business, determined to apply for graduate school if I'm still interested by December. Turns out I am, so I start looking for graduate programs. I discover that educational consulting is a "thing" back East. And here I have been giving advice for free! I start looking into turning my new passion into a career.

2010

I leave my costuming job and pursue an MBA while working full-time at a utility company (regular hours and more money). I commute two hours, each way, on the weekends to school at Mount St. Mary's in Los Angeles. While it's difficult, I'm determined. I also enroll (because I'm crazy) in the University of California at Irvine's certification program for educational consulting. I complete the certification with a 4.0. Yeah! I open up my consulting business with a business partner and immediately close it when she moves to New York.

2011

I lament the killing of my soul in the corporate world and continue with my graduate work. I spend the year helping students part-time.

2012

I finish my MBA, restart my business part time, have a baby (one day after finishing all of my coursework—is that timing or what?), and start thinking about a book. Crazy.

2014

I take a huge leap of faith and leave my corporate job to help students full-time.

2015

Thriving in my new business, I've found that this myriad of experiences helps me to better help students like you. I use my experiences, research, and cavern of usually useless knowledge in my brain to help students prepare for the modern world and workforce. After all, who wants to be in one job for the rest of their life? Or feel trapped in a job they hate? NO ONE. So let's not let that happen to you. Trust me, you'll feel your soul dying in a job you hate.

PART **1**

Put Yourself
to Work

Advocate for Yourself

In life, you don't get any extra points for doing just the bare minimum. Sure, you can show up at school and take the minimum number of units you need every semester to keep up your financial aid. You can show up in classes *most* days, earn passing grades, and eventually walk across the stage with a diploma.

That's what going to college is all about, right?

Wrong.

If you're just showing up and just doing your work, you'll be a mediocre student, and you'll probably be a mediocre employee. If your goal in school is just to get by, you will be missing the opportunities you have each and every day at your college or university. Opportunities that will allow you to get more out of college—and life.

If you want to put college to work for you, first you have to put yourself to work.

Plead Your Own Case

Sometime about the middle of your high school career, you start getting letters and emails and phone calls and slick brochures from colleges and universities. They all want to tell you what great opportunities you will have if you come to their school—opportunities for research and meeting important alumni and studying abroad and finding a great job. They make it seem like all those opportunities are waiting for you just as soon as you step onto their beautiful campus.

And those opportunities are waiting for you. But you won't find any big billboards on campus or neon signs that flash "Opportunity Here!" In fact, you may miss out on the most fantastic opportunities unless you learn to be an advocate for yourself and *ask* for what you want.

The first question you may be asking is "What is an advocate?" Well, *Merriam-Webster's Collegiate Dictionary* (11th ed.) says an advocate is "one that pleads the cause of another." So, when you become an advocate for yourself, you're pleading your own cause; you're asking the right people the right questions so you can find the right opportunities for you.

ad·vo·cate *noun* \'ad-və-kət, -'kāt\

1: one that pleads the cause of another; *specifically*: one that pleads the cause of another before a tribunal or judicial court
2: one that defends or maintains a cause or proposal
3: one that supports or promotes the interests of another

Synonyms: exponent, advocator, apostle, backer, booster, champion, expounder, espouser, friend, gospeler (*or* gospeller), herald, hierophant, high priest, paladin, promoter, proponent, protagonist, supporter, true believer, tub-thumper, white knight

You may be used to someone else advocating for you—your parents or your coaches or your teachers or your high school counselor may have told you (or at least recommended strongly) what classes to take and what activities you should be involved in. They marked a path for you that could lead you to a good college and made sure you knew right where to walk.

But now it's time for you to step up and become your own advocate. Otherwise, you're going to wind up disappointed and maybe even bitter.

{ Kat's Tales from the Real World } When I started at Santa Clara, I wanted the full college experience, even though I was a transfer student who would only be around for two years. I wanted to meet the people in the alumni association—hobnob with the *alumnirati,* as it were—have internships, figure out what I wanted to be when I grew up, participate in research projects, study abroad, you name it.

Did I tell anyone about my expectations? No. Did I dream about them? Yes. Did I expect the college would just magically make an internship appear for me? Did I think a professor would call on me and declare that I would be part of a research project?

Embarrassingly, yes. I believed that.

It was partly because of an idea that I had been given as a kid: Work hard, get good grades, go to college, and you'll have success. So, somewhere in my young mind, I believed that if I worked hard enough, surely someone would notice, right? Someone would notice and give me an amazing opportunity, which would blossom into another amazing opportunity. By the time I was done daydreaming, I was rubbing elbows at the Oscars and taking Oprah out to coffee.

Did any of this happen? No. (Well, not yet, anyway.) Do you know why? Because I never asked.

At some point, I did go to the career center and ask about jobs, but did I ask about other resources they might have for me? No. Did I make an appointment with the career counselor? No. I was too shy or too intimidated, or too something to even ask.

Did I ever go to an alumni event? No. Did I ever ask about study-abroad programs and how I might be able to apply? Nope. Nada. See you later, good-bye, thank you very much.

Just Ask

You don't gain anything when you don't even try for anything. As Wayne Gretzky once said, "You miss 100% of the shots you don't take." The same is true for making things happen for yourself in college and beyond. You're going to miss everything if you don't speak up for yourself. You're the one who has to ask if you can get into the class you want or if you can be on the debate team or if you can apply for that semester in Paris.

Seriously, the worst thing anyone can say is *no,* which means you're no worse off than you were before you asked. Is it a kick to the ego to be turned down? Maybe. But it's worth the risk if we're talking about your future happiness.

So ask. Go to the career center and ask what they can do for students. Ask to make an appointment with a counselor. Ask a professor if she needs a research assistant. Ask fellow students about the study-abroad programs they attended. Ask the alumni office if you can volunteer at the next nearby alumni event.

Ask. Even if it's terrifying.

Ask.

Ask.

Ask.

Ask.

It's the single most important thing you can do for your future and your career. Seriously. What if your career center has information about an exciting job you've never heard of? What if the professor says yes? What if you're heading to France to study next semester? Or on a research trip where you might discover something incredible?

Ask.

Practice the Ask

You'll love yourself later if you gather up the courage to do it now.

But I'm not going to lie to you; the first time you step outside of your comfort zone to ask someone for something, it's going to be terrifying (and I mean *terrifying*).

The best thing that you can do is just start practicing. The first few times you do it, you're going to be completely and utterly self-conscious; you're going to sound awkward; and you might want to slide under the table, desk, or counter, depending on where you are and who you're asking.

Here's the trick: know what you're going to say before you start talking. There's nothing worse for your nerves than bumbling around, looking for words. Write yourself a little script if you have to, or at least write out your opening lines.

Practice introducing yourself. Practice being confident. Trust me, the more you hone your skills, the sharper they will become.

College students have a built-in arena to practice these skills: the classroom. When you're in class, speak up; make sure the professor knows who you are. Then it will be even easier to approach him after class or in his office.

Learning how to advocate for yourself is so important because in the world of college and beyond, you're going to have to ask for a lot of things. So take advantage of this time and place where people *want* to help you and start practicing asking right now. You'll seriously become a pro by the time you finish senior year, which is perfect because you'll be sauntering out into the real world, ready to ask for what you want.

> **TIPS AND TRICKS**
> ● Always remember, when you're in college, most of the faculty and staff are there to help you. That eases the fear of asking a little, doesn't it?

And if you're not sure what you want, read on. Chapter 2 is going to help you figure that out.

{ Kat's Tales from the Real World } Recently, I took a workshop on how to cold call because it was something that has always been one of my deepest darkest fears. If you don't know what cold calling is, you should know that it strikes fear into the heart of pretty much everyone I've ever met.

A cold call is when you get onto the phone, usually calling a corporation or business, and you call someone you've never met before and never talked to you before. You then try to talk them into either buying or considering your product. Most people say no. Some people are very rude. And a small percentage buy the product.

Sound terrifying? I'm actually learning the ropes and getting more comfortable doing it. I don't cold call random people, but if you've ever seen me speak, that was probably the result of a cold call that led me to get the engagement. It's terrifying and energizing at the same time.

2

Discovering Yourself

Before you invest the next four years (or more) of your life and thousands in tuition on one major or subject area, don't you think you should spend a little time making sure that you're investing in something that's going to make you happy? I see too many students investing time and money on a major that is "guaranteed" to make them rich—only they later find out that they hate their jobs.

How do I know this personally? Because it's what I did.

Popping Bubbles

When I was in high school, I spent a lot of time dreaming of the career that would make me (1) a millionaire and (2) respected in my community. Medicine and engineering were the two career fields that spoke to me the most, probably because everyone would react well when I would tell them what I wanted to be. In eighth grade, when all of my friends were getting braces, I heard my parents comment a lot on the cost of braces and how much orthodontists must be raking in. Naturally, with that single piece of information, I decided I was going to be an orthodontist.

I swore I could picture myself in a lab coat, saving lives—one pair of braces at a time. I could work a few hours a week and have my fancy car, huge house, and horse ranch. My dream abruptly ended when I started asking what an orthodontist actually does during the day. After a few Internet searches and a conversation with my dentist, I decided that wasn't what I wanted to do day in and day out. There went that dream. Naturally, I started looking for another.

» Abrupt Landing

Aerospace engineer came next, mainly because I loved studying space and the idea of space exploration with my dad. I read about the moon landing, Apollo 13, and the stories of brave people at NASA solving incredible problems on a daily basis. After a little more research, I declared that aerospace engineering was definitely for me. I'm sad to report that just like orthodontics, reality crushed my dream. All it took was one trip to the NASA offices at Edwards Air Force Base in California.

My biology teacher in high school happened to have a brother who worked for NASA. Being the overachiever and future brilliant scientist that I was, I had joined our biology club and landed myself the title of vice president. (Truth be told, biology is still the only science subject that comes naturally to me.) Upon finding out this little tidbit about our biology teacher, I got her to inquire about a tour of the base and a private tour of the NASA offices. Once her brother agreed, we arranged everything for the trip—all five of us. Yes, we were nerds excited to go on a trip to a NASA office. No, we didn't have pocket protectors.

The tour was fascinating. We were given the general tour of the base including a tour of the hangar where they had historic planes and war machines. We were shown pictures of the space shuttle landing on the base. Then, in the afternoon, we were taken "backstage" to meet my teacher's brother.

An intelligent and friendly fellow, he took us on a tour none of us would forget. He explained the computer systems, the projects they were working on (the nonsecret ones he could mention), and demonstrated one of the wind warehouses where they tested various material. Finally, one by one, we were put into a flight simulator and told to not only navigate the plane into the air, but to navigate the landing onto an aircraft carrier. I'm proud to report that I was the only one who didn't crash her plane.

While the trip was fascinating, I couldn't help feeling that all of my classmates were far more interested in what we found there than I was. I wasn't as interested in aerodynamics or the math of the projects they were doing. That was when my teacher's brother mentioned that the math skills required went beyond calculus four. The rest of my classmates looked excited at the possibility. Me? The thought of spending the rest of my life doing math—no. Oh please, no. My soul died a little just thinking of it.

When I returned to school, I did more research on aerospace engineering. I learned quickly that my personality and engineering weren't going to mix. Specific details and data? Not particularly interested. Technical knowledge, materials, construction? Nope. Math? Nope, nope, nope. I even went so far as to look at the classes that I might have to take in college. None of them sounded even remotely fun, nor did they spark my interests.

» Vet Crash

So, I turned my attention back to medicine. Having spent the majority of my time in equestrian sports growing up, I was familiar with veterinarians and what their day-to-day looked like. I'd shadowed with them for a day or two, and by my late teens, I was skilled in giving vaccinations to horses, cleaning out wounds and applying wrappings, and even cleaning out abscesses (yuck). Thinking this was my ticket, I plunged into the pre-vet curriculum.

Again, I wound up realizing that my chosen field wasn't for me. While trying desperately to avoid taking organic chemistry, I looked at the veterinary school requirements that I'd have to meet my senior year of college to continue into graduate school. Not only did I have to take organic chemistry (boo) but I also had to log hours of volunteering at a veterinarian's office. I contacted the veterinarian who took care of my horse and all the horses at the stable where I worked, applied, and was accepted to intern at her office.

I lasted two weeks.

It wasn't the blood and guts. It wasn't the job, as such. It was seeing how people treated animals. Horses would come in emaciated—skin and bones—and she'd either have to nurse them back to health or put them to sleep, which is what happened most of the time. We saw abused dogs and abused livestock. Situations that my heart couldn't take. I knew, deep down, I couldn't do this day in and day out.

Don't Get Stuck

That's why it's so important to take into account your skills, interests, passions, and purpose before you declare a major. Don't do what I did and wait until you're in college to start finding yourself. You're going to spend far too much time and money doing this, declaring a major that sounds good, only to find the job associated with it is completely different from what you envision.

I have college classmates who either completely changed their career paths after graduation, went to graduate school in a different field, or are stuck in jobs that make them miserable because they misunderstood the reality of their chosen career.

There's no shame in not knowing what you want to major in or what you're going to do for a career when you first get to college. But you don't want to be clueless about it when you graduate. And you don't want to get yourself stuck on a road you don't enjoy.

{ Kat's Tales from the Real World } After I abandoned veterinary science, I continued to try to figure out what I wanted to be when I grew up. This went on for YEARS. I applied for whatever job openings I saw (before the economy crashed), hoping to find something interesting. Don't get me wrong, I learned a lot about myself in those formative years, but I also felt like I was constantly behind. I was in my twenties with no plan. I had no goals, and I wasn't working toward anything.

One day that changed. I decided to start doing something about it. In fact, around New Year's (how cliché, right?), I decided to study a new topic for the whole year. We're not talking about intense studying or any research papers, but in my free time, I would make an effort to look at an article online or read a book about that topic. Do you know what happened? I realized that I was stuck in my situation because I hadn't been doing anything to change my situation.

You see, I was the only one who could do that. Why was I miserable and complaining about my job situation when I wasn't doing anything to change it? I wasn't taking control of what I could control, nor was I creating opportunities for myself. I was complaining. I was making excuses. I was the whiny version of Luke Skywalker in *The Empire Strikes Back.* When I realized I was getting in my own way, my Yoda appeared, and I started living my adventure. I started planning, I started working. Pretty soon, I was a Jedi master.

Although it took me a long time to recognize it, eventually I saw that there were forks in my road, different options I could take, options that continued to grow and branch out. Many people, when the economy tanked in 2008, found out quickly that they didn't have any forks or other branches to their paths; they were stuck traveling along one tired, pothole-ridden highway with someone else in the driver's seat.

Choosing Your Route

So let's make sure you're doing the driving. And that you're traveling on a road with more than one alternate route.

I'm going to take you through a few exercises to help you start thinking about what you're really supposed to do with your life to make you happy. Is it different for everyone? Yes. Does it mean you're going to be a starving artist, miserable because you don't have any money? Or a wealthy bond trader, miserable because you have to spend every day looking at numbers in Excel charts? No, unless you're willing to go that far in either direction.

This is about moderation and finding that middle ground so that you can do something you enjoy and still have some financial

In addition to the worksheets in the Resources section, you can download worksheets and bonus material at www.mymarchconsulting.com/PutCollegeToWork for this section. Print them out and treat it like a fun assignment. You'll have a lot more clarity when you're finished, I promise.

security. What kind of work that will be and how much money you need to feel secure is different for everyone. That's why you need to figure out your route based on your own personality and preferences, instead of mechanically following a route created by someone else's GPS.

Are you ready? Climb into your dream car and let's start driving.

"A career is a job you love, right? That's what a career should be. If you're in a job that you hate, you should quit. That's the way I look at it. I'm in a job that I love, so I'm going to make it my career."
—Cameron Sinclair

What You Hate

If you ask yourself what you love doing or what your dream is, you'll get mixed answers from yourself. For some reason, when put on the spot, your brain will start telling you what you love, while at the same time, telling you why it's a bad idea to pursue the things you love. I've seen this with most of my students when I ask them about their dream job.

So, instead of focusing on that absolute dream of yours that doesn't seem tangible yet, let's get something else out of the way: what you hate. Ask yourself what sorts of things that you would absolutely abhor doing. Tasks or jobs or workplaces where even millions of dollars of salary wouldn't be enough to make you happy about showing up to work every day.

Think about the subjects you *don't* like in school. What volunteer positions do you *not* like? Clubs? Activities that you're involved with? If you aren't involved in activities, think about school events or situations that you don't enjoy. Do you hate going to dances? Why? Is it the social pressure? The pomp and circumstance of it all?

Really try to get into the nitty gritty of WHY exactly you don't like being in certain situations or doing certain things. Concentrate on the skills required and what makes you consider a particular task tedious or frustrating. When you are ready, turn to the Resources section at the back of this book and fill out Exercise 2.1.

Great! Now we've identified a bit about what you DON'T want to do. Are you starting to get a little clarity about which jobs and situations you should start avoiding? And why?

» What Are You Doing Now?

For the next few weeks, I want you to think about your daily decisions, tasks, and choices. Yes, there are some things that we don't like to do that we have to do anyway (for me, it's cooking or cleaning). But you don't want to prepare for a career that will require you to spend a significant amount of time every day doing things you hate to do.

If you found it hard to fill in the blanks on the "most hated" chart, start getting involved in different activities and situations where you can learn more about what you like doing and don't like doing. It will help you identify your major, decide where you want to work, and understand what tasks and chores you want to avoid if possible.

> **"It's not hard to make decisions
> when you know what your values are."**
> *–Roy Disney*

Identifying Your Values

You never want to be a part of a group that doesn't share your values. No one does. This can pose one of the biggest problems for people when they are looking for a job—they don't check to see if the company they're joining shares their personal values. Without that match, you will wind up trading your time for money in a place that isn't working toward what you hold most dear.

Talk about depressing and soul-crushing.

Let's start with your values. To be technical, values are a person's principles or standards of behavior—your judgment of what is important in life.

These are the core principles that you believe determine a good person versus a bad person. Though some values are universal, people prize certain values over others or deem certain values more worthwhile than others. Your personal values determine the decisions you make, the actions you take, and the kind of person you are. They are the principles that you hold your own behavior to, your inner compass.

Sometimes it's hard to recognize which values mean the most to us, which can be the reason we make decisions or take jobs that make us miserable. We don't understand that we have violated our own values because we haven't taken stock of what we value most. So, take some time right now to turn to the Resources section and complete Exercise 2.2.

> **"Over the years, I've learned that a confident person doesn't concentrate or focus on their weaknesses–they maximize their strengths."**
> *–Joyce Meyer*

Your Strengths

Now that you know what you hate to do and recognize your most deeply held values, let's examine your strengths.

Asking yourself what you're good at can be daunting. When I'm placed on the spot, I find it hard to think of anything, let alone the list I've compiled for myself. There are many different ways to discover what you're truly good at doing, but we're going to go concentrate on a few particular ways you can uncover your strengths.

Why is it important to know what your strengths are? Sometimes we get so down on ourselves that we concentrate only on what we're not good at doing—and then we spend all our time trying to compensate for those shortcomings. Knowing what you're good at doing can help you to really get the most out of your talents and weave them into your future life. Pinpointing your strengths also makes you aware of your true weaknesses, which can show you areas where you'll need additional help—and professions you should avoid.

» The Myers-Briggs

First and foremost, do you know how you think? People can be more technical or strategic in their thinking, more process-oriented or spontaneous. One way to get a better understanding of how you think is to take what's called the Myers-Briggs personality assessment (http://www.myersbriggs.org). There are full assessments conducted by professionals that will cost you money or you can find free online assessments that aren't as detailed but give you a place to start. One free version is available at http://www.humanmetrics.com/cgi-win/jtypes2.asp. This is the Jung-Myers-Briggs assessment administered through Human Metrics.

Most schools will allow you to take the full assessment either for free or a small fee in their career centers. Some public career centers also offer them to members of the community. A quick search might turn up a certified coach in your area. Or, if you prefer, you can contact my office, March Consulting, and we'll administer the assessment to you as well. Look for contact information at www.mymarchconsulting.com.

After you take the Myers-Briggs assessment, you will get a four-letter label describing your personality type. If you want to know more, you can always Google your combination of letters (horoscope fashion) to see more about your personality type.

» Your Excellent List

Next, take a moment to list the things you excel at. For example, I'm good at communication, public speaking, and recognizing nonverbal cues. Turn to Exercise 2.3 in the Resources section and give it your best—and worst—stuff.

» Friends and Family

Your next task—and this could be the most daunting one—is to reach out to friends and family and ask them what they consider your strengths and weaknesses. Sometimes we don't see the whole picture of ourselves and need an outsider's perspective. To get this, you're going to have to do some digging (and digging means you're going to have to put some work into it). Ask people you know well to name three of your strengths. Hopefully, they're going to be amazingly positive, but I also want you to ask them to name one of your weaknesses.

You can do this in person, create a SurveyMonkey poll, post it on Facebook, tweet it out to your followers (provided that they know you well), or do what I did and send the questions by email. You can email them something along the lines of:

Hello!
I'm doing an assignment to identify my strengths and weaknesses. If you have a chance, could you please reply back with three qualities or skills that you consider to be my strengths? Also, could you list one quality or skill that you believe is a weakness?

Thank you in advance for your help!

Sincerely,
Tony Stark

Once the responses start flooding in, begin looking for similarities in what your friends and family have said. Do you see a trend? Do certain characteristics get listed repeatedly? Do you see words that describe the same quality? For example, someone might say you're driven, while another says you have drive, and others say you are determined, or have determination. All four are basically describing the same quality.

How do the weaknesses measure up? This is going to be the hard part, since no one likes to hear that others recognize weaknesses in you. I can say with all honesty, though, that if you don't know the bad, you can't improve. So put on your big-kid pants and take that criticism. But consider the following:

> Do you agree with it?
> Do you not agree with it?
> Why?
> Is it something that you want to improve?
> Can you improve it?
> Finally, ask yourself which of your actions led someone else to think of that negative quality in you.

{ Kat's Tales from the Real World } A friend of mine said I was always late. I was offended by it at first, because I consider myself to be a punctual person. Reflecting back, however, I realized that every time this friend and I had gone out to do something, I had been late.

In my defense, I never considered the times we agreed to meet as a "be there or else" sort of time deadline. In her mind, however, it was.

Taking that into consideration, I made adjustments to arrive 10 minutes early whenever going out with friends, because I didn't consider lateness one of my weaknesses that was impossible to change. Later, I thanked her that she was brave enough to criticize me so that I could remedy that problem.

"It is sooooooo necessary to get the basic skills, because by the time you graduate, undergraduate or graduate, that field would have totally changed from your first day of school."
–Leigh Steinberg

Your Skills

Ah yes, we can't forget your actual abilities! Your skills are what you're able to *do*, what you're capable of doing, and what you really excel at doing. They go hand in hand with your strengths, naturally. You're probably used to seeing skills listed in job descriptions.

When you're deciding what major or career path to choose, you want to concentrate first on your strengths, and then your skills.

But they are connected, and in the next exercise, you're going to list your skills as they relate to your strengths, then describe how to relate those to different jobs. Don't be scared; it sounds like a lot, but I'll guide you through it.

You'll be surprised at what skills you can mold into different categories. For example, let's say you're really good at making friends. That doesn't seem like a skill that would be listed on a job description. However, when you dig a little deeper, you can probably see that you're good at making friends because you are good with people. Why are you good with people? Because you know how to make everyone feel at ease.

Now that's a skill a lot of businesses would want; they would love to have an employee who can instantly put customers at ease and listen to their needs. Now that you can relate your strength (making friends) to a skill (being good with people), you can mention this skill in your interview, especially if the job has to do with customer contact or customer service.

To help you figure out your skills, complete Exercise 2.4 in the Resources section.

> "All of this plays into the development of your personal brand.
> Passion is energy. Feel the power that comes from
> focusing on what excites you."
> –Oprah Winfrey

Rock Your Passion

Ahh, your passion. How many times have you heard things like: "Live your passion!" "Work your passion, and you'll never work a day in your life!" "Pursue your passion!" Do you notice how no one ever really instructs you *how* to live, work, or pursue your passion?

Well, for starters the path to passion is different for everyone, and it's extremely personal. There is also no real method to figuring out what your passion is. But you can start by considering the hobbies and activities you enjoy and why you enjoy them. If you start thinking deeper about things that seem to come naturally to you, you can start uncovering those fundamental passions that you've had your entire life.

So, turn to Exercise 2.5 in Resources and list the activities you love. These activities could be playing video games, hiking, reading, sewing (that's mine), visiting museums, going to the beach. Everything and anything you love doing.

Why is it important to know your passions? Why can't you simply skip this section? Well, it's through our passions that we come alive. It's through our passions that we stop being another number in throngs of people and start standing out as individuals with interests, loves, and expertise. So go on; flip the pages and create your list!

> "Setting goals is the first step in turning
> the invisible into the visible."
> –Tony Robbins

Your Goals

Now we're finally ready to look at where you're going and where you want to be. Defining your goals and knowing your purpose in your major and career will help you better communicate with future employers, giving them an idea of where and how you will fit in their organizations.

There are two types of goals you should be setting for yourself: short-term goals and long-term goals. Short-term goals should be milestones that you want to hit in less than a year. Long-term goals are usually on the five-, ten-, or twenty-year mark. What's that you say? You're not sure what your goals are? Let's define them now.

» Long-Term Goals: Your Bucket List

These are the milestones that you want to achieve throughout your life. A lot of people have these types of goals, such as visiting a foreign country, being a CEO of a company, or having a summer home in the Hamptons. It's sometimes referred to as a "bucket list," or "things that you want to do before you die." I know that may sound a bit morbid, but it's really more about living than dying. Deep down, you have ideas of things you want to achieve or experience at some point in your life.

Take a moment to consider where you would like to be in 20 years. Iron out in your head what that looks like. Are you in a huge city? A small town? Do you have your own house? Apartment? Summer home? Are you painting your own art, running a company, or working in your own business? What does your day look like? What does your weekend look like?

Now turn to Exercise 2.6 in the Resources section and use the space provided there to get your thoughts onto paper.

» Short-Term Goals

The best thing about short-term goals is that they lead to the long-term ones. Instead of starting where you are now and figuring out how to get to your long-term goals, start at the long-term goals and work your way backward. List the big milestones and then the steps you need to get there. For example, your first milestone goal is to be a CEO at a gaming company. The steps to get to that milestone fall below it.

CEO at a Gaming Company

> *Getting into management at a gaming company*
> *Getting hired at a gaming company*
> *Meeting people at gaming companies*
> *Doing well in classes that will build skills for working at a gaming company*
> *Going to gaming conventions to find out what classes and major I should consider*

Now, turn to Exercise 2.7 and try this with a couple of your long-term goals. Decide on your milestone and then list the steps you need to take to reach that milestone.

"Many people have a wrong idea of what constitutes true happiness.
It is not attained through self-gratification but through
fidelity to a worthy purpose."
–*Helen Keller*

Your Purpose

Take a good look at your long-term and short-term goals, thinking about how they fit in with the work you've done so far with your values. There's one last soul-searching exercise that you're going to have to go through, and that's to define (or at least touch upon) your purpose in life. This is that ultimate "what does it all mean and what do I have to do with it?" sort of question.

I want you to concentrate less on the materials in your long-term goals and look at the meaning you're going to be bringing to your life. How are you going to be giving back or helping people? Will you be helping people through your company, giving them a solution to a problem through a new product, like a tennis shoe? Supplying them with a new yummy snack to give to their kids?

Maybe you're volunteering in your spare time to help other students discover their talents. Maybe you have the means to give money to your favorite charity or you're teaching somewhere.

What's the one thing that you can imagine yourself doing that is going to make you feel good about yourself? Fill your soul? Make things worthwhile? If you get stumped, think of things you've already accomplished in your life. Which ones make you feel like you've lived your purpose in life? What does that look like?

Now turn to Exercise 2.8 in the Resources section and answer the questions there, which can help you recognize your deepest desires for purposeful living. You can spend a lifetime trying to identify your purpose, so don't get too down on yourself if you find this exercise is the hardest. Most people do. The secret is to be aware that you're searching, because then you will be more likely to eventually come to your own answer.

"Very little is needed to make a happy life; it is all within
yourself, in your way of thinking."
–Marcus Aurelius

Now What?

We've explored what you hate, your values, your strengths, your skills, your passions, your long-term goals, your short-term goals, and your purpose in life. You've done a lot of work discovering yourself, so give yourself a pat on the back. No, honestly. Reach behind you and pat your shoulder. You deserve it.

Go on.

How do you feel? Surely you feel as though you know more about yourself now than when you began this chapter. Take the next few weeks to think about the decisions you make on a daily basis in light of all the things you've learned about yourself. Do they sound like you? Why do you make them? When you say *yes* or *no*, what does that mean? Why do you enjoy one subject over the other? What about your favorite subject appeals to you?

For example, you might like philosophy because you enjoy reasoning through an issue and constructing an argument. You might enjoy math because you like the technical steps and straightforward way that you can go about solving a problem. You might like leading your study group because you end up explaining concepts in different chapters to fellow students in a way that's similar to teaching them a topic or an expertise.

Considering your passion and all that you've discovered about yourself, look at the pattern that has been created. Does it scream office job? Becoming an expert in one particular area? Starting a new venture and taking a lot of risks to earn the reward of making an impact?

Everything that you've written down in the exercises for this chapter was for a reason and a purpose. Read between the lines and see what speaks to you. Start investigating new opportunities.

Research different careers and paths online and see how they match up to all of this information you've gathered about yourself.

You've done the hard part—discovering what you bring to any job or career you decide to pursue in the future. Make sure that whatever you do aligns with the following:

> Your values
> Your passions
> Your strengths
> Your goals (both short-term and long-term)
> Your vision of success

That's it! That's the big secret. As you continue in this book, you will find more information about how to research specific industries or career fields and make the contacts you need in those fields. But knowing what you're looking for gives you a head start on most of the people out there who will still be wandering around aimlessly hoping to stumble into their dream job.

And in the next chapter, you're going to get tips that will give you an even bigger head start because you're going to figure out how to manage your time so that you can be more productive!

3

Manage Your Time, Maximize Your Productivity

There are two reasons that most students don't put college to work to their full advantage. First, they don't realize how valuable their university services can be to them. Second is because they're too busy to make the best use of those services. The thought of adding one more task to their schedule is exhausting. Most students give up before they even begin.

But if you put yourself to work first and learn a few tricks to help manage your time and be productive, you can employ all the services your school has to offer so that you can excel in college *and* beyond.

"The problem with trying to balance your social life with your studies is you can't do it all. Trust me, something is going to suffer. So before you agree to ALL of the social committees or join *every* club, take a good look at your calendar and your school obligations. Choose wisely. Maybe you can just attend an event instead of being on the board? Having a social life during college is a fundamental part of the experience, but putting your social calendar above your school calendar can be detrimental to your success. Unless there is free pizza–go to EVERYTHING with free pizza."

–Jenny Maddern, image consultant and owner, Snappy Casual Consulting; also a chronic underachiever and over-socializer turned successful entrepreneur

How to Create Time

There's a parable that I heard in graduate school that I've used ever since when I'm thinking about wisely using my time. It's a rather famous illustration in the business world.

You have a jar. Your task is to fit a set amount of sand, water, large stones, and small pebbles into said jar. If you put the sand in first, followed by the large stones, and then the small pebbles, you'll find that half the pebbles won't fit and there's no room for any water—the jar is too full. But if you put the large stones in first, followed by the pebbles, then you will be able to add the sand and the water. You can fit in all of the ingredients.

Picture that for a moment. Each of us is given twenty-four hours a day. How is it that the Bill Gates of the world can create incredible things while running companies while we feel overwhelmed by sixteen credits of coursework?

Well my friend, it's all about how you're filling up your jar. Set your large stones in your jar first: your coursework, obligations, study time, and sleeping hours. Next add in the small pebbles: club activities, time with your friends. The sand is the time that you have for career exploration. The water? That's the time you have to take action.

While it seems simple, it requires you to be very systematic about your time, wise with your priorities, and willing to take action. Let me say that again: you have to WANT to take action. That's the crux of everything. I can tell you until I'm blue in the face (or my hands are numb from typing this on my laptop), but until you're ready to get up and do something, there is nothing I can do to really help you. This has to be your idea.

TIPS AND TRICKS

● This chapter includes many of my tips about how you can accomplish more during your time at college. If you find that my tips don't work for you, there are thousands upon thousands of time management tips out there in the world.

I would highly recommend the book, *Getting Things Done*, by David Allen, if you want a developed system for managing your time. There are more recommendations in the Resources section.

The tips in this chapter were how I got through college alive. Looking back, I don't know how I was able to juggle my three jobs, full class schedule, and have time to study and enjoy life in college.

{ Kat's Tales from the Real World } When I started charting how I was spending my time, I realized that a lot of it was spent checking Facebook, Twitter, and my email a thousand times a day. Seriously, clicking through those sites gave me a way that I didn't have to be present or do anything, since I could find plenty of ways to busy myself. While I think part of it was habit from working too long in the corporate world, a lot of it was also procrastinating.

DOING something would put me in the position to be criticized for what I had done. So I would make up a lot of busy excuses why I couldn't take action.

For example, in writing this book, I had to force myself to sit down and write. Every day. Do you know how hard that is? Well, it is. Just making myself sit down and get it done, regardless of how I felt that day.

I wanted to write when I felt inspired, not when I had to. But inspiration rarely struck when I had free time. The lesson here is that not only did I have to make myself be consistent, but I also had to block out the time in my schedule to write. Not easy considering I have a full business, a toddler, a house, and husband, and that I would like to have a social life as well.

But you're holding my book now, so there's proof that it can be done!

» Discover Where Your Time is Going

To discover where your time is going, you're going to want to actually log it. Hour by hour, record where you're spending your time. Do this for a few days so you can see what you're doing on different days. You'll be surprised at where most of your time goes. I certainly was.

I'm guilty of underestimating the amount of time it takes to get anything done, underestimating how much time it takes to get my work done and how much time I spend doing things like watching Netflix, browsing around online, or just being unproductive—

period. I would say the good ol' Internet is the biggest time suck of my day. I can sit down for one task, and pretty soon, the afternoon is almost gone, and I haven't opened that tab to start researching yet. You know how easy it is to get sucked into something that you enjoy, especially when you're procrastinating.

Spend a week evaluating how much time you're spending on your hobbies and nonwork activities. I guarantee you're going to be surprised at the amount of time you're spending doing various things.

» Concentrate on Quality and Not Quantity

Now look at your time logs. In college, I would imagine you're either studying or you're in class for a lot of the hours of your week. My question is, *how well are you using your time when you're not in class*? Do you spend more time procrastinating doing your homework than actually doing it? Not being fully engaged when you're studying, which means it will take longer?

You'd be shocked at how much you can get done when you concentrate on the task at hand and bust it out. Give yourself deadlines to get things done. Especially the crappy things that no one wants to do. If you give yourself a time limit (for example, I'm going to spend ten minutes cleaning), it won't be as big of a deal, so you won't spend so much time avoiding the task.

The same goes with your study time and any other tasks that take concentration. Tell yourself you're going to fully focus for a set amount of time. That means during that time there will be no music that will tempt you to sing along, no checking your phone, no going online. Then reward yourself with a little break. After that break, return to the task and again give it your full attention.

You'll see that you can concentrate more and get more done in less time when you do things that way. Give a task your full attention.

» Block Out Time

The thing that's brilliant about taking classes at college is that the building blocks of your schedule are arranged for the quarter or semester. That means that each week, you know where you're supposed to be and what you're supposed to be doing on a particular day and time.

Do that for the rest of your schedule. Block out time for studying, for classes, for social hour, meals, etc. Be somewhat flexible, too, meaning you have some padding if your roommate wants to catch Taco Bell. Blocking out time means that you've made a date with yourself so that you can get certain things done. As in, done done. As in, you'll have time to investigate your career, have a social life, and keep your grades up too.

» Keep to Your Schedule

Blocking out your schedule is only useful if you actually stick to it. Otherwise it's just color-coded squares on your calendar, which do look pretty on your wall. Hold yourself to your schedule. If you slip for a few days, get back on the wagon. Don't give up. It actually takes twenty-one days to develop a habit, so remember to not be too hard on yourself. Try it for a month—and I mean really try it. Commit.

Time Management Tips

You'll find that some colleges will actually require you to take a class on time management and productivity, wanting you to be as successful as possible your freshman year of college. These can be great resources, but I've found my best productivity tips and time management tips by trial and error, finding what works best for me by trying out a number of techniques I've heard about or read about.

What works for me might not work for you, so keep an open mind. I'm going to provide a variety of tips and give you a glimpse of my own routine in this chapter. Hopefully, something will work for you. Try a few at a time; if they're not working for you, move on to something else. Know that it might take some time to find your own method and rhythm.

» Start Your Day Knowing What You Have To Get Done

Take fifteen minutes at the start of every day to plan out what needs to happen and decide what you're going to achieve. Name one, two, or even multiple things that you absolutely have to do, regardless of what happens that day. This could mean finishing a term paper, doing research, cleaning your dorm, studying for a test, reading a book—you get the idea. Identify these things first and write them on a whiteboard, a piece of paper, or even a Post-it note.

Now, do these things on your list FIRST. Then, no matter what happens the rest of the day, you will know that you got the most crucial tasks done and that your day was a success. There's something amazing about knowing at the end of the day that you got your most important tasks done. Trust me, it's the best feeling in the world, like you're actually moving forward instead of treading water.

» Focus

This is the hardest for me, honestly. I don't want to sit in silence, focused on the task at hand—I want to have my phone next to me, something streaming on Netflix; I want to have Facebook open, be checking Twitter, chatting with a friend, and keeping a few tabs open in my browser, all while I'm trying to get something done. This task could be anything—like writing a book—or homework, studying, you name it.

The problem is, when you have multiple attention-demanding streams going at once, you're not really devoting your full attention to what you're doing—you're only giving part of your all. What will happen when I get past the first draft of this book? I'll turn everything off and start editing, because the book will need my full attention.

The same is true with anything you try to do. It deserves your full attention in order to be good.

Put away your phone and put it on silent. Find a quiet place where there won't be any distractions. Close your browser window and don't look at Facebook or any other websites that are unrelated to what you're doing. There are apps you can put on your computer to actually block out the Internet for set amounts of time, so when you're tempted to cheat on yourself and sneak a peek at Twitter, the app won't let you do it. It keeps you honest.

After you've dealt with all the incoming distractions, you still need to truly focus. Concentrate on whatever it is you're doing and pretend as though nothing else exists. It might take a bit of time and energy to get yourself focused, but once you do, you're in the zone. Stay in the zone.

> **TIPS AND TRICKS**
> ● Put on some music if it helps you focus. But by music, I mean something that you're not going to start singing along to. Ambient music or classical music is great when you're focusing. I use Focus@Will, an app on my phone and a website that lets me choose a genre of music and set it for a certain time or frequency, depending on my mood or what I'm trying to do. Check it out.

» Start Your Day Early

I can already see you rolling your eyes and hear you groaning. Getting up early is hard, torture—and nearly impossible when you're in college, I know. But, there are students who get up at the crack of dawn to go running or go to the school gym, athletes who start at four in the morning before anyone is up, and others who get in a few more hours of studying before everyone else wakes up. Most college students I know aren't morning people, and I can't say that I was one either, until I was older.

But getting up early means you have more time in your day. I can't explain why I feel like I have more time than most people in the early hours of the morning compared to later morning, but it's true. When everyone is starting to wake up, I've already completed my main tasks for the day, meaning I got a head start. I feel like I have more time to relax and that I can DO more. I feel like Superwoman when I get up early.

Consider this typical college-student schedule: You get up at nine in the morning, go to class until three, start your homework, hang out with friends, and read/browse the Internet/watch Netflix/hang out until late in the evening, collapse into your bed late, only to do the same thing the next morning.

Compare your typical day to this one: You get up at five in the morning, while your roommate is still asleep. You either slip off to the gym or you stay in bed and study or start on that paper that's due next week. Or you do a little research. By eight a.m., you've already accomplished the three things you HAD to do today. Your roommate gets up at eight, and you're already done. You go to class, get the rest of your homework done, and you're done for the day. Now you can feel no guilt if you nap or catch a movie or read something for fun because you're already finished for the day.

Imagine that feeling. Now start going to bed earlier.

» Start Early on Everything

Procrastination—where your brilliance goes to die. I myself am a professional procrastinator and never seem to have enough time to get things done in the way I want them done. Part of this lies in the fact that I'm also a perfectionist, and my procrastination is a cover. If I don't have enough time to do something, then I have an excuse when it doesn't turn out as good as I wanted it to. Sound like you?

The way you combat this tendency, naturally, is through discipline and planning. Consider yourself a rebel instead of a super-organized person, and you have it made. Instead of having a paper done the night before it's due, give yourself your own deadline. Say that you're setting your own deadline because you don't want your professor telling you what to do! Just make that deadline a few days before your professor says the paper is actually due.

Then map out another deadline for having the rough draft done. Add yet another deadline for starting, and you have it made. Of course, the hard part is sticking to it. Get up early and get the biggest part of this task done first. You'll be amazed at how much better you'll feel about yourself in general.

For example:

> Your professor's deadline: Friday
> Your deadlines:
> Paper due by Wednesday
> Rough draft due by Monday
> Outline/research due by Friday

Naturally, you should also reward yourself for the work you've done. If you meet your deadline, celebrate a little (don't go overboard). This means you have a little more spare time, so you can reward yourself with your favorite snack or even a little nap in the afternoon. Something to celebrate the fact that you set your goals and achieved them. Remember however, to keep your rewards simple. You're not going to achieve your goals the next day if you stay up all night binge-watching your favorite television show on Netflix.

» Give Yourself Time Limits

Don't let your hobbies or your default activities or fear of starting work (or laziness) get in the way of being productive. Give yourself time limits on your hobbies or use them as rewards. I've found that I can make a deal with myself by working for fifty minutes and giving myself ten minutes of online time. When I've finished my work completely, I can reward myself with one or two episodes of my favorite show, or going out with friends—you get the idea.

I especially like to give myself a time limit when I'm working on tasks I just don't want to do—period. It makes it less torturous. If you hate your math class and everything to do with it, make a deal with yourself that you're going to work on your math homework for a half an hour. Just a half an hour. If you do that (you're bargaining with yourself), you'll find that you'll be more productive in that half hour and you won't spent four hours avoiding the fact that you have to spend a half hour on your math homework. While you're doing that half an hour of math homework, make sure that you're focused that full half an hour (see *Focus,* above).

» Lump Similar Tasks Together

If you have an essay due next Monday, a project due next Wednesday, and a dance due at the end of next week, don't assume that you have to work on each task separately and in order. Rather, do the research for both your essay and your project at the library on one day. Use the dance studio after class to work on your dance, and then go back to your room and work on your project and essay. Try to put similar tasks together, so you don't need to go to the library four times over the course of the week or backtrack as you're working. Group similar tasks together so you don't have to reprogram your brain as you keep working.

Do this with your calendar as well. Batch out time to work on things and you'll find that you'll be more productive. Even if it's assigning Tuesday as laundry/cleaning day.

» Figure Out What's Important and What's Urgent

This is one of the hardest things to manage in college because it seems like everything is both important and urgent. When you start your day and you determine which tasks have to get done before the day's out, those are your *urgent* matters—things that have to happen. The *important* tasks are things like calling your mother, spending time working on your career goals, and taking care of your mental and physical health.

Does this mean that your paper should wait because you need to hit the gym? No, but it does mean that you should make sure you're scheduling time to take care of the important things—like yourself, your family, your friends, and your mental health.

TIPS AND TRICKS
● There's nothing worse than my phone dinging, telling me I'm not doing something or that someone needs me, or that I just received a new email. Don't let your phone rule your life. Put it on silent—not vibrate, not low—*silent*. Nothing on your phone can be so urgent that it disrupts your entire day.

Use Focus@Will if you want to keep yourself on a timer. The music will stop after a certain amount of time, providing a much more gentle reminder that your hour (or two) is up and it's time to go to the next task.

When you are aware of the important tasks in your life and make time for them, you'll see that you're moving forward toward your goals. You'll learn how to schedule times for the most important things, like working toward your personal goals and aspirations and building relationships.

» Say No

This is the hardest thing to do. You're going to want to say yes to everything because you want to be included, you want to help your friend, or you want to get out of your room. But saying yes to everything means that you're compacting your schedule and stomping all over your precious time. Your time IS precious.

When someone asks you to do something, ask yourself if it's the best use of your time. What would you gain from saying yes? Is it a step toward your career? Your goals? Your aspirations? If the answer is no, then move on. You don't have to be rude about it, just say something like: "You know, I would love to help you but I'm overwhelmed right now. Thank you so much for asking, but I really can't. I wouldn't be able to dedicate the time to (insert task/position/activity here) that I think it deserves."

That's it. You don't have to be a jerk about it; you can say no gracefully.

» Under-Commit and Over-Deliver

Under-committing and over-delivering means that you'll always shine when you turn in anything—essays, project, assignments—and when delivering on promises. This doesn't mean that you should be flaky or wishy-washy when committing to things; just don't promise the moon. Keep a few ideas to yourself and over-deliver on what you promised. It'll always make you look good when you deliver more than you promised in the first place.

This extends to everything in your life—activities, assignments, and organizations. This will be key when you get that first job and you want to impress your boss and co-workers.

» Get Organized

Make sure that you're organized—whatever that might be. This includes your room, your bathroom, your book bag, your life, and your calendar. (Ugh, I know, the dreaded cleaning talk). The more organized you are, the more you'll feel like you're in control of your destiny. I know that doing the dishes or cleaning the toilet isn't part of your destiny (or doesn't seem to be), but you'll be amazed at the brain space you'll clear up when everything in your life has a place.

Set out your clothes the night before if your appearance is important to you so you're not wasting valuable time each morning debating over which shoes to wear. Take five minutes to pack your book bag for the next day. Print out your paper (remember, everything is going to be done before the deadline, so do this ahead of time). Staple your papers and walk to the student store to buy your scantrons before class. You know that if you wait till the last minute to do these tasks, something might go wrong to make you late. If you eliminate that possibility entirely, you won't have to worry about it.

Have a place for your important documents (insurance papers, bills, class syllabi, etc.), a place for your assignments, a place for your clothes, etc. You get the point. Don't waste time looking for things; know where everything is. Put everything back where it belongs. It'll help clear your mental space, make things easier in the morning and around bedtime, and make you look like you have your act together (because you totally do).

» Make Use of Dead Time

How much time, exactly, do you spend waiting in line, waiting for class to start, or traveling (not driving)? That is time you can be using to do things! Your phone is great for this, if you don't surrender to the habit of checking Facebook, Twitter, and the like every time you have a few seconds. What's also amazing is that you'll find the daily stresses like waiting in line or waiting for your friend, or being in traffic (you're not driving, remember) will melt away as you're doing something productive with your time. You take control of that time and you own it. There are a few apps you can use to help you with this.

Evernote. Evernote is amazing. It lets you clip articles on your computer, tablet, or phone to one account that you can access from any of these devices. Not only that, but you can record voice notes for yourself, make to-do lists, or pull up notes that you've typed in. Evernote is great for keeping you organized; using this app, you can study a bit while you're waiting in line, or check in and do some research knowing that when you get back to your computer, all of those articles will be waiting for you.

Flashcard apps. There are some great ones out there where you can enter in information and then use that information to quiz yourself on your phone, while you're waiting for your latte at Starbucks. Enter the info and get some studying in, especially if you're memorizing species or the like in your biology class.

Indeed. Indeed is a career search site that you can browse when you have some dead time to see what jobs are out there, where they're hiring, and what requirements and qualifications they're looking for. It's a great way to research new industries and possible careers. You won't want to stay on this site longer than a few minutes, so it's the perfect app to have on your phone while you're doing a little more research on your career.

GRE/GMAT/MCAT apps. Are you looking to go to graduate school? You'll most likely have to take an exam to get there, much like you did the SAT and/or the ACT before you applied to college. Start studying for those tests by downloading an app that's designed to help you sharpen your knowledge.

If you start in your freshman year and just look at it while you're in line at the grocery store for the next four years, you'll probably get a better score and be more prepared (as long as you go to the grocery store regularly, that is).

News and career sites. Professional development is paramount, as is keeping up with your industry and what's going on in the world. Get a few of your favorite news apps on your phone to keep up with what's going on, even if you just read an article or two while you're waiting for your class to start.

You'll be amazed at how much more aware of the world this will make you. And you'll be able to say to someone in a conversation: "You know, I was reading an article lately on. . . ."

» Don't Multitask

Multitasking used to be the number-one skill that employers said they were looking for in potential hires. But scientific research has proven no one can truly multitask well. (I'm not going to cite that research—a good Google search will provide the studies for you.) We do better when we're focused on one task and not a whole mess of tasks at a time.

Again, read the *Focus* section above. Working on one thing at a time will pretty much double your productivity—so don't try to write a paper while you're watching Netflix, talking to a friend, and tweeting at the same time.

Set Step-by-Step Goals

Making better use of your time every day won't do you much good if you don't figure out what you want to do with the time you're not wasting. One of the best ways to be more productive is to frequently review your goals.

We're talking about life goals here, daily goals, career goals, project goals—big goals, small goals, all kinds of goals. Just like you block out time and identify what you're going to accomplish each day, you're going to want to set your long-term goals and then give yourself smaller goals to get there. (See Exercise 2.7 in the Resources section for more advice on how to do this.)

If you're only setting the big goals, or telling yourself that someday you'll do something, it's never going to happen. Think about the number of people who always say, "Someday I'm going to have that house on the beach." Think about that. Is there a due date to that goal? A step-by-step plan for how they're going to actually obtain that house on the beach? No. And since it's not set in step-by-step short-term goals, that long-term goal will always be a someday dream that will never happen.

Imagine taking that goal of a beach house and setting structure to it. For example, you might say, "In five years, I'll have a house on the beach." Now let's get more specific. Where on the beach? What town? What neighborhood? What do houses cost in that neighborhood? Do some research. Now determine how much money you'll need to buy that house and what kind of salary you should be making.

Then work backward from there. By year three, you would need to have a set amount of money. By year four, another set amount, so that by year five, you have enough to buy that house. Work backward until you get the point where you know what you have to do tomorrow or next month to start making that beach house dream a reality. See how that makes the goal more tangible? And if you hold yourself to it, you'll find yourself sipping lemonade in your new beach house, enjoying the view in five years. All because you made it happen.

Setting goals and seeing how you're going to get there, step by step, helps make them a reality. They're suddenly not as daunting when you know what your next step will be. Besides, the more goals you reach (even mini-ones) the more motivated you'll be, thus the more happy you'll be. You'll be avoiding that awful feeling of being stuck or not knowing what your next step will be. You won't get sidetracked and you'll know your purpose, and you'll accomplish more in your years at college than most people do in decades.

Becoming known as the one who gets things done can become a part of your image—part of your personal brand, which we'll discuss in the next chapter.

{ Kat's Tales from the Real World } When I was working in Los Angeles, some actor friends of mine took the concept of goal-setting and visualizing their goals to the next level. On the wall in their little apartment, they cut out a paiper-maché tree (the kind you'd see in a second-grade classroom), and labeled the branches with their milestone goals.

At the very top of the tree was the main goal: being the lead in a feature film. They started at the roots—which was moving to Los Angeles—and worked their way up with smaller goals leading to the top. Lower steps included acting classes, getting a manager, and getting an agent. Naturally, when I met them, they were achieving the goal of getting an agent, because I was working for the talent agency that took them on as clients.

They could literally see each step of their main goal in easy, digestible pieces, and it motivated them when things got rough or they didn't make progress as quickly as they thought they would. They could see on the tree what the next step was and also could see how far they had climbed (which is important when you get down on yourself).

What was the end result? Well, I lost contact with them, but I did see one of them a few years later as a lead in a feature film. So I'm guessing their tree of goals worked out pretty well for them.

Do you have to put a tree on your wall? No. But if it helps, do it! Make your goals your own and have fun with them. They're yours, after all.

4

Personal Branding

Branding? What do cows have to do with college? (Insert cheesy '50s educational video music.) No, Jane, not that type of branding. Personal branding.

Chances are, you've already started developing your personal brand. Are you always late or always on time? Are you a hard worker? Straight-A student? Are you creative? Do you play the guitar? Have you reached an expert level at a certain video game? Do you always wear designer-label clothes? Do you never wear designer-label clothes?

All of those qualities and many more make up your *personal brand,* something that you'll carry with you and continue to develop as the years pass. So let's dive into this so-called "branding" and how you can use it to your advantage—in college, in your career, in life.

What Is a Brand?

A brand on a cow marks that cow as belonging to a particular owner. A brand name shows you that a product comes from a specific store or manufacturer. The brand name, logo, and other distinctive features wind up representing a business, and you eventually come to equate all the things you think about a business with its brand. For example, with Starbucks, you might think green, coffee, warm, inviting environment, friendships, hipsters, etc. Those impressions reflect your thoughts on its brand.

Starbucks spends a lot of time and money to create those thoughts and impressions through its actions, services, and the environment it creates in their stores and with their products.

What Is a Personal Brand?

So how does this apply to you? You're not a company, right?

But whether they are aware of it or not, people wind up with personal brands. Companies work hard to create and maintain their brands, while many people create brands without even realizing it.

Let's look at two different people and compare their brands. Jennifer and Monica went to the same high school and were hired at the same time at the same coffee shop. Jennifer, who always arrives on time, dresses in black slacks, nice (yet comfortable) shoes, and a black button-up, pressed shirt; her hair is always neatly pulled back in a bun. To feel a little more dressy, she wears simple earrings. When working, she tries to remain positive even on the worst and most busy days, and she finds things to do that involve organizing or cleaning when the café isn't busy. Whenever someone needs to trade a shift for a day

Creating a Brand

Lots of companies work hard to create their "brand." Take Wal-Mart as an example. What's the first thing that pops in your head? Is it low prices? Blue? Or other qualities about the store or products? All of the impressions that fill your head are all reflections of Wal-Mart's brand.

Your impressions of the brand could be positive or negative. Do you think "low prices, blue, walking away with a cart full of great stuff for a little money"? Or do you think "low wages, mega-stores, and the *People of Walmart* website"? As you might guess, Wal-Mart would not want you to associate the *People of Walmart* site with their brand, for obvious reasons.

Compare your thoughts about Wal-Mart with Target. They're different, aren't they? With Target, you might think of red and white and their bull's-eye logo. You might think of the nickname Tar-zhay or colorful displays. Those impressions are different than your impressions of Wal-Mart because Target's branding is different than Wal-Mart's. Branding is unique to each company.

off, Jennifer can usually be counted on, unless she's out of town or busy with her friends that night.

Monica is more casual. She wears dark jeans, a black T-shirt, and her hair always seems messy, even when it's pulled back. She's usually about five to ten minutes late and sometimes calls in at the last minute to say she's unable to come to work. She gets grumpy or short with customers when they ask for extra things; if the café isn't busy, she's on her phone. Monica is usually the one asking Jennifer to trade shifts, because she's always going to a concert out of town or attending a party with her friends. While she does what is asked of her at the café, she rarely finds more work for herself.

As you can see, Monica and Jennifer are two entirely different people. When you think of each person, can you start to spot their branding? Jennifer is always well put together, professional, reliable, and hard-working. Monica is more relaxed, borderline messy, and doesn't go above and beyond. She can't be bothered with extra tasks and sometimes can't be bothered to show up at all. She's unreliable.

What's important to realize is that these actions and appearances that Monica and Jennifer display are their brand signatures. Monica might not really be a messy, irresponsible person. She might be great! But her *brand signals*—the things she does and the attitude she displays at work—make it hard for her co-workers to see what a great person she is. Instead, she appears to be someone who doesn't care. Jennifer, on the other hand, maintains an impeccable brand and would

Be Aware

Being aware of your personal brand is so important. The actions you take, the words you use, and the attitude you have all form what someone else sees as your personal brand. The good news is that you have control of your brand.

In fact, you're forming that brand right now, whether you're in high school, college, or at a part-time job.

Your brand is very important while you are in college and when you start applying for jobs, and it will make or break your career. What you do, how you dress, what attitude you display, and what skills you choose to focus on are all part of your brand. Your brand is someone's perception of you. That's it, that's the big reveal.

likely be hired and/or promoted over Monica. All because of the little things she does.

As Jeff Bezos, founder of Amazon famously said: "Your brand is what people say about you when you're not in the room." Your brand is how your employer, professor, classmate, or friend perceives you to be. While you don't have complete control over that perception, you do have control over the actions you take and the attitudes you display which affect that perception. That's why it's so important to be strategic about developing your personal brand for your college years and your future career.

How to Develop Your Personal Brand

You're thinking now that you can't control how someone thinks of you, right? Wasn't that what you were taught in school in self-esteem training in health class, or through all of those teen movies? Well, that is true to a certain extent, and it may be more true in the jungles of high school. But in the college and professional world, there are things that you can do to control and develop your brand.

First we're going to look at how you *want* to be perceived. There are four key areas that you should focus on here:

> Appearance, which includes your body language and clothing
> Personality, your mannerisms, the way you communicate with other people, your attitude, and how you react to situations naturally
> Differentiation, which is a fancy business word for what makes you different from other people
> Skills and abilities.

» Appearance

What is your style? Now, more importantly, what is your *professional* style? Are you an Armani suit-wearer? Or business casual with the latest fashions? How put-together do you usually look? What perceptions do you want people to have about you based on what you wear?

Now, turn to the Resources section and create a few lists. In Exercise 4.1, I want you to list five things you want people to think about your appearance. Then you're going to write two ways you can make each item on your list happen with your clothing or the way that you put outfits together. For example, I want everyone to think that I dress professionally and yet causal and true to my own style. Two ways I can do that would be to wear outfits that look the part (i.e., professional and true to my style) and to make sure my hair is clean and styled every day, no matter what.

Your body language is important here too. What do you want people to think about you when you enter the room? If you want to be seen as confident, you want to make sure your body language matches. People won't see you as confident if you're hiding in a corner, hunched over, not willing to interact with anyone.

» Personality

Again, turn to Exercise 4.1 in the Resources section and list five things you want people to think about your personality. Do you want to be perceived as being fun? Helpful? Caring? What are some ways you can express that in the way you talk with or help people? List two ways each quality can communicate your intention.

If you want to be seen as a helpful person, you can offer advice, tips, or help with projects that people offer in conversation. Naturally, you would want to communicate this in a positive manner so you don't sound like a know-it-all. Another way you could demonstrate helpfulness is by offering to actually physically help someone.

Your personality will always be one of the hardest to change because it's an integral part of you. But making a list like this will help you focus on what you want other people to see—and make a plan for how to showcase your best qualities.

» Differentiation

Differentiation is a business term for how you're different from other people or companies. It's what makes you completely different, a quality that no one can copy. Take a moment and think about what makes you different. Then turn to Exercise 4.1 in the Resources section and list three items that set you apart from other people.

At first you're going to come to the conclusion that you're just like everyone else. With more digging however, you'll start to see your own qualities. For example, what makes me different from other educational consultants is my odd path through college. Because of a car accident my junior year of high school, I actually ended up graduating early and starting at junior college, bypassing the usual four-year track that I had already started planning for. Instead, I had to navigate the college admissions process as a transfer student. Because of that, I have experiences that few other consultants have.

What makes you different from your classmates? What can you bring to an employer that will be different from what anyone else interviewing for the same job will bring? Look at your list you created in Exercise 4.1. Those three items are going to help you stand out in college and after graduation. Embrace them and be ready to talk about them immediately when you're looking for an internship, research position, or job.

» Skills

Ah yes, we can't forget your actual abilities! Your skills are what you're able to do, what you're capable of doing, and what you really excel at doing. You're probably used to seeing skills listed in job descriptions. For your brand, you want to concentrate on your strengths, also.

Look at the list of strengths and skills you created in Exercises 2.3 and 2.4 in the Resources section. Review the section in Chapter 2 that discusses strengths and skills, if you need to. Now choose three items from your list of skills that you created in Exercise 2.4, and list those in the last section of Exercise 4.1. These are the skills you want to emphasize, the ones you want your professors, classmates, and potential employers to know that you have. These are the skills that should become a part of your personal brand.

The Current State of Your Brand

Now that you know what you *want* your brand to look like, let's check in on the current state of your brand. Yes, remember that you do have a brand, no matter if you're in college, high school, or wandering around your parent's basement.

» Seek Feedback

First, you will want to discover where your brand stands right now so you can start to improve it. To do this, you're going to have to do some digging (and digging means you're going to have to put some work into it) and ask people to name three qualities that come to mind when they think of you. (Remember the exercise from the "finding your strengths and weaknesses" section in Chapter 2? I hope you liked it because you need to do it again; feedback is essential to perfecting your brand).

You can create a SurveyMonkey poll, slap the question up on Facebook, tweet it out to your followers or email them. You can write something along these lines:

Hello!
I'm doing an assignment to identify my impressions on people. If you have a chance, could you please reply back with four qualities that instantly come to mind when you think of me? I'm supposed to collect three positive and one negative.

Thank you in advance for your help!

Sincerely,
Tony Stark

Once the responses start flooding in, start looking at the positive and negative qualities for similarities. Do you see a trend? List your responses in Exercise 4.2 in the Resources section.

How do the negatives measure up? This is going to be the hard part, since no one likes to hear bad stuff about yourself. I can say with all honesty, though, that if you don't know the bad, you can't improve. So put on your big-girl panties and take that criticism.

Consider it. Do you agree with it? Do you not agree with it? Why? Is it something that you want to improve? Can you improve it?

{ Kat's Tales from the Real World } A friend of mine said I always looked slightly standoffish when I was with a group of people I didn't know. She had noticed that my body language and my face are protective, or closed off, to other people. At first, just like when one of my weaknesses was pointed out, I was offended. I consider myself to be a very approachable, nice person.

Reflecting back on a few networking events however, I realized that my nerves and my shyness were being misinterpreted and I was being seen as aloof and closed off. At our next event, I took that into consideration and made adjustments by not crossing my arms, making sure to smile even when I wasn't particularly smiling at anyone, and trying to keep positive thoughts in my head, so my overall mood was happy.

It made a huge difference. I was approached by more people, actually felt less nervous, and had a better time at the event than at previous gatherings. My personal brand had been representing me in a way that I didn't want it to—a way that was getting miscommunicated.

Later, I again thanked my friend for being brave enough to point out this negative impression so that I could fix it.

Negative criticism will always be tough, but if you can remember that your personal brand is under your control, it doesn't sting as much.

» Make a Master List

The next step you're going to take is to list the top five qualities from the feedback you've received that you feel best represent who you are. These are the qualities that you are going to emphasize in your personal brand, the qualities that you're going to want to polish so that they shine through whatever you're doing. Remember the list of values you created in Exercise 2.2? Make sure that all the qualities you decide to emphasize are in line with your values.

Now turn to the second half of Exercise 4.2, and create a master list. List the top five qualities you want people to recognize in you. Then come up with two ways you can demonstrate these qualities through *action*. For example: If you have *trustworthy* on your list, you'll want to demonstrate that quality by not gossiping about other people and by keeping the secrets of others.

Next, do the same with the negative qualities. List five negative qualities that you *don't* want to represent you. These may be impressions you need to change, or just characteristics that you never want to develop. Examples could be lateness, negativity, or disorganization. Then list two ways you can demonstrate with action that these characteristics do *not* apply to you.

After you've created your master list, copy it and put it somewhere that you will see it every day. You can put it on your bathroom mirror, or on your desk. Maybe the wallpaper on your phone, if you're really ambitious.

Living Your Brand

The most important part of developing your brand is living up to your brand. You have to decide that you're going to demonstrate every day through your actions and words the brand that you've developed. Make sure you're aware of what you're saying, doing, and the decisions you make, because they're all part of the world's perception of you.

You're going to start putting a lot of stock into your brand, an investment that takes hard work, awareness, and time. You don't want to blow it halfway into your senior year and ruin everything that you've worked so hard for.

Thinking about creating a personal brand does not mean you won't be a sincere, genuine person. And your brand can always change too, as time goes on. Being deliberate about a personal brand simply means that you're going to be consciously developing yourself, thinking about the impression you make on people, and actively trying to influence that space you take up in their mind when they think of you.

Your Brand Online

Once you've determined what your brand is going to be and how you're going to manage it, you'll want to take a look at your social media profiles. Google yourself and see what pops up. Do you have pictures of you doing inappropriate things? Tweets, Facebook posts or Instagram posts that don't represent this new brand?

Believe it when you hear that employers are now looking at social media profiles of potential employees. Since you might be a representative of their company, they want to make sure that your branding aligns with theirs—and that includes what you post online.

> The best thing you can do is start being conscious about your online presence now, and clean up the less-than-savory, early-high-school mistakes you made online. Yes, I'm talking about that online drama you had with so-and-so's boyfriend/girlfriend where you got into an all-caps screaming match.

Use a professional picture of yourself. Before you graduate college, have a professional photographer (or a photography student) take a good headshot of you that looks professional. Dress up, look nice, and have that picture taken. Nothing will ruin your new professional brand faster than a bad picture from a party. While you're in college, you can get away with your high school senior picture. Crop it to show just your face and shoulders and not you leaning against a tree or something (you know how senior pictures are). Use it on all your profiles, if you can.

Speaking of pictures, sanitize your pictures on Facebook, Twitter, Instagram, etc. Remove from your profiles any pictures of that inappropriate gesture, your new tongue ring, you half-dressed, and any crazy party images that go

TIPS AND TRICKS

● Be careful about any postings or messages that look like "text speak." You want to prove to future employers that you can write like you would for a professor or your English class. Again, you will potentially be representing their company, and they need to know you can write professionally.

Beyond what employers might think, you don't really want to be known for that either. It's embarrassing in the professional world to be known as the girl that writes: *lol I will totes b there, j/k.*

against your brand. Do the same with old status postings that are no longer relevant and reflect badly on you.

» Use Your Privacy Settings

I know that most of this sounds sanitized and lame, and even when you want a professional personal brand, you don't want to look like a stick-in-the-mud to your friends. So, remember that you can adjust a lot of your privacy settings, and be more casual in places that only your friends should see. But even then you have to consider that you don't have full control. What if one of your "friends" decides to share your unkind but very witty comment in a public space?

Just remember that anything available to the public could be published in the newspaper, front-page center, for your grandparents to read. It puts things in a different perspective, doesn't it?

How to Use Your Personal Brand

Now that you've developed this personal brand, how are you going to use it? What value does a brand have? If we're talking about businesses, I encourage you to Google "Interbrand," a company that actually measures the worth of a company's brand each year. In 2013, Interbrand named Apple as the most valuable brand in the world, valued at $98 million dollars. That's not the actual company or any product that it might sell; it's simply the dollar amount assigned to the perception of Apple. Insane, right?

With that in mind, how much do you think your personal brand would be worth? Practically speaking, it's your brand and your abilities that professors choose for plum internships and research projects and employers hire. If you're going to be an entrepreneur, it's these abilities and qualities that will win you customers and make people want to work for you. If you're going into the workforce, your brand will make employers choose whether to hire you.

Your branding and your experiences combined equal your salary. It can be measured in opportunities, job offerings, salary negotiations, and relationships (both professional and personal).

» Clarity

You've already clearly defined what your brand is by doing Exercises 4.1 and 4.2 in the Resources section. Your social media profiles are scrubbed. Your appearance and personality reflect your brand, and you're ready to go. You want to keep this clarity in what you stand for as you move forward.

Don't get me wrong—you're going to have to keep updating your brand, as you move from being an underclassman to an upperclassman and then a college graduate and a career professional. None of this is permanent. It will require effort at first, but soon, with practice, you'll find that it's easier to clearly show people what you represent. This is especially true when using social media.

! TIPS AND TRICKS
● How do you use your personal brand? You need to keep it in mind when developing relationships, when you're completing your coursework, when you're applying for jobs, and when you're leaving comments online. You want your actions to represent your brand so that others will always think of that brand when they think of you.

When that happens, then your brand will be working for you. The keys to putting your brand to work for you are to be clear about what your brand is, be sure your actions are consistent with your desired brand, and make your brand visible to the people you want to see it.

» Consistency

Make sure you and your brand are always in step. Your brand won't represent you as an organized person if you frequently show up to meetings or class late, miss appointments because you didn't have them in your calendar, arrive at events without your notes or your business cards.

Take a strong stand to make your actions match your desired image, and your brand will follow wherever you go. Be consistent and diligent because it takes only a few wrong decisions to destroy all that you've struggled to build.

» Constancy

You're never finished. You're always going to be in the process of communicating your brand to the people you want to reach. This is important to remember when going to class, club meetings, networking events, industry events, trade shows, or any general situations where you may encounter current acquaintances or future employers. Your brand should always be working for you, communicating to the right people with the right medium at the right time.

Your brand must always be working for you.

Get it? Always.

PART 2

Succeed in School

When I first went to college, I had no idea what was going on most of the time. I went to class, got good grades, and did what was expected of me. Unfortunately, that didn't get me very far. Yes, I had some incredible professors and learned a lot, but I did not put my university to work for me in all the ways I could have. When I graduated, I had an expensive piece of paper and some on-campus work experience that could relate to real-world experience, and not much more. I missed so many opportunities while I was in college that it took me about ten years to figure out what I wanted to do and how to do it.

I figured it out eventually, but I want you to have it easier. I know there's an easier path because I found that road by the time I got to graduate school. Instead of diving head-first into the deep end on a major, I spent an entire year investigating what I wanted to study. I read books on business and entrepreneurship, listened to podcasts, started reading about business in newspapers and websites, and tried to teach myself a little finance. When I decided that business school was the next step for me, I started researching programs and making visits. When I found my perfect program (one cohort, weekend classes, challenging academics, and an environment that felt like home), I applied and scheduled my interview. It was the perfect program for me and I could explain to them exactly why.

My graduate experience was completely different from my undergraduate because I knew what I wanted to accomplish and learned how to use my school's resources to reach my goals. I carried a different outlook into my classes, utilized our alumni network, developed strong professional relationships with my professors, and really got to know my classmates. I used my career center and got acquainted with the key players at my university. I did pretty much the complete opposite of what I had done in my undergraduate studies, and it paid off. I managed to get a promotion after graduation thanks to the support and suggestions of the faculty and the career center. I tried out theory while I was working, noticing different case studies at my current job that helped me to understand the practical aspects of theory and how it relates to the real world (and real people).

This is the path I want you to take in the four years that you have in college as an undergraduate, no matter if you know what you want to do long-term in your career or not. The important thing is that you're going to start considering your future in your freshman year and planning for it until you have an answer and a route mapped out.

In the last section, we talked about putting yourself to work: being your own advocate, considering goals and dreams based on your personality and preferences, using your time wisely, and building your own brand. In this section, I want to help you learn how to take advantage of the many resources you will find in your college or university. Resources that you're paying for. Yes, let me repeat that: You're already paying for these. USE THEM.

Putting your college's resources to work can help you be successful IN college, which can lead to success AFTER college. This section introduces you to some of the best resources you'll find at your school and provides some handy tips on how to start utilizing what they offer.

5

Your Coursework

We're going to start off by looking at your coursework. After all, no matter what movies and TV try to tell you, college is actually all about the classes. To put college to work for you, you have to find the right courses—and that involves more planning than just trying to avoid 8 a.m. classes for four years.

Choosing the right courses in the right order can mean the difference between graduating in four years with a degree in a field that fascinates you and graduating in five or six years with a degree in the only major you could scrape up enough credits to complete. After you get into the right courses, then you have even more chances for learning and developing relationships that will carry you through college and beyond.

What's My Major Again?

To Declare or not to Declare—that is the question. While I always advise students to declare a major as soon as possible, there is merit to not doing so—confusing, right? I'm going to present both cases and you can make your own decision based on your personal path. If you find yourself in the "I've already declared, and I'm happy" camp, then that's awesome. Keep reading to learn how you can enhance your major and make yourself a thousand times more likely to get a job out of college. If you're in the "I have no idea what I'm doing" camp, read on and use the tips here, the ones in the first section, and the exercises in the Resources section to help you figure that out as soon as possible.

I went to junior college right out of high school with the idea of majoring in journalism . . . I wanted to be a sports writer. My first year in college, I got a part-time job as a sports writer covering high school football for the local paper. After a few months of low pay and LONG nights, I realized that I might want to look elsewhere for a career.

Having no idea what I wanted, and no real counselors available, I just took classes that interested me with no real focus. Near the end of my two years there, I made an appointment with administration to see how I could graduate. The "counselors" they had were just teachers who volunteered to help as they could. The fellow who looked over my transcripts said, "Well, you have enough credits to graduate with an AA in fine arts." I didn't even know what "fine arts" meant, but it sounded good to me.

–Ken Brinkley, former adjunct professor of English at California State University, Bakersfield, and current senior engineering estimator for Pacific Gas and Electric

» For the No-Idea Crowd

As you may—or may not—already know, most schools are going to require you to take certain general education courses no matter what your major is and additional courses for the major you choose. There are a few exceptions to this rule (Brown University, I'm looking at you), but for the most part, this is the way it is. You'll have to take classes from "areas of concentration" or whatever your school labels them—meaning you will be required to take a few courses in math and science, history and politics, writing and literature, etc. Colleges mandate these general requirements to make sure you become a well-rounded individual who has a wide range of knowledge to help you carry out your role as a good citizen. General education courses are designed to give all students knowledge outside their specialized fields so they can make better decisions, solve problems, and relate to people from a variety of backgrounds.

Your general education requirements are either on the paper handed to you at orientation, on your college website, at the counseling office, with your counselor, or in the student handbook or catalog, usually in the front few chapters. It's usually very easy to find a list of these requirements.

Most college students take their general education requirements their first two years of college, panic when they discover they haven't settled on a major yet, and pick one based on which general education class they liked best. This means they're picking the subject matter they liked and not the actual career associated with it. This is the reason there are philosophy majors. (No offense, philosophy majors; I think you're wicked smart and you could easily transform your critical thinking skills into a variety of different careers.)

You want to avoid this method of choosing your major if you're not going to a school that magically transports you to a time before the 1990s. Back then, companies would take time and money to train you for a specific position, meaning you could do almost anything with a business degree and a company would train you to go into some area of business within their ranks. Now, because bachelor's degrees are much more prevalent than they were 30 years ago, that era has passed. Employers want candidates with specialties, who have trained themselves or come from programs in college that trained them, so they can put you in a position and you'll be able to start providing value (read: making them money) in the first few months.

So, if you're reading this chapter and worrying about how to choose a major, stop! Go back to Chapter 2. Read that chapter again (or read it for the first time) and complete the related Resources exercises. Think about your values, passions, strengths, goals, and your own vision of success. Consider which careers square with those characteristics; now figure out which majors lead to those careers. Simple, huh?

If it still isn't clear to you, think of your favorite classes in high school, consider which classes in the college catalog look interesting to you, take some assessments in your career center. Explore fields by talking to people in those fields.

Don't pursue any major that doesn't lead to a career that squares with your passions, strengths, and goals. Period.

» For the I-Got-This Crowd

If you have declared your major and you're positive this is the field for you, take a good look at your general education requirements. You will most likely have a choice in the classes that you take. Now, think about your future career choice and what you want to do with it. Are you going into medicine and considering private practice? You might want to take a sociology class or a psychology class to fulfill a general education requirement because you'll be studying people's behavior and marketing your services to them. Going into business? Look into taking business calculus or a basic business course. If you're going into tech and don't know how to code, taking a general coding class will only benefit you in the future. Try to match as many of your general education courses as you can with skills or knowledge bases that you'll need for your future career.

I highly recommend that you take a couple of business classes no matter what your major or future career choice because every career field you go into is related in one way or another with business.

Choosing Your Courses

Registration! Perhaps one of the more harrowing parts of the college process, but I found it to be the most exhilarating. That's probably why I'm in this field now—I loved

---

TIPS AND TRICKS

● Don't get swept up in the latest "must-have" major. I'm tired of hearing everyone tell me that they want to major in engineering because you make money and can get a job. About seven years ago, we heard the same thing told to people about being in the pharmacy tech field: get your degree and you're guaranteed a job with an amazing salary. Do you know what happened? A flood of pharmacy techs hit the market about four years later. There was no longer a shortage of pharmacy techs; people couldn't find jobs, and salaries were no longer as high because companies knew they had an abundance of candidates to choose from. It's the old rule of supply and demand.

You don't want to be in this position. No one does. If engineering is your passion, and you want to do it, fantastic! But don't pick that or any other field of study just because you heard it makes money. Take the time to examine yourself, so that you can choose a major you will enjoy studying in college and enjoy using after college. If you put yourself to work and put your college to work, you will find ways to make your major work for you when you graduate.

poring over the course schedule and catalog, planning out different areas of study for myself. It was like living multiple lives where I could be a chemistry genius or the most skilled philosophy student at the university.

To put your courses to work for you, you need to put registration to work for you. That means having a plan going into registration. Why plan? Because you want to take all the courses you *must* take and include some of the courses you *want* to take without having to take any extras.

Naturally, you don't want to take extra, expensive classes that you don't need. One extra class means more time, studying, papers, tests, and book fees. And let's be honest, no one wants to have to shove in a required chemistry class at the last minute, replacing that awesome photography elective you were looking forward to taking.

» Your University Catalog

Let me introduce you to the Bible of your university: your school's catalog. It can be obtained online or in the student store or bookstore, and it is your guide to all of the classes, majors, and requirements for graduation from your school. Your catalog might also include your student handbook, which lays out disciplinary measures, rules, student conduct, etc. There's probably an academic calendar in there somewhere, as well as information about fees and other college policies.

Spend some time looking at your catalog. Look at the general education requirements, which are usually found in the beginning. Usually you'll have a required English or writing class, a math requirement, a Constitution or United States history requirement, a science with a lab, some sort of humanities (philosophy, sociology, psychology, history, classics, etc.), and a reasoning requirement. These will be different depending on your school. If you're at a place like Colorado School of Mines, you won't have humanities requirements at all—they'll mostly be math and science classes. If you're at an art school, you'll probably not be required to take a large amount of science and math classes.

Which brings me to another point. Depending on your major, there might be different classes that cover the same general education requirements. For example, your school might try to bring more of the humanities into the sciences by offering humanities-based courses in the science department. Courses like ethics of game design or science in the age of the Enlightenment work to bring major subject matter into the humanities—or vice versa. Engineering departments sometimes offer a completely different path for students because they have so many major requirements for their degree that it would be otherwise impossible for them to finish general education and major requirements. Which is what you're going to look for when you flip to the department or major that you're considering.

Look at the requirements for that major. Usually there will be information about lower and upper division classes, requirements for a specialty, and electives that you can choose from. Here's the trick: look at your major requirements and compare them with your general education requirements. There should be some overlap. Circle those that overlap and watch how your general

---

TIPS AND TRICKS

● Something you definitely need to know about your catalog: the requirements listed there in the year you enter school are the requirements you must meet through graduation. Meaning that if your school decides in your sophomore year of college to require all English majors to take three years of calculus, you don't have to do it!

You are bound by the requirements listed in the catalog that was in place the year you started school. So, you can argue that those three calculus classes weren't part of the original requirements for your major and therefore, they do not apply to you. While that's an extreme example (calm down English majors, you won't be required to have calculus at all), you should definitely keep this information in mind as academia is always in flux and requirements do change. You don't want to be told in your senior year that you're missing a required class that you didn't know about. It's happened, trust me.

In fact, it happened to a good friend of mine. When he started his freshman year, his school was considering adding a new requirement in humanities. By the time he was ready to graduate, the new humanities requirement was mandatory. Because my friend didn't know to look in his catalog and challenge the requirement, he ended up having to take a history class the fall semester after he graduated to fulfill the requirement. He wasn't pleased.

education requirements go from many to few. This is double counting your requirements, and we'll talk a little more about this in a moment.

Within that catalog, you'll see the class requirements and class electives for different majors (electives meaning choices you can make in one class over the other). Beneath that information you'll find course descriptions. Make sure that you pay particular attention to the prerequisites—classes that you have pass to take other classes. For example, if you're thinking of enrolling in a Calculus 2 class, you will find one of its prerequisites will be Calculus 1, which means you must take Calculus 1 before you can take Calculus 2. All of this information will be included in the course descriptions in the catalog.

» Double and Triple Counting Requirements

While harder to achieve in some schools than others, it is still possible that a few classes can knock out two, perhaps even three, general education requirements. For example, I took a world religions class that knocked out a humanities requirement, a religion requirement, and a multicultural requirement all with one class.

Look at your requirements sheet and highlight the classes that count in multiple areas. Take these classes if you're trying to get the most for your money and make room for other classes you might find more interesting. You might find those requirements interesting, you might not; the point is, you'll feel better if you're being smart and saving yourself almost nine units of coursework with one measly little course. You're not going to want to spend your time taking five classes if you can fulfill the same requirements with two. That's why it's so important for you to have a game plan and cross-reference requirements.

TIPS AND TRICKS

● If you happen to be at a community college, course descriptions will also tell you whether or not a class is transferable to a four-year institution. For example, if you're at a California Community College, the course description will read something like this:

BIOL B3A General Biology I[1]

5 units

Prerequisites: MATH BD or MATH B70 with a grade of 'C' or better and Reading—one level prior to transfer.

Description: Introductory course for students majoring in the biological sciences or pursuing pre-professional programs of study such as pre-medical, pre-pharmacy, pre-dentistry. Emphasizes scientific processes and methods of biology including original research. Explores unifying principles of micro- and macro-evolutionary processes, biodiversity of organisms, systematics, principles of ecology, animal behavior and plant biology. Field trips required.

Hours: 54 lecture, 108 laboratory

Transferable: UC, CSU and private colleges, IGETC 5.B; IGETC 5.C; CSU GE B.2; BC GE B.1-

Let's break this down. Naturally, you can see the course name and level, the number of units. Next are the prerequisites, meaning you'll need to have passed either of those math classes and reading level to register for this course. (If you have met your prerequisites but the online system won't let you register, contact a counselor. Sometimes glitches happen or you have to be approved for the course.) The description follows, telling you the basic outline of the course and all the knowledge you'll gain (this could be Christmas or torture, depending on whether you like the subject or not). The hours are the amount of time over the semester or quarter that you'll spend in lecture and lab (if the class has a lab).

Last but not least, since this is a description from a community college, you'll see that this course description makes it easy for students to check to see if it's transferable. This class is transferable to the University of California System, the California State University system, and most private colleges. Following those statements are the specific areas of concentration for the IGETC (a transfer agreement between the community college system and the University of California System), the CSU transfer agreement, and this particular college's requirements.

---

[1]A challenging but awesome class that actually exists from my old alma mater, Bakersfield College: www.bakersfieldcollege.edu.

Formulating a Game Plan

Imagine knowing exactly when you're going to be taking most of your classes in college. Imagine having alternatives, so if one class you want is full you can substitute a required class instead of filling your schedule with fluff classes just to make your unit requirement for being a full-time student.

Imagine having a plan.

Imagine having a backup plan.

Imagine being Batman.

Okay, I digress. The point is, you want to map out what you're going to want to take and when, starting with your final semester of your senior year and working backward. Start with the most advanced classes and look at their requirements. Then map out backward what you will have to take—and when—in order to get into those classes. This will save you tons of stress when registration pops up the week before finals or during that week when you have 9,813,545,678,928,739,648,293 exams, a 100,000-page paper to write, and your roommate just broke up with their significant other. Maybe not that dramatic, but if you map it out now, you won't have to do it at the last minute when registration surprises you every semester or quarter.

So put together a mock schedule starting from your senior thesis or capstone project, backward. Make sure you get all of your requirements in each semester (this is a great time to look online and see if your department has a guideline for what you should take in which semester). Once that's done, choose a few of your double- or triple-counting general education requirements; then, finally, put in a few classes you might enjoy.

Pay particular attention to required classes that are only offered in the Fall/Spring or Fall/Winter/Spring—these can really mess you up if you're not careful. Do you need to take French 3? When you see that it's only offered in the Spring, you'll know you need to make room in the Spring of your sophomore year to take it. Costume design? That class is only offered once every two years;

if you really want to fit that in during your college years, you need to plan for it carefully. Many classes like physics, foreign language, and math classes require you to take the first of the sequence in the fall, the second in the spring (or winter), and if you miss that fall class you're going to miss the spring class because of prerequisites, forcing you to wait an entire year to start the sequence. So make sure you're aware of classes that are labeled A or B, 1–3, or following the 101, 102 sequence.

See what I mean?

Don't get screwed over by the calendar. Know what you're going to need to take each semester. Which leads us to this:

» Have Alternatives

What happens if you can't get into that Calculus 3 class because it filled up before you could register? Can you put it off another year, or is it imperative you have it this spring in order to get into Physics 4 in the fall? Knowing this information can either make or break your schedule. If you REALLY need to get into that class now, make an appointment with a counselor or your academic adviser and explain the situation. In those cases, professors and counselors can sometimes make exceptions (especially if you're an upper-division student).

TIPS AND TRICKS

● When asking counselors or professors to admit you into a class that has a waitlist or that is full, remember that you will gain more from sugar than from vinegar, so to speak. Do your homework; be able to present a full business case as to why you need that class, and be respectful.

Don't walk in entitled or try to bully your way into things. Simply be professional and explain the situation. Show them your schedule plan and how not being in the class will throw things off. Most people will help you if you can prove to them why they should help you.

What if you can't get into your first choice of classes, but there's no emergency? Fine, just know which alternative requirement you can shove in there instead. Have that mapped out, as discussed above. I recommend heading into registration each semester with three options for alternative schedules; that way you have a plan A, B, and C.

If you're going to study abroad, be sure to fit that into your college-long calendar as well. You don't want to have to make a choice between going to Paris in the spring of your junior year or taking that last class of the physics sequence.

Alternatives to Classes at Your University

Like life, there are usually a lot of loopholes and options at college. Because some universities can't offer enough classes for the amount of students going there, students are becoming more and more creative when it comes to getting their coursework done. Here are a few alternatives when you find you can't score the class you desperately need.

» Take Classes at a Junior College

While this won't help you if you need a specialized upper-division class, it can be very useful when you can't get into that general education math or English class that you need. Taking classes at a junior college is usually permissible, as long as the course is what is considered "transferable." Meaning, your university will accept credit for it. Most state universities have nearby community colleges that feed into the university. In California, the entire community college system is built to feed into the University of California or California State University system. Because of this, most classes from California community colleges are transferable into those systems.

I would highly recommend that you speak with one of the counselors at your university to check out what you need to do to make this happen. Likely they will tell you to enroll as a student at that community college and enroll in the class. Once the class is done, you'll collect your official transcript from that community college, showing your grade, and deliver it to your university along with a few forms, so that they can amend your transcripts to show you've got credit for the class.

Note that your official transcripts have to be requested and sometimes sent directly to the university, so know where it should be sent when you request the transcript. There might be specific forms that your college wants, so do your homework before you enroll for the class—you'll thank yourself later.

You can also take classes online through some community colleges, nonprofit colleges, like National University, or other universities. While going to another university should be used as THE VERY LAST RESORT, taking an online class can be a great option—if your university will accept it as credit. Check with your counselor or adviser BEFORE you sign up to make sure you can get credit for the online course.

And know that online classes are not for everyone. It sounds simple—like playing a video game. But online courses take a lot of time and energy. Some students are great at them; some are not. Don't bank your grade point average on a half-dozen online classes until you're convinced you can be successful at them.

» Testing Out of Classes

You can also end up challenging classes and testing out of them, another alternative that can save you time and money—and this goes beyond your high school AP classes. If you're well-read on a subject or have taken a class like one being offered at your university, you can request to challenge the class and receive credit or move into a higher-level course. This procedure depends on the policies at your university, so make sure you know the details. If you're doing this to move ahead, make sure that you understand the course material so you don't get lost in the more advanced classes.

You can find out about challenging classes from your counselor or, generally, the head of that department. They will test your knowledge in the subject by examination or by asking you to include a paper or a project that proves your knowledge base—like I said, the process varies from university to university. It also varies as to how many classes you can challenge. These rules and guidelines can be found in your student handbook.

Be smart about challenging classes, too. Don't challenge everything in the hopes that something sticks; be strategic if you're going to do this and know what you're trying to gain.

Don't Go the Easy Route

Pick classes that challenge you. When you research your professors as you decide your schedule for the next semester, don't just go for the "easy" ones. Pick at least one class that you believe is going to challenge you. Talk to your peers; be strategic. You'll be amazed at what you'll learn.

There is one key to succeeding in your classes: participating. While it seems obvious and simple, you'll be surprised at the amount of students who *don't* participate. They sit back in their chair, looking bored, doing the bare minimum while pretending that they don't care about their grade (which you should, if you're paying $400+ per unit for the class and another $400 for your book—let's be real).

There are a few reasons why you might fail to participate in your classes.

1. You don't care. This probably means you don't care in general about your grade, the information in the class, or you hate the professor. Fair enough. But if you look at your classes and realize this is the case in all of your courses, then there's a problem. It's like dating. Maybe it's *you* and not the class.

2. You're scared out of your pants to talk in class. You would rather die than give an incorrect answer to a question, let alone in front of an entire group of people. You'll only talk in class if it's required, and even then you will do only the bare minimum.

The problem is that showing up isn't enough. You have to participate and speak up. You have to be part of that class, go to the professor's office hours, learn the material, and be ready to discuss it. Otherwise, you're just another cog in the machine: going into class, going out of class, doing homework, regurgitating information onto a test, moving forward, and forgetting said information. The pattern goes on and on.

Don't train yourself to do this in college. It'll bleed into the rest of your life, and someday, you'll wake up and realize that you missed most of it by just doing the bare minimum. You can't get ahead doing that, and you sure as heck can't do that in college and get your money's worth from your classes.

Participating in class, putting effort into your assignments, visiting the professor's office—all these are the keys to boosting your GPA—and enhancing your personal brand that you're carrying with you through college and beyond. It will also help you develop the kinds of relationships with professors that will open doors for you. More about that in the next chapter.

6

Professors

It's the first day of class, you've turned over a new leaf, and you're determined to make the most of your college years. Yet you're terrified. You look around and watch other students filing in. Finally, your professor arrives. This person could be the key to all of your future happiness—or just another instructor in a class about a subject you're not particularly jumping up and down to learn.

Either way, if you want to put college to work for you, you must start with your professors. Utilizing opportunities with your professors is the best way to get the most value out of your education.

Developing a good professional relationship with your professors is more than important. Not only to do your professors offer expert insight into the subject that you're studying, but they also have professional experience in the field, are constantly working on new projects and research, and have connections in the industry that you're thinking about entering into. Professors can also be great people, too. Some of my best professors became my best mentors later on in life. In fact, I still talk with some of them to this day.

How do you start developing that kind of relationship? I'm glad you asked. I've gathered this advice for you from my time teaching, acting as a teaching assistant, and being a college student in general. These are tried and tested methods that won't fail you.

Make Sure They Know Who You Are

This advice might seem terrifying to some of you, but you must make sure you're not completely anonymous to your professors. You want to be sure that they know your name, can identify you in the halls, realize that you have asked a few questions or led discussions in different topics, and recognize that you're an all-around good student who is there for the right reasons.

How do you make sure your professors know you? Ask questions in class about the material. Participate in class. Visit your professors during their office hours. I guarantee that if you're bordering between one grade and another, your professors will be much more likely to bump you up if they know you've been making an effort.

» Work Hard and Do Your Assignments

This should be obvious, but you're not going to score points or be the first choice for extra opportunities if you're not doing more than the bare minimum—or the bare minimum at all. Put effort into your assignments. Take everything a step further, and it will really make you shine.

TIPS AND TRICKS

● Most professors will post optional or recommended reading—meaning not required. While your time is probably limited, make an effort to try some of that recommended reading. Every now and then, you'll get an exam question drawn from this "optional reading" (I've had a few professors do this but they are few and far between).

But even if you're never tested over the material, the recommended reading can provide launching points for good conversation when you're visiting during office hours. And your professor will be impressed twice—that you came to office hours and that you've done the extra reading.

» Read Your Syllabus

I can't tell you how many times I was surprised by things listed in the syllabus of the course that were never mentioned in class. Papers, quizzes, tests, extra study materials. Your syllabus is your complete guide to your course, so make sure you read it carefully. Professors are not high school teachers—they aren't required to go over every piece of information they expect from you. This is where you can prove you're an adult and you're making an effort. Highlight important things in the syllabus and make changes as professors mention them (and date those changes) in class.

» Work Ahead and Do Your Reading Before the Next Class Session

If there's one important tip that I could give you in regard to class discussions, it's this: do the assigned reading one or two class sessions BEFORE the class session it's scheduled for in your syllabus. Chances are it's exactly what you'll be talking about in class, and your professor will recognize whether you've done the assigned reading when you start engaging in the discussion and asking questions.

This is what you're supposed to be doing in college! Alas, few people seem to do it. It's a great habit to form, as you'll always be a class or two ahead. Keep this habit and you'll thank yourself later.

» Go to Your Professor's Office Hours

This is one of the key moves you can make to help yourself out. You can ask questions here that you might not feel comfortable asking in class. Not only that, but this will give you a chance to talk to your professor. When I visited my professors, we'd engage in lengthy discussions about the topic (and sometimes off the topic), and I'd always come out of the meeting feeling like I was much more prepared for an exam or knowledgeable about a topic.

Be respectful and make an appointment or drop by during scheduled office hours. Always knock; always be respectful—it goes a long way. If you're meeting your professor because you're worried about a bad grade or you're having trouble in a certain area, make sure you don't shed tears or offer any sob stories. Professors get this all the time; it's no longer original. But if you're facing problems like health difficulties or family problems, explain the situation and ask the professor for suggestions on what to do. Go about it like an adult, and they'll treat you like one.

Ask For Help If You Need It

This might seem like the most obvious advice, but you'd be amazed at how many students don't ask for help when they need it. Most colleges and universities have a writing or tutoring center that is free for students. You can get help and editing suggestions for papers, tutoring in math and science classes, and even free workshops to help you develop better study habits or learn how to cite research correctly in your papers.

Your professors are there to help you, as are teaching assistants. There are literally dozens of people at your college or university to support you, so don't think you're all alone. Reach out to a friend if you're too shy to ask a professor for help. You're going to need your peers and your college resources during at least one of your classes, I guarantee you.

Make sure you get help and get it as early as possible. Don't wait until after the midterm to try to raise a failing grade to an A.

» Ask for Opportunities

Your professors are not mind readers. They don't know that you're hoping for that next research project or internship. They won't know that you're genuinely interested in the subject unless you participate in discussions or show an interest beyond poring over your books outside of class. Ask your professors about research opportunities in their fields. Ask about projects that they're working on. Show an interest in their studies and their topic of expertise and ask them questions.

Go to study groups, ask advanced questions about the topic at hand. Visit your professor's office hours more than once. This is really important. Your professor should know who you are and know that you're interested in the subject you're studying.

This comes with a caveat though, too: don't waste your professor's time! Go in for a genuine discussion or to get pointers on your last assignment or to ask about how you can improve on your next paper. Don't just show up and waste their time.

Don't hesitate to talk with the secretary or administrative assistants at the department office, either. You'll be amazed at how people can point you in the right direction if you simply ask. But you have to put in the effort; no one is going to do it for you.

Be Someone You Would Want to Help

Okay, this should be obvious, folks. If you haven't shown up for class for several weeks, don't show up on the last day and expect to get a grade bumped up. It's not going to happen. Use your common sense. If you want help, if you want to know more about this subject, if you want that research opportunity, be the kind of student you would want to help or to hire as a research assistant.

What's in a Title?

It is PARAMOUNT that you use the correct formal title when you address your professors—even (or especially) if you're just shooting them a quick email. Realize that you should be formal unless your professor has specifically asked you not to be.

Your professor spent a lot of time and effort to earn the degree or degrees that go with their titles. You show respect when you use that title, and many professors are sensitive to the implied disrespect when you DON'T. Since you're trying to show your professor that you're an awesome person, make sure you show the proper respect by knowing what title to use. Here's a guide:

- If your professor has a master's degree: *Professor* _____. For example, I have an MBA (master's of business administration), and you would call me Professor Clowes in the classroom.

- If your professor has a PhD (doctoral degree): *Dr.* _____. ALWAYS. For example, if your professor is William B. Smith, PhD, you would refer to him as Dr. Smith. Getting a PhD requires years of study—probably at least six to eight years of graduate school—and lots of hard work. They have earned the right to that title. Use it.

- If your professor has a medical degree: *Dr.* _____. This is a different type of degree, but he or she is also a Dr. Most people don't seem to have such a hard time remembering to use this one.

What if you don't know what kind of degree your instructor holds? When in doubt, go with Professor. Or take the time to find out—a little respect can go a long way.

Another important point: make sure that you ask for what you want in a polite and professional manner. Don't demand. Don't send emails to your professor the night before the big paper is due and expect to get a response. Never call professors by their first names unless they have asked you to.

Realize that your professor has a life outside of your classroom— they may have a few hundred students every semester, so don't be offended if they don't remember your name the first time you show up for office hours. Or when you show up two years later asking for a recommendation.

TIPS AND TRICKS

● Here's a list of common-sense actions you can take to develop relationships with your professors.

- Show up to class on time
- Add value to the discussion
- Do your homework
- Put effort into your assignments
- Know when assignments are due
- Take advantage of office hours
- Be polite and respectful
- Be someone you would want to help

Professors can be your best allies in your college years and long beyond if you take the time and effort to cultivate a good relationship. Treat them with respect and show enthusiasm for their subject matter, and most will be more than willing to help you navigate requirements for your major, help you find an internship, or write recommendations for graduate school, jobs, or scholarships.

{ Kat's Tales from the Real World } I learned early on that I *had* to participate if I wanted to get the most out of my classes and really get help from my professors. You're paying big bucks for these classes, and the only way to get your money's worth is to join the discussion. Plus, let's be honest, it really helps out your grades too.

I began learning this huge lesson on one of the first days of a philosophy class my freshman year of college. Me, a seventeen-year-old overachiever, arrived bright and bushy-tailed in my jeans and Converse sneakers, girly T-shirt, ponytail, and glasses. Seriously, I was a nerd straight out of a bad '80s movie. I took my usual preferred front-and-center seat, got out my book and notes, and waited.

My intelligent philosophy professor, a former Marine, entered and started class. We were reading Kant. He asked the class of forty what Kant was trying to say in the passage we'd read. When he received crickets, I raised my hand, knowing I had the answer. I knew I had the answer, mind you, because I'd taken notes on the homework the night before.

When he called on me, I gave a brief and brilliant summary of what Kant was demonstrating and discussing and the strengths in his argument. In my mind, it was the perfect, packaged, five-paragraph essay-type argument that I'd learned so well in high school.

The room was silent as the professor stared at me. Reaching out an arm as if to shake my hand, he shouted, "No!" His booming voice carried a trace of amusement at crushing my soul. "Next."

I sat there in shock. I had never, *never* been in that situation. All of my worst nightmares had come true and publicly! Fighting back tears, I took more notes as every single person he called upon failed to give him the answer he was looking for. Furious, he left class, telling us to complete our assignment before coming back to the next class meeting.

I pored over those eight pages like a woman on a mission. Actually, that's a bit of an understatement. I went through and outlined my argument again, highlighted a bunch of new stuff, and thought I understood it this time. When I arrived at class the following meeting, I felt as though I was on top of the world. My professor walked in; everyone grew silent, and he asked the same question again.

My hand shot up. This was my redeeming moment, and I wasn't going to waste it. When he nodded to me, I offered another argument for what Kant was saying, this one more elaborate and better planned than the first. When I finished, I looked up at him, knowing I'd nailed it. Nailed it.

"Wrong," he said again, voice booming across the class. "Next."

That time, my eyes grew glassy. Never having been one to cry in public, I choked back tears, even more mad and embarrassed, and angrily took notes. That was it, I thought. I was writing a bad evaluation. I was going to the dean, I was going to tell them exactly how this professor wasn't teaching but humiliating. By the end of class, however, my hot head and embarrassment had cooled somewhat. When class was over, I ignored my classmates' "man, I'm dropping this class" mutterings and decided to visit the professor in his office hours. Marching in, I waited for him to get settled and asked him exactly why he'd decided to not answer his own question while embarrassing everyone who tried.

He looked at my calmly—perhaps noticing my red face—and said he didn't understand why everyone expected him to do their work. "The point is for me not to do the assignment for you. It's for you to take the time to ponder what Kant was really asking. You're in a philosophy class. You have to think."

It made me pause. In his subtle way, he was challenging me. And in that moment, I decided I wasn't going to back down. I was getting an A in this class, plain pure and simple. It was happening. "Okay," I said. "What are your office hours?" I would spend every minute of his office hours going over this assignment if I had to.

"Come back tomorrow," was all he said.

I was back the next day with a new idea. This time he said I was on to something, but he wouldn't tell me what it was. This went on for the *entire* semester. We started having discussions during office hours, and I was getting more bold in class, challenging him if I thought his point wasn't clear or if I didn't agree with his assessment of the assigned reading. Let me tell you, sixteen weeks of this made my classmates want to run for the hills, and most of them did. A good half of the students who started the class dropped it before the end of the term.

With finals fast approaching, four of my classmates and I decided to meet at Starbucks to study. Offhandedly, during one of my office visits, I'd mentioned the study group to our professor and even given him the date and time, although it never occurred to me that he'd actually show up.

But he did.

The looks on our faces! These days we would probably have been made into some lame Internet meme as we watched him walk in, order a coffee, and plop down at our table. We were all silent for a moment before I took the initiative. "We decided to start with Kant," I explained, handing him my outline. "And work our way through Mills and Hume." I showed him on my notes what we were studying, the content, and the pattern we were following. He must have looked at it for thirty seconds, but I swear it seemed like hours.

"I'd take note of what she says," my professor said, taking a sip of his coffee. "I'd let her lead the study group, if I had such a thing."

My jaw dropped as he walked away, and I realized it was probably the first time he'd ever said anything to me that wasn't abrupt or downright mean.

Needless to say I passed the final with flying colors. Or, at least, I pulled an A- (which I celebrated, thank you, very much). When I went to his office hours after finals (because, heck, why not), I didn't fine the same grumpy professor who I had bothered the entire semester. He was actually in a good mood. "Learn anything?" he asked. I can still remember the smile on his face. It was unnerving.

I shrugged. "Yeah," I answered noncommittally. Because I was a teenager still, and man, I couldn't pretend to care about anything, could I? Besides, this guy had made me work my butt off in his class for a good grade.

"Good," he replied, turning back to his desk.

"You realize that there were only like fifteen brave souls left in your class of forty, right?" I asked, still bothered that I couldn't figure this guy out.

"I don't give out grades, and I don't think for other people," he said, turning to look at me. "If people can't handle that in my class and they don't want to participate in the discussion, they don't need to be taking my class. You're not in college to be spoon-fed information; you're here to learn. Part of philosophy is thinking. You spent your entire semester learning how to think. You in particular, because you and one of your friends were the only two who had the nerve to come to my office hours every day to discuss the material. You learned not to accept my answer as right or wrong. You learned to think into a bigger sphere and to put pieces together. You learned how to persist in the pursuit of knowledge. That's why you got an A in my class. You went above and beyond and did more than the minimum. You got your money's worth. Congratulations."

I took that lesson with me the rest of my four years of college and into graduate school. Best money I ever spent on a class.

7

Financial Aid

Ugh, the financial aid office. I know, I know. More forms and signatures and just a big chunk of time that you could be doing something else, something more productive, something—different. But since financial aid is probably a huge part of your university experience, we're going to discuss ways you can be more prepared and make this the least painful experience possible. Getting the details right can save you time and money—possibly a lot of money.

Learn everything you can about financial aid of all forms—grants, scholarships, loans, work study—and you're likely to succeed in school and be more prepared for whatever comes next. So let's figure out how to put the financial aid office to work for you.

Workshops

Did you know that most financial aid offices provide workshops for students? Workshops on grants, scholarships, budgeting, personal finance, and more. These workshops can be gold when it comes to your tuition, getting scholarships, learning how to budget, and how to interpret the rules and regulations regarding your student loans and paying them back.

Most colleges that I visit have workshops run by the financial aid office that are free for students. Make sure that you find out about them—go to the office and ask—and attend. You'll thank yourself.

In the business world, you'd have to pay top dollar to take a budgeting workshop or class. So take advantage of the fact that you've already paid for these. Use them.

Workshop schedules will be posted either in the office itself or announced in emails from the financial aid office. Most schools are also utilizing Twitter, Facebook, and sometimes even Instagram to inform students about events, meaning you might get wind of a new workshop on your trusty phone while you're scrolling mindlessly, waiting for class to start.

Want another secret? The school website is gold for this kind of information. Visit once in a while and see what's on the calendar.

> **TIPS AND TRICKS**
> ● If you go to the financial aid office at your school, the first person you're likely to encounter is the student working at the counter. They're probably working part-time, doing homework on the side when it's not busy, trying to gain valuable experience—and a paycheck.
>
> No matter what mood you're in—or they're in—remember that desk jobs are boring (unless you're super passionate about financial aid, and I have yet to meet a student worker who is). The person you're talking to would probably rather be doing a lot of things other than listening to demanding parents and students.
>
> Long story short? A smile goes a long way. A nice tone goes a long way. A compliment goes a long way. Just make it genuine. You'll get a lot more information by being nice to the bored student worker than by trying to be a bully.

Talking With Financial Aid Advisers

Your financial aid award probably was one of the top considerations when you chose your college. But you need to know that award is not set in stone for the next four years. If your financial status changes, if you're not sure how to afford college next year, or if you're wondering how you can apply for more scholarships, it's time to pay a visit to your financial aid advisers, who will be the best resource in these circumstances.

Financial aid advisers/counselors are there to help you. If you're facing significant changes in your financial situation, are looking for more scholarships, or want information on your student loans, schedule an appointment, bring your questions, and ask for advice. Financial aid advisers are a wealth of information who can give you answers specific to your situation and the school you're attending.

Aid Variables

It's important to remember that the outcome of your financial aid package might change over the next four years. You have to refile the Free Application for Federal Student Aid (FAFSA) EVERY YEAR. When January comes around, after you've recovered from the holidays, it's time to sit down and complete your financial aid paperwork. Get it done early. You don't have to have your taxes completed for the year that just finished in order to file your FAFSA, but you will have to update it once those most recent tax returns are completed.

A lot of grants (i.e., free money) and scholarships are issued on a first-come, first-served basis, and you'll benefit from turning in your paperwork early. Completing your FAFSA way before your university's deadline should be your goal. The deadlines vary from state to state and school to school, but March 2nd is the typical deadline in California, where I'm from. The FAFSA is available starting January 2 every year. Turn it in early!

The number used as the base for your financial aid award—your expected family contribution or EFC—could change if there are changes to your parents' income, number of household dependents, etc. Say you're the oldest and you started college first. But after a couple of years, your sister also starts college. Your expected family contribution actually will decrease because your sister is now in college too, and your parents deserve a bit of a break.

For example, let's say your EFC was $20,000 before your sister started school. After she starts, your EFC drops to $10,000. That drop could make a huge difference in the amount of need-based aid you qualify for. It pays to pay attention.

Your financial aid status will also change if you turn twenty-four or get married (congratulations!). While these events might not change the numbers in your bank account, they will change your financial aid status. At twenty-four you will no longer be claimed under your parent's tax returns, meaning if you're not making a whole lot of money, you will qualify for financial aid based on your OWN tax returns. The amount of aid you qualify for could significantly change—and probably for the better, if you're broke.

If you take a break, join the military, and then come back to school, you will see huge changes in what aid you qualify for and who is paying for your education. The GI bill, your possible veteran status, or being an active duty member could all affect your financial aid award.

The lesson here? Things change, and when they do, you could qualify for more money (or less) depending on the situation. So keep those financial aid advisers informed of your situation and make sure you get your paperwork in early. Which leads me to. . .

> **TIPS AND TRICKS**
> A few financial aid dates to remember:
> - Federal Application for Student Aid (FAFSA). Available Jan. 2nd most years. Submission deadlines vary by schools and states. In most California schools, it is due by March 2.
> - State grants. Applications are usually due the same time as the FAFSA; some states use the FAFSA as the qualifying documentation. Check in your state for more details.
> - University deadlines. Check your school's website and don't neglect any emails from your financial aid office.

» Get Your Paperwork In Early

Like I said, this is a first-come, first-served sort of thing. Schools have deadlines for when everything has to be turned in, and they've heard countless tear-jerking stories about why students missed the deadline. Don't be that guy. Keep up on important dates—most of which are posted on the financial aid website.

Scholarships at Your School

The alumni association is actually one of the best resources for scholarships, as past students who love the school provide money for current and future students that can be renewed each year. Contacting your alumni center is a great way to get started. Your financial aid counselors are going to know these scholarships, too, and can guide you to the application.

As when you were a senior in high school, the adage of "apply fast, apply early" still holds true. Keep track of scholarships that are offered at your school and department and their deadlines. You HAVE to apply to get scholarships. Let me repeat that: *you have to apply to get scholarships.*

You may have to write an essay, fill out an application, get recommendations, and turn everything in on time—all while keeping up with your studies. I know how hard this can be, but you need to make sure that you do it; otherwise, all of that free money that you could have gotten with scholarships won't be in your bank account. *Capiche?*

Scholarships Outside of Your School

There are other ways to get scholarships as well. You'll need to search for them. Use resources like www.fastweb.com to search for "scholarships for current college students." If you're in a specific major or have a specific career path, apply for scholarships in those areas. Network with community organizations in your hometown or your college town. Although they won't provide a full tuition ride, you can make a major dent in your tuition bills if you lump together a few smaller scholarships that most students won't take the time to apply for.

Start local and branch out from there. Write one main personal statement and edit it to answer the essay question for each scholarship. Keep a spreadsheet updated with upcoming scholarship dates, essay topics, etc. In fact, visit our website at www.mymarchconsulting.com/freebies to download a free spreadsheet to help you do just that.

This is going to require research and effort, no doubt. That doesn't mean that you have to spend hours upon hours researching. Set aside a half hour three days a week in the summer to do this. Make yourself some tea or grab a Mountain Dew and sit down at your laptop and do it. Turn off Twitter, Facebook, and Reddit and concentrate just on your scholarship search.

As a girl who has a small vacation home's worth of student loans? Go for the free money. Your future wallet will thank you.

• • • • •

Jodi Okun, former senior assistant director of financial aid, Occidental College, and founder of College Financial Aid Advisers has this advice:

The people who work in the financial aid office are very approachable. They're willing to answer any questions. They are the people who are in charge of looking at each student's financial aid application, whether it's the free application for federal student aid or if a particular school uses the CSS profile. They are in charge of analyzing the application. Each college has their own section of financial aid on the college website. So a great place for students to start is on the financial aid website. There are resources, such as a net price calculator, so that students can figure out how much it costs them to go there and also what resources they have. It also will give them deadlines for their application forms and how to contact their financial aid officer. So my best advice always is: contact your financial aid officer because they will be your friend for the next four years. Filling out your applications is the number one way to get started in applying for financial aid.

Financial aid is based on what the parents and the student earn or are eligible for that year, so if that changes, then maybe their financial aid will change. The student should always let the financial aid officer know what's happening in their family financially.

There are regulations, so college offices are awarding students based on regulations that are passed down from the government. ... Students who go to private school, if (the school uses) the CSS profile, (it) will use institutional technology to award students. So, sometimes (students) going to a college that uses institutional methodology might get a different award than students on federal methodology. So that's why awards might look different.

(Students) should compare their awards as continuing students, making sure that they're consistent throughout the year and everything stays the same. As incoming freshmen, they should ... (take) a look at what's really going to work for their family in the cost of college. ... You can look on the College Board website (for more information) on how to pay for college. They have a list of all the colleges that use the CSS profile in alphabetical order.

On Increasing Financial Aid Packages

Continuing students are pretty much receiving their financial aid right now, so continuing students get their letters after the incoming freshmen. They'll receive a package based on if they applied last year; it will be relatively the same based on if their parents brought in the same amount of money so their financial aid will be relatively the same. If they're looking for more scholarship grants, then it's a great idea for them to either go online, look for private opportunity for them to apply for scholarships, or even their own community is a great place to start. Whether it's a community organization or a church or a temple or maybe a local club. Those are always great places for them to start. They can also introduce themselves to the financial aid officer if they haven't done that and let them know they're interested. Maybe in their specific major they can look for foundation grants or other kinds of grants that can help them increase their award letter.

Grants at the School Level

There are different kinds of grants. Some officers have grants that they can award students ... based on their own criteria. ... Financial aid officers can lead them to a different kind of scholarship, or their department adviser can let them know about specific scholarships for their major.

Renewing Financial Aid Awards

Some colleges will only require the CSS profile freshman year. ... I always have (students) check application deadlines or how to apply, and that will tell them exactly what to do if they're continuing students if they need those other applications again. Now, as far as scholarships, some schools have scholarships forms, so if they were awarded a scholarship, they need to get it from the website that indicates what the student needs to do in order to keep that scholarship in good standings.

What to Take Advantage of While You're in College in Terms of Financial Aid

I think monitoring their finances and expenses; they're beginning to take ownership of those, so that when they graduate, it won't be the first time they're looking at their checking account or looking at their expenses or what's going out or what's coming in. While they're in college is a great place to get super comfortable, so when it is time that they graduate and are going into their career, this isn't the first time that they're looking at "what do I owe?", "what do I pay for?", and "how do I do it?"

Broke Student Discounts

Ahh, beautiful student status, when you have an .edu email address that you'll likely never have again. If you're on a budget, your student status can help you get a variet y of different discounts on things you never even dreamed of! Asking for a student discount is always a good idea, because you never know if you can save an extra dollar or two on something. While you probably know you can get a discount on movie tickets, here are more to consider as you make your way through college.

Amazon.com: Shipping costs on textbooks or other material through Amazon.com can get costly. Amazon Prime, an amazing way to get free shipping and free instant video streaming, among other perks, can be expensive for a student. However, if you are a student with an .edu email address, the annual price is slashed in half, for a yearly cost of around $49 dollars. You're welcome.

Microsoft Products: Although Google Docs may be slowly taking over, there's nothing worse right now than NOT having a version of Microsoft Office—particularly Microsoft Word on your computer. I learned in graduate school that I could get Microsoft programs for free or at a deep discount with my .edu email address. Software like Adobe, Quickbooks, and other often have student discounts as well. Check for student discounts through their main website too.

Travel: Wondering how you're going to get home for Christmas with the price of flights always climbing? And what about that all-important flight to start out your study abroad semester? Well, your student status may make cheaper tickets available to you and only you (okay, maybe to graduate students and faculty members too). Before you book tickets, check out http://www.studentuniverse.com/, which offers discounts particularly for students from major airlines, hotels, train tickets, cruises, etc. You also might want to check to see if your school has an agreement with any local travel agencies.

Apps: If you're using apps like Dropbox, you can often get extra storage if you're a student—for free. Dropbox in particular gives an extra 500MB of storage for free to students.

Traditional Discounts: Of course, you have your usual discounts with a student ID for fast food, movie tickets, haircuts, stationery, clothes, and the like. A number of local establishments around your university might offer specific discounts, such as 10% off of pizza or free breadsticks. Ask around and always have your student ID ready.

8

Learning Centers

You can get loads of assistance, such as tutoring, writing help, study tips and more at your university's learning centers—for free. It might have a different name at your school, such as the tutoring center or even just student services, and some schools advertise these services more than others. But virtually all colleges and universities have such help available, and most should at least mention it at orientation.

With services like these on campus, there really is no reason why you shouldn't be acing all your papers and tests. Okay, maybe a few reasons—like your class is so challenging you wonder whether a course in rocket science might be easier—but learning center services can help you vastly improve papers, grades, and learn a few things about yourself in the process.

Let's look at some ways you can put your college's learning centers, writing centers, tutoring centers—or whatever they're called at your school—to work for you.

Writing Centers

Granted, you can only take advantage of the help available in your university's writing center if you actually write your paper before the deadline—and I don't mean hours before the deadline. In high school, you're taught to develop flash cards and outlines and other such nonsense (or so you think at the time) before you're allowed to turn in a final draft of a paper. Outline, rough draft, then final draft.

In college, most professors only ask you to turn in a final draft, so most students simply skip all of the preparation steps their high school teachers so painstakingly taught them and go straight for the final draft—which usually ends up being the first rough draft. I'm guilty here too. However, be glad that you're not reading the first draft of this book.

When you're simply vomiting information on a page for a grade, the information tends to be disjointed and full of BS and fluff in order for you to meet your minimum page count. This is what you also learned in high school. The fluffier the better. It helped to keep your word count/page count up, and if you happened to prove a few points along the way while using your SAT vocabulary, you earned an A +.

College is different (though not by much). Your first writing class will attempt to bring you to a college level of writing where the fluff is replaced by actual arguments that prove a point. The four- and five-paragraph essays are long forgotten, replaced by term papers, research papers, and proper Modern Language Association (MLA) or American Psychological Association (APA) formatting.

It can all become more than confusing, even to a seasoned citation veteran. No longer are you judged solely on whether or not you could simply prove a point without misspelling something; now you're being graded on your argument, content, spelling, grammar, punctuation, citations, and how well your research meshes with class materials.

Your professor may not even assign a particular topic. I had a few who would tell us to simply take a topic from the class materials and write something about it. In fact, one of my communication professors had us observe people in a public space, record all that we witnessed, and then turn that into a research paper. Talk about something that can't be done the night before!

This is where the writing center comes in. Most universities have one staffed with folks who are experts in anything and everything to do with writing.

At some centers, you can make a one-on-one appointment with a tutor; at others, people are available during school hours in a workshop-type setting and you can just walk in and ask questions. Make sure that you check out your writing center's website or drop by to explore its hours, services, and how it works at your university—*before* you are in desperate need of help!

TIPS AND TRICKS
● The writing center can help you:
  • Narrow down a topic
  • Organize your thoughts into valid points
  • Consider which areas to research
  • Develop an outline and thesis statement
  • Develop a solid rough draft
  • Create and edit citations
  • Integrate your research with the topic
  • Check your spelling and grammar

Most writing centers offer a spot where you can write peacefully, which is a major advantage in my opinion. I was a student who wouldn't write a paper unless I forced myself to do it, and my dorm room was full of excuses not to do my homework. I needed to disconnect from the Internet and take my laptop to the writing center or the library to force myself to write my papers—mostly because there was nothing else to do.

TIPS AND TRICKS
● Plagiarism is an instant way to get into some major academic trouble in college. So you need to make sure that you know how to quote and document your sources in accepted ways.

The writing center often offers classes on proper citations. Tutors can always help you when you're not sure how to quote from sources and document research to avoid plagiarizing.

Seriously, this has become a *huge* issue, so don't mess around with it. Professors are relying on online programs like TurnItIn.com and other tools to check for plagiarists, so don't even consider going down that road.

Use the writing center. If your grade is bordering between pass and fail or even an A and a B, use the writing center to help you polish your writing. Even if you know your latest research paper is the best thing you've ever written, let someone else read it and see if it flows the way you want it to and whether you get your point across. It could make a huge difference in your grade.

But like I said, to do this, you're going to have to give yourself time to do it. Use the time management tricks we discussed in Chapter Three—especially the ones about creating your own deadlines—to your advantage.

Tutoring Centers

The tutoring center can truly be your best friend in those general education classes that you're required to take and pass even when you're not especially good in the subject. I utilized every bit of my tutoring center when it came to my math classes. Whereas you might have had to pay for a private tutor in high school, most colleges have some sort of free tutoring services on campus that you can utilize. Often, you can get one-on-one help at least one hour per week with either a student or graduate student who was successful in the subject that is bedeviling you or a general studies tutor the school has hired.

Take full advantage of this. Tutors can sometimes explain things in a manner that is different from your professors, and perhaps in a way that makes more sense to you. Also, many of the student tutors will have taken the class you're struggling with and can provide pointers about the subject matter, the professor, and how to get a better grade in the class. It's a way of networking and studying at the same time, really. You're asking people who've already taken the class for information on how to better learn the subject matter. It's a win-win.

Math Centers

Many universities will also have math tutoring centers in addition to general subject tutoring, making it available to you more often. Like the writing center or tutoring center, the math center—or whatever your university wants to call it—allows you to seek out help from either a learning facilitator or a knowledgeable student.

This kind of help can be vital if you're struggling in your math classes—or even if you need encouragement to do daily math assignments. You can schedule yourself to visit the math center directly after math class—or after your classes have ended for the day. Treat it as another class you have to go to, an obligation. Making yourself do this is a great way to guarantee you'll do your math homework each day, and you're also guaranteed to get help on those problems you're not sure how to complete.

Language Centers

The same advice goes for language centers. Many times, universities will have additional resources to help you master your foreign language classes—whether it's additional tapes, MP3s, videos, or tutors in Spanish, French, Latin, Japanese, or whatever language you may be studying. Tutors can help you practice your pronunciation and help you with your written grammar. If you're simply looking for additional practice, they can provide that too.

Specialty Help

The help doesn't stop with the ones I've named so far! Different departments within your university will often have study sessions, clubs, and other ways for you to prepare for classes. Keep your eyes open in the hallways for posters and fliers, check your email for announcements, and keep your ears open in class for ways you can find additional study help.

9

Learning Differences

Too many students don't realize that colleges offer a great deal of support for students with learning differences. The support can vary depending on the university and program, but you should find some help at every school based on U.S. legal requirements.

If you have been diagnosed with dyslexia, ADHD, or another such learning difference, the school can make accommodations to help you. You may be given additional time to take tests, help taking notes, or other support based on your particular situation.

The most important thing to remember is that you must be an advocate for yourself! No one is going to know how to help you if you don't tell them that you need help. There's nothing embarrassing about asking for help, nor should you be self-conscious at all. If you're not sure what your university offers, make an appointment with the counseling center and ask there first. They can refer you to the program at the university or give you more information about the policy and services.

{ Kat's Tales from the Real World } One of the most rewarding jobs I had on campus was a simple one that required little extra work on my part and yet made a huge difference in the life of another student and helped me form a friendship that I'll never forget. A fellow communication major, Kevin, had been involved in a horrific car accident in high school that left him paralyzed from the neck down. He came to class each day with his specialized wheelchair, complete with a breathing machine much like the one used by the late actor Christopher Reeves.

Kevin had the best sense of humor and was hard to oppose in a debate because his arguments were better and more logical than mine were back then. We had most of our classes together, since this was a smaller liberal arts school, and after the first quarter, he approached me about taking class notes for him, which I was happy to do. I would take notes on a specialized carbon paper that would create two copies, turn them into the learning center that day, and they'd be typed up for him within hours.

While I wasn't paid for this job, it benefited us both. Naturally he received the notes from class, which were a benefit to him, but I also took better notes because of I knew he would be seeing them. We became closer, even when other students weren't exactly sure how to act around him.

Kevin is a great example of someone who advocated for himself. He approached me to take notes for him, which helped him achieve what had seemed impossible after his car accident: he graduated from college with the rest of our class.

Comprehensive Program

Universities that have a large program catering to learning differences usually employ a director, counselors, and specialists to help provide the support you need to be successful. Sometimes these programs are included in your tuition and regular school fees, and sometimes there are extra fees; you will have to ask about that. Schools often have programs designed to help you transition into college either during the summer before classes start or in the fall of your freshman year.

Because the services offered in these programs vary so widely between schools, it's hard to say exactly what you will get at your school. But programs built for students with learning differences often have drop-in hours or allow you to set up weekly meetings. The programs could also include workshops and structured hourly sessions with other students to help you focus on where you need assistance.

All of the programs geared toward students with learning differences will help you create strategies to be more successful in all your classes. These strategies can revolve around time management, structured study time, counseling, or communicating your needs with your professors. Many times you'll meet with a counselor, a specialist who helps with your particular learning challenge, who might act as an advocate or liaison between you and the faculty.

Some of these programs are run as a specialized institute or program within the university and require their own admissions process. But all are designed to be extremely supportive and help with a variety of learning differences.

Robust Services

Other universities—particularly smaller ones—may not have a comprehensive program but do provide robust services, meaning that they have accommodations beyond the basics, employing a few staff members to make the accommodations process easier. They don't offer workshops or services but will provide help you if you need additional test-taking time, someone to help you take notes, or other such accommodations similar to ones you received at the high school level. These types of programs are designed for you if you're pretty independent and simply need a little support advocating for the services you need.

You will need to have a documented disability in order to access these services, and the services that will be offered you will be based on that documentation. If you need these types of services, ask for them! And then use them!

Basic Services

The programs in some schools are not robust by any means but they do meet the minimum standards required by law. These types of programs are best if you know you need only a little assistance and are used to advocating for yourself so that you simply need someone to approve the process. In a support program like this, you'll be working mostly to negotiate accommodations with your professors.

If you need help beyond this level, you might want to look at colleges with more services and programs to help you.

Again, I can't emphasize enough that self-advocacy is key here. If you need accommodations, ask! Take advantage of what's offered to you! That's the only way you'll be able to put all of your college's resources to work for you! If you fail to get the services you deserve, it will affect you, and no one else.

Typical Accommodations

Here's a list of some accommodations that your university might offer students who have documented learning differences.[1]

- Alternative test-taking formats
- Note-taking services
- Foreign language requirement substitution or exemption
- Finals adjustment to prevent multiple finals (or exams in general) in one day
- Priority registration
- Classes with professors who are more accommodating to your style of learning
- Coaching or counseling to help improve your time management, organization, and assignment completion
- Text-reading software and/or audiobooks for textbooks
- Recordings of lectures
- Reduced course loads

[1] This list was suggested by Rachel Sobel, of College Possibilities, at the 2013 Summer Training Institute of the Independent Educational Consultants Association (IECA).

10

Counseling and Medical Centers

When you hear the words "counseling center," the first thing that might come to your mind is a bunch of offices, some motivational posters, and a few schedule changes. But the counseling center in college is much different from what it is in high school.

College counselors offer a variety of services, including personal counseling, group counseling, crisis management, and more. There are different types of counselors, different ways to utilize counselors and their advice, and a variety of services that college counselors offer that you should learn about so you're ready to put them to work for you.

I confess I didn't have much use for my counselors in community college and only met with my counselor once while at Santa Clara. Fiercely independent, I thought I had everything figured out, and when I needed help, I didn't know it was available to me. I thought that a counselor in college would be like my high school counselor, who managed my schedule changes and arranged things with a specialist after my car accident. In fact, Santa Clara's counselors could have helped me cope with the depression that continued to linger into my college years because of my car accident, deal with the issues that came from being two years younger than most of the students in my class, and adjust to life as a young university student.

I wish I would have known that there were different types of counseling in college. When I needed emotional help, I didn't realize it was available. I'd also convinced myself that what I was feeling was normal or that I was alone in the problem I faced. And I felt that talking to someone would make me seem like I was crazy.

This is entirely not true.

In fact, not seeking out help for my own personal issues in college allowed them to stick around and hurt me in my adult years. Don't be like me! Being aware of the help you can get and seeking out someone to talk to is only going to benefit you.

Most counselors in college counseling centers are licensed psychologists, and your visits there will be confidential.

If you're overwhelmed your freshman year, don't hesitate to make an appointment. If you're feeling depressed, make an appointment. If you're

Different Types of Counselors

In high school, you probably had one type of counselor at school who handled everything from schedule changes to emotional meltdowns. In college, there are several types of counselors; some handle your academic needs while others can take care of more personal needs.

Academic counselors/advisers. These are the advisers who are strictly there for your academic needs, meaning declaring a major, choosing courses, double-checking your prerequisites, and planning your schedule. Depending on your college, they may be found in your department or college or in a division of student services.

Academic advisers can help you plan out your course study, take full advantage of the coursework for your major, or answer general questions. They can also help you change majors, declare a minor, or double major. They help you with everything academic, really. I would highly advise that you meet with your academic adviser at least once a semester or quarter just to check in, make sure you're on the right track, and ask any questions that have popped up since your last meeting.

Counseling Center counselors. The other type of counselors on campus are typically licensed counselors, psychologists, or psychiatrists who can help you with any mental or emotional issues you might have. They may be able to prescribe medication or help you find a provider who can write a prescription if they think you need it.

having trouble adjusting or if you're fighting with your roommate, make an appointment.

Mental Health Is Important

We often spend a lot of time worrying about the health of our bodies, making sure to eat right and working out. However, we may spend little time making sure that we're taking care of ourselves mentally, especially in college. But it's not unusual for students to need some help making mental tune-ups in college.

» Yours

Not only have you gone through a major change just in attending, but now everything is a little different. You're away from home, you're living on your own (or with a roommate), you're making new friends, you're adjusting to a new way of learning, and you're trying to find time for yourself too. Meet with a counselor from time to time in a sort of tune-up for your mind. There's no shame in it. No one has everything figured out—even if they think they do. Don't let the pressure build up.

TIPS AND TRICKS

The counseling website for the University of Texas, Dallas, says its counseling services can help if you're having thoughts like these:
- "I often feel sad and don't know why."
- "My mind goes blank during tests."
- "It's hard for me to talk to people."
- "My partner just left me."
- "I have no confidence in myself."
- "I don't know if college is for me."
- "I can't get my work done on time."
- "My partner is pressuring me to have sex."
- "I'm having a hard time juggling work, school, and family."
- "I'm having trouble trusting my partner."
- "I have a friend who drinks too much."
- "My partner is hitting me."
- "I worry too much."
- "I can't decide whether to stay or leave the relationship I'm in."
- "I'm having panic attacks and don't know what to do."

» Your Friends'

In addition to monitoring your own mental health, you should also look out for the mental health of your friends in college. Encourage them to use counseling services too. Be accountable to each other for a mental tune-up here and there. If you're noticing dramatic changes in their mood or behavior or you fear that they might harm themselves, speak up. Sometimes they can't speak up for themselves when they need help.

There are tools out there available to you and your classmates. Since it's hard for anyone to admit that they need help or want help when they get depressed, anxious, or are experiencing any number of feelings that cause behavior or thoughts to change, look out for one another. Look out for your friends and roommates. Don't just assume that someone is okay.

Crisis Management

Colleges and universities are paying more and attention to crisis services these days, although many students may not know about them. Suicide prevention, sexual-assault counseling, and other such services are often available to you too.

Temple University, for example, offers the following information on its counseling website related to sexual assault: "Temple students who have experienced sexual assault, partner violence, childhood sexual abuse, sexual harassment, and/or stalking. Our mission is to link students to additional resources for ongoing support and assist in establishing a sense of safety for those who are survivors of violence, to provide a space for them to find their voice, tell their story and feel heard, and to restore their connection to themselves and their community."

Most counseling departments will also offer services for LGBQT students to help them strengthen their identity and give support.

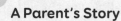

A Parent's Story

Although I think most college counseling centers offer wonderful services, I want to remind you that, sometimes, the help you need might not be on campus. If you're not connecting with a counselor at school, ask for therapy recommendations in the area and seek help there.

Keep your friends and roommates in mind too, and encourage them to look for help until they find what they need. The following story is an example of a time the college counseling office wasn't providing what a particular student needed. If only one of his friends had recommended he get help from the community or recognized that his falling grades, mood changes, and other indicators meant he was having a rough time.

My son was a senior in college and sought help through the counseling center at his university. After a very rough semester with a lot of changes, including a bad break-up, he started meeting with a counselor to discuss his concerns and depression. During one of those meetings, he had expressed that he was feeling suicidal. Unfortunately, the counseling center—either because he didn't use the right words or they didn't hear him correctly—didn't do anything to help him and didn't report that he was suicidal, or leaning toward those tendencies, so he could get immediate help. The following Monday, he attempted suicide and was taken to the local medical center to be held for his own protection. Because he was hospitalized, he has a involuntary psychiatric hold (code 5150) on his medical record, which could affect his future rights, job prospects, etc. Had the counseling center intervened when he started using suicidal language, the entire situation could have been avoided.

I wanted to share this story because sometimes, there are signs out there that students need help and as a parent a few cities away, I wasn't aware of how much he needed help. I assumed that he was getting the support he needed. After help with a professional in town, he was able to return the next semester, but now he has a mark on his record, and he has an entire semester lost.

—Anonymous concerned and loving parent, CA

This story might be a bit of a downer, and you're probably wondering, "Kat, why are you telling me about counseling services while giving me an example of a time when counseling services failed a student?" Because sometimes, everything you need might *not* be readily available. Sometimes you have to question services, professors, and what you're learning. Look out for one another and don't be afraid to speak up if you don't think you're getting what you need. This lesson could be one of the most valuable you will ever learn!

● ● ● ● ●

The University Medical Center

Ah, the university medical center, how I loved you. As a hypochondriac, I swore every year I had the flu, or whatever ailment was going around campus. You may be just the opposite, never thinking about your medical center except as a place you pass on the way to the gym. But most campus medical centers offer more than you might think, and learning how to use them effectively can help you stay healthy enough to excel in school and beyond.

» Basic Health Care

That health fee you're paying with your tuition is nothing to snivel at. Most universities are now providing some type of insurance for their students, and at the very base level, will give you a few free visits to the university health center. Check with your university to see if they offer insurance. Some do and cover emergency care; others do not. If they do, you might need to fill out some more paperwork, so it pays to investigate. Most of this information can be found on your university website or through the center itself.

Some facilities are more extensive than others, but you should visit even if yours seems limited. Your university health center is great if you think you might have a sinus infection, want to get your flu shot before finals season, or are having any basic medical problems. Some have doctors on campus; others have a trained nurse who can refer you to doctors or health facilities in the area.

Your university health center should be able to help if you have a cold, cough, or the flu, provide basic antibiotics, and administer immunizations.

» Personal Care

Many universities offer specific assistance to men and women, depending on what's needed. Physicals, yearly check ups, and the like may be offered, along with STD testing. Although it depends on your university, your medical center might be able to assist with birth control.

If you've run out of a medication prescribed by your primary care doctor, some university medical centers can help you renew your prescription or fill your prescription if you're unable to have it shipped to you. This applies to allergy and asthma medications. If you're going to a school in an area that has different grasses and trees, you might develop new allergy symptoms. Go to your health center; they probably know all about it.

Other Health-Related Services

Universities are now realizing the importance of wellness for their students, and many have developed nutrition assistance for students, including nutrition classes to help students make healthier choices in their daily diet. Since I lived off of the vending machine in college around finals each quarter, I probably needed this service the most.

If you're planning on traveling abroad, your university health center might be able to help you with vaccinations and other medical awareness topics that will come up depending on the country that you will be visiting. Again, if you're going to be studying abroad and will need a few months' supply of your medication, the health center may be able to help you with that.

Some universities also offer emergency services, meaning you wouldn't have to go to your local emergency room in the community if you need stitches or other injury care. Again, check out your university health center's website and see what it covers, how to make appointments, and what's included in your health fee. You might not only save yourself money in a future emergency, but you'll know what to do if the flu creeps up on you during the winter term.

11

Summers

Summer! **The time of year** when you can get caught up on your sleep, tan, and have fun with your friends. Right? Wrong, unfortunately.

In this day and age, gone are the summers you see in the old '60s beach movies like *Beach Blanket Bingo*. If you want to do really well in college *and* land an amazing job after graduation, you're going to have to put in some extra work—year-round.

But if you put your summers to work the smart way, it doesn't have to feel like work for you. Summers can be a great time to undertake internships, sign up for specialty work, and get temporary full-time jobs. Or you could use your summers to study abroad, participate in research programs through the university, or take a few summer school classes to get a leg up on coursework and certifications.

Study Abroad

Perhaps the best way to travel and gain college credit at the same time, study-abroad programs can give you an incredible view of the world and make you aware of other cultures and how people live in different areas of the world. Studying abroad is almost guaranteed to broaden your horizons and open your eyes to a completely different way of looking at the world, and it doesn't have to cost an additional arm and a leg.

In fact, most study-abroad programs are the same as regular university tuition, with a few extra fees, and you can receive credit for the classes that you complete abroad. Naturally, you're going to want to check with your school to see how it handles study-abroad programs, but the cost is usually akin to taking summer school classes.

I don't want you to think of studying abroad as a vacation. The point is to broaden your perspective, to experience a culture outside of your own, and perhaps see how things are done differently in other parts of the world. Take a language class, step outside of your comfort zone (safely), and try something new. You'll be amazed at what you can find out.

As the world becomes more globalized, having experience in another country can help you gain better career opportunities, especially if the career you're vying for involves travel or interaction with other cultures. Learning a new language and being able to practice it in another country can be rewarding not only for yourself, but—if continued and practiced—can help you gain that international opportunity that you were dreaming of at Company X. Networking and building friends in other countries can always help in future career moves, too.

Plus, you might not get a chance like this again. While we all say we want to travel some day, that becomes harder and harder as you gain employment, a mortgage, a family, etc. Consider taking that study-abroad opportunity when you can, even if it's just for one summer.

TIPS AND TRICKS

● Studying abroad doesn't mean you're going to be simply traveling around on vacation. You'll be taking some sort of classes at a local university or with the professor who comes with you on your trip.

Taking classes though another university can be a great way to study something specific that your university doesn't offer. For example, if your passion is working with excavations in Ireland or researching the early Irish people, taking an archeology class or history class at the University of Dublin would probably be a dream come true.

With the proliferation of study-abroad and student exchange programs, this is entirely possible, and for much the same price as your regular tuition (although airfare might be up to you).

College Exchange Programs

Another option that might be available to you would be the chance to take classes at another university through a university exchange program. If there are specialty classes or areas of study that your university doesn't offer but an affiliated university does, you can apply through the exchange program to take those classes and have them count toward your degree—depending on your school.

Even if you never considered applying for universities like MIT or Stanford, you might be able to take classes there based on a domestic exchange program through your university. Usually this program is handled through the same department that handles study-abroad programs, so I suggest looking there first for guidance.

This kind of program could help you not only get the credits you need to graduate, it could also help in your upcoming job search. If you're looking at a particular area of the country or considering a particular company, being at a local college wouldn't be a bad idea in terms of networking opportunities. Your dream company might have programs or recruiting events there at the college or might offer workshops or internships for you to explore. It's worth looking into.

Certifications

Professions that call for certifications in certain specialty areas can be frustrating when you're applying for jobs after college, and requirements for odd certifications here and there can put stall your career path progression if you're not aware of them ahead of time. But if you do your prep work while researching different career paths, you should be able to earn these certifications while you're in school. Summer, naturally, is a great time to do this.

While certifications don't have to be completed at your university, your school might offer certification classes either to undergraduates in the summer or through university extension programs offered to post graduates to help them keep up on industry standards, certifications, and other career-related specialties. While it's important to know about these programs after college, you may also be able to gain access to them online or in person while you're still in school.

For example, let's say you're an engineering student and you notice you're going to need AutoCAD certification or experience to start your career in the area that interests you most. Currently, your university offers an introduction course in AutoCAD but nothing more for undergraduates. However, your university extension program does offer certification for AutoCAD. Use your summer to invest in that certification.

Don't quit if you can't find the program you need right away— just keep looking for another avenue. Remember, you're going to have to advocate for yourself and your career. No one else will. And you're not going to have long summer breaks in the future when you will have the time to tackle a new certification program, so put those summers to work for you while you can!

TIPS AND TRICKS

● Having certifications in hand will be another way to stand out from the other graduates in your field when it comes time to start applying for jobs.

If your university doesn't have an extension program, look to your local community college or other university extension programs for the certification you need. Or talk to the head of your department about starting a certification program or ask how the university might help you achieve that certification.

Ask your career center, your professors, your admissions counselors. The worst they can say is no, the best they can say is yes. Pursue it, even if they say it's impossible. Formulate a business case about how offering a particular certification would help you as a student and would also help future students and make the university look better.

PART **3**

Succeed *After* College

College should not be *all* about getting a job when you get out. I don't want you to spend so much time fretting about your future that you forget to enjoy your college experience! Don't forget to take a few courses just because they look interesting or because you've heard the professor is fascinating.

But don't forget your future either. I don't want you to walk across the stage, pick up your college diploma, and think, "Now what?" And you won't—if you put your college to work for you while you're still a student.

If you make the most of your college years, you'll find ways to meet alumni, participate in special programs, find out what people really do at their job all day, work as an intern or as a volunteer, and even attend a career-building conference or competition. You should be able to find all these types of resources at your college or university, and in this section of the book, I'm going to help you figure out how you can employ them to get a head start on a great career or graduate program.

No matter what you think you want to do when you graduate— and especially if you don't have any idea—your first stop should be the career center, so let's head there now.

12

The Career Center

The career center. That ominous, hidden department somewhere in the depths of your university where you occasionally hear about a workshop or a job posting. My career center might as well have not existed when I went to college. I knew little about what it could do for me, didn't know what to ask, and never put it to work for me in the ways I could have to get internships, jobs, and opportunities to get ahead in my career.

All I knew about my career center, at the time, was that I could use it to find jobs on campus. Literally, that's all I used it for, which is embarrassing! I missed so many workshops and job fairs that could have helped me get ahead before I graduated—maybe even set me up for a cushy job in the Silicon Valley, regardless of the economy at the time.

You HAVE to put your career center to work for you. Well-established professionals hire coaches all the time to do what most career centers do for free. Think about that. You're already paying for the services that the career center offers, so take full advantage of them!

Make it a point to visit this area of campus and ask questions. You'll be amazed at the wealth of information available to you. Here's a rundown of some of the services offered in most college career centers.

List of Job Opportunities

Yes, this one should be obvious, but it wasn't to my undergrad self. The career center will announce job opportunities it's aware of for current college students and future graduates. It's in your university's best interest to make sure that you're successful after college—they want to brag about how amazing you are so they can entice other students to come to the university to be just like you. So all schools will look to actively partner with employers to present job opportunities to students.

For engineering majors, this might mean opportunities with companies like Lockheed Martin, Boeing, local engineering companies, big utilities, oil companies, and the like. For business majors, it might be financial companies, accounting firms, consultants, computer companies, or start-ups. You get the idea.

If you're a humanities major, you're going to have a little bit of a struggle because opportunities aren't as clear-cut for you. You're going to be responsible to create your own opportunities by researching your field extensively and talking to people who have careers that you're interested in. Although it may be a bit harder to match humanities students to ready-made positions, the career center will help you in every it can. Be prepared for this, and be ready to take advantage of every bit of help you can get.

The career center usually has some sort of email list you can sign up for or server you can log into every day that will show new job opportunities that match your search criteria.

Résumé Help

Do you know how to put together a proper résumé? Your career center (and yes, I mean yours—I have yet to find a career center that doesn't do this), provides some sort of workshop, guideline, or private coaching about how to put together a résumé.

I suggest drafting one and then making an appointment with one of the career counselors in your career center to discuss its strengths and weaknesses. Start this your freshman year and go back yearly, adding items as you progress through college. This will help you identify the holes in your résumé and give you four years to work on filling them.

If you start drafting your résumé a month before graduation, you're already working against yourself. However, if you do find yourself in that situation, go get help from your career center.

There's a lot more information in Chapter 22 about creating a winning résumé. You can turn there before you visit the career center.

Workshops

Most college career centers sponsor workshops every semester/ quarter/ month on a variety of topics geared to helping you succeed in your career (of course). Much like your financial aid office will help you with personal finance or budgeting, career center workshops will help you prepare for interviews, learn how to apply for internships, and give you tips on how to narrow your job search.

And you never know, you might meet some like-minded, forward-thinking fellow students who can help you brainstorm about your future or provide invaluable tips. If you're a pre-med student going to a pre-med career workshop, other pre-med students might have some insight into areas you haven't explored yet. Or maybe you can share tips you've just picked up about applying for a particular school.

TIPS AND TRICKS

● Campus career centers generally offer a wide range of workshops every year. With one cursory Google search for career center workshops at a university, 2014, I came up with the following at UC Berkeley and Indiana State:

- Fundamentals of Résumé Writing
- How to Work a Career Fair
- Writing Effective Cover Letters
- Careers from Chaos
- Pre-Med Career Lounge

There's really no excuse not to go to these free events. Yes, the weekly workshops might be offered during your one evening class or your hours at your library job one semester, but I doubt that's going to happen throughout your four years. But if you just can't get to the workshops, remember that you can always reach out to the career counselors or the staff at the center to schedule a private, one-on-one appointment.

Career Counselors

Your career center has counselors who work for you! You can schedule one-on-one appointments to discuss declaring a major, to discover career and internship opportunities, and to get guidance on your next step. This is already offered by your university, so use it!

Most career counselors can help you no matter where you are in the process: first-semester freshman or about-to-graduate senior. They can help you discover majors, point you to programs to enhance your skills, administer assessments, and help you further identify your aptitudes, values, and passions—like the ones you looked at in Section 1 of this book. Take the results from those exercises into your career counselor and discuss them with him or her to get another perspective.

Developing a good relationship with your career counselors might help you in several ways in the long run. If they're aware of what you're looking for, your experience, and your goals, they can let you know of new opportunities that come along as you progress through college. If a new job opportunity surfaces or a new program is developed, your counselor might email you or give you a call to let you know.

When you first meet with a counselor, explain where you are in the process and what you hope to get out of the meeting. Be clear about what you want and be respectful. Career counselors can help you a lot more if you're clear about your goals.

College isn't about having it "all figured out." We are socialized and programmed to think that we have to know exactly what we are going to do from the time we leave high school until we retire. But that's not how it works.

College is your ticket. When I majored in psychology and communication, I thought it was taking me to law school. I thought that I had it all figured out. I grabbed my ticket, and then it took me into a sales career that I thought would pay for law school.

Law school never happened. Instead, I advanced very quickly
from a sales position to president of a multimillion dollar company
by the time I was twenty-seven years old. And then later,
that ticket helped me get a master's degree in psychology.
Eventually, that ticket helped me start my own business.

College is a first step to the rest of your life. It's the ticket that will
open a door that will take you to your next step, which could be a job,
starting your own business, graduate school, or even meeting the love of
your life. Your job is to grab that ticket and know that it's the perfect
next step, even if you don't have it all figured out yet.

–Ursula Mentjes, best-selling author of
Selling with Intention and founder of Sales Coach Now

Assessments

You can pay a lot for career and personality assessments later. But
most college career centers offer them for free or for a small fee.
Take full advantage of this, and put these resources to work for
you. There are tons of assessments out there that can help you get
a better idea of your skills and aptitudes, and that can help you
figure out what you want to do, how to talk about yourself in ways
that will make your career advancement easier, and help you mesh
with others in the workforce. Here's a little bit about some of the
assessments you might find in your career center.

» The Myers-Briggs

We've covered the Myers-Briggs in Chapter 2. But if you can take a
full version of this assessment through your career center, go for it.
Results will tell you a lot about your personality, how you process
information, and where your strengths are. The full Myers-Briggs
assessment will also tell you what career paths are most and least
enjoyed by your personality type.

» StrengthsFinder by Gallup

The StrengthsFinder assessment focuses on what you're really
good at doing and how you can further strengthen those skills. It's

an easy exercise that doesn't require a lot of thought but provides quick insight into your natural strengths.

» True Colors Career Assessment

The True Colors system categorizes you into four different color types by your personality, mentality, and attitude. Based on how you answer the questions, you'll be assigned a primary and secondary color related to four categories of a temperament scale created by David Keirsey. The four categories are the idealist (blue), the rational (green), the guardian (yellow), or the artist (orange). You'll be assigned a primary and secondary color that best relates to you.

These are only a few examples of the thousands of personality and career assessments out there, so visit your career center and see which assessments it offers. No matter what they offer, register to take them. You'll always come out ahead in the long run by knowing more about yourself.

Internships

Your career center makes an active attempt to match students with internships, which are discussed in much more detail in Chapter 22. Whether internships are for college credit or money, the career center (along with your professors) can help open the gate to the massive world of internships.

Internships are a great way to get your feet wet without actually joining a company. They're also a great way for you to gain experience to list on your résumé and meet people in a given field. Start your search for internships in the career center. And read Chapter 22 to learn more about how to get internships and how to make the most of them when you do.

Job Fairs

Your campus career center holds the keys to help you make the most of the often overwhelming job fair. Although stressful, job fairs can help you in a variety of ways beyond just getting a job.

They're an opportunity to learn more about various industries and see which careers relate to those industries. You can also find out what employers are looking for in current graduates so that you can better prepare for your senior year.

Job fairs are also a great way to network with other career-seeking students, get interview tips, and get the most out of the workshops and seminars your career center might be offering on that day. Last but not least, job fairs give you a great opportunity to practice your professional networking skills, get used to talking about yourself, ask questions about a company, and meet hiring managers for that important first career.

Learn more about how to put job fairs to work for you in Chapter 20. And be sure to visit every job fair your career center holds— even when you're a freshman.

Put your career center to work for you while you're in school, and you will be well on your way to a great career by the time you cross the stage to pick up your diploma.

13

Alumni

First, let's talk about using your alumni network while you're an undergrad, something I did not do. Thankfully, I didn't lose out on this opportunity completely as I can still use my alumni network even though it's been more than a decade since I graduated. But I want you to put this valuable resource to work much earlier than I did.

What exactly do I mean by alumni? According to *Merriam-Webster*, an *alumnus* is "one that has attended or has graduated from a particular school, college, or university." *Alumni* are more than one *alumnus*.

The alumni office at your university keeps track (or attempts to keep track) of every person who has graduated or attended your institution. For example, I graduated from Santa Clara University, meaning that I am a Santa Clara University alumna (a female alumnus). Santa Clara considers anyone who attends there for at least one year as an undergrad to be part of the alumni association (this might differ from school to school). I receive emails and mail—usually in the form of a magazine—from the university, keeping me in the loop of what the university and other alumni are doing. They might also call once in a while and ask for a donation for a scholarship or some new project.

I am also an alumna from Mount Saint Mary's University in Los Angeles, where I attended as a graduate student as a part of the MBA alumni association and the school's general association.

Which equates to more magazines and funding requests (and possible contacts—more on that later).

The nice thing is that, once you're in the alumni club, no one can ever take that away from you. The alumni office becomes your gateway to the world of your past university and the many perks that come with that. Let's first look at all the cool things the alumni office can offer you while you're in school, and then we'll examine all the awesome things your alumni office can offer you once you've graduated.

Do Your Homework

First and foremost, the best way to get to know what your alumni office can do for you is to visit its website. The next best thing? Actually visiting the alumni office. It's a good idea to do a little research about what services your alumni office provides before you head into the office, mostly so you don't sound *too* ignorant (you don't want the office staff shielding all the good alums from you).

Each office is different and offers a wide variety of services to its school's past and current students. The alumni office page on your university website should let you know about events that are upcoming, reunions that are planned, discounts on services, workshops, mentoring programs, etc. Familiarize yourself with what they do and what's coming up. For example, if you surf around the University of California, Berkeley, alumni page, you might find that the university offers the Cal Alumni Student Association, which plans events and workshops that allow alumni to connect with current students.

Then, actually go visit the alumni office. Make an appointment or walk in and talk to the person at the front desk. Ask how you can get involved, what the alumni office can offer to current students, and if you might be invited to attend any events. You might be surprised by what you learn. Leadership or mentoring programs, a large electronic database of alumni contacts, special events, and alumni recruiting opportunities are just some of the services or perks that your alumni office might offer current students.

Ask if there is an ambassador program and how you might become an ambassador for the school—a current student keeping alumni informed of all the news and events. You might be asked to make phone calls to alumni to remind them about donating to scholarships or participating in other fundraising activities. Instead of looking at this as a hassle, think of it as a great way to keep connected and build your network.

Take Advantage of Your School's Graduates—Forever

Why should you be thinking about your alumni office and your alumni network even before you graduate? And what's this network I keep mentioning? Have you ever heard the idiom, "It's not what you know, but who you know"? Your success is going to be at least partly associated with your network and how you leverage it. For example, I'm sure somewhere along the path of your education, you've asked a bunch of your friends for something—be it information, a ticket to a concert, an invitation to a party, or a simple favor—and someone made it happen for you. The same is true in the business world. If you keep your network robust, you're going to know someone who knows something about what you want to know. Or you'll know someone who knows someone in the company you want to work for. Sound confusing? It can be, but this little secret is what makes successful people successful and others . . . not.

The biggest advantage that your alumni office can offer you is a presorted, selective network. Everyone who has ever attended your institution has already been vetted—meaning they applied, were accepted, and generally share

Want to Know a Secret?

The faster you gain meaningful, successful employment after college, the better your college looks. College is a business, and your college faculty and administration want you to look good so you will make them look good.

That's why many schools are offering more ways for current students to gain connections and possible job offers even before they graduate. One way they do this is by providing chances for students to connect to past graduates and other businesses connected to the university.

at least some of your values, because you went to the same school. Furthermore, you already have something amazing in common with them—your school. Knowing you have this in common can help break the ice because it gives you instant conversation starters.

This alumni network is what can make an Ivy League college a gold mine. Since those schools tend to be very selective, the quality of their alumni lists is also extremely high, and that list can help you gain access to some of the highest ranked and most well-respected leaders in the country. This doesn't mean you don't have alumni advantages at any institution; merely that if you're at

TIPS AND TRICKS

● Let's make sure that you don't embarrass yourself when you're talking to an alum. After all, this person could be your connection to your first job or a future employer. Or they could be someone really important (like Bill Gates). First and foremost, remember that the hardest part has already been done: you have something in common! There's more information about networking in Chapter 21, but here are some specific tips to keep in mind when you're approaching alumni.

- Introduce yourself. Alumni know what you're going through, both in life and school because they've been in your shoes. Smile and be confident.
- Don't go into the land of awkward pauses and glances after your introductions. Just ask them when they graduated or what they majored in while they were in school.
- Are you in the Greek system? Asking if they were in a fraternity or sorority might give you an instant conversation starter.
- Other questions you might ask: Where do you work? Do you like your job? What did you spend your time doing on campus when you were in school here? What's changed about the school? Do you have any advice for future graduates? What did you do once you graduated? Did you think that you'd be in the career you're in now when you were a student?
- Don't forget to mention what you're looking for in the future! If you're looking to get a job at Google, mention that. They might have a connection there. Or they might know about the business structure there or some other useful tidbit.
- If you're interested in what particular alumni have to offer, don't be afraid to ask if you can contact them later. If possible, you should have a specific issue or problem that can be the focus of this second meeting or conversation. Mention that specific idea when you invite them for coffee or lunch, so that they know you're focused and you value their time.

an Ivy League college, make sure you take advantage of its alumni network. All colleges and universities create an alumni network that you can put to work for you.

You'll want to start making contact with the alumni office and the alumni network even before graduation because it will take time for you to build meaningful, professional relationships. I admit, it can sometimes be hard to find time to do this work and build these relationships while you're still in school.

Fortunately, the alumni office on campus tries its best to make it easier for you to connect with alumni. Remember that helping current and past students make connections is the reason the alumni office exists.

» Social Media

You can always connect with alumni through social media; it's a great way to reach out to people all over the world who may be in companies or industries you're interested in. LinkedIn is a great platform for this, and it's especially easy to connect with alumni there. (See more about using social media for career advancement in Chapter 24.)

If you go to your school's page on LinkedIn, you can see specifically who lists your university on their profile. Reach out— politely—to any alumni you would like to connect with. State that you're a student at their former university, and ask if you could talk with them about their company or industry. You can do this by Skype, a phone call, or in person if they're still in the area.

If they say no, make sure you thank them for their time anyway. If they say yes, you've made another possible great connection. The alumni office can help you make these connections as well.

» The Old-Fashioned List

Naturally, your alumni office will have a full database of all of their alumni. Now, the question is: how do you access it? Well, you could simply ask the alumni office for connections in the field you're thinking of going into. Start building a list of your own by considering which organizations you'd like to gain information about, skills that you would like to develop, and possible careers you might want to shadow or consider. Take that list to the alumni office, and they'll probably hand over a list of alumni in those fields, and also include contact info, graduation year, etc.

Starting with that information, do some research on that person. Use the same research techniques as the ones you would use to prepare for a job fair or interview (see Chapters 20 and 23 for more details). This will also help you to be more comfortable if you talk to or meet the alumni on your list, as you will know things to talk about. Plus, you'll get extra points for knowing whether they've been in the news lately, etc.

» Alumni Events

This is perhaps the easiest and most nerve-wracking part of building your network. You'll have to meet people face to face at some point. Where can you easily connect with alumni? Alumni events.

The alumni office will offer reunions for different classes of the university and other special events to honor alumni. Volunteer to work these events. This gives you double benefits. Not only will you make more grateful contacts in the alumni office, but you'll have the opportunity to meet with dozens (or sometimes hundreds) of professionals who are proud of your school and want to help promote it any way they can. That includes helping current students—like you—succeed.

Volunteer for these events. It's an easy networking opportunity. If it's a reunion, do a little research about your school's accomplishments and the current big players on campus—that can be great material to help you start up conversations. You'll find a lot of donors to the school among the alumni who attend these types of events—they're the ones who are more than willing to help students and want to see the school succeed.

» Speaking of Donors . . .

Another advantage of being heavily involved with the alumni office and hobnobbing with the alumni: most of these people make up the alumni scholarship committees. You know, scholarships that you can apply for during the year to reduce the huge amount of money that you're paying for school. It's definitely worth putting in the extra work and allowing committee members to put a face and a name to your application (which is probably in a stack with everyone else's). Knowing the scholarship committee chair on a first-name basis can only help you.

If Going to Events Terrifies You

If you're an introvert like me, the thought of going to an event with a huge number of strangers makes you want to lock yourself away in your dorm and watch Netflix instead. Rest assured, there are opportunities to get involved with alumni that aren't massive group events. As I mentioned above, the University of California, Berkeley, has an entire program for a small group of students that offers workshops, lectures, and one-on-one mentoring programs. The University of Kansas offers mentoring programs that match you with one former student—something far less terrifying.

Whatever the opportunity, make sure you take full advantage of it. Don't wait for others to make all the moves. Be involved, stay in contact, and be polite and professional. If you're looking for networking opportunities on a smaller scale, don't be afraid to ask—or take it upon yourself to start something at your alumni office.

» Special Alumni Recruiting Events

The Ivy League schools really excel in this particular area, but other schools also arrange these types of events. In conjunction with the career center, the alumni association might bring employers on campus for recruitment events where they target the future graduates of your university (i.e., *you*). Companies with connections to your university—and who hire a lot of alumni—believe they have an idea of what they're getting when they hire you.

They know the education you've received, and in a way, you've already been vetted by being accepted to this particular program or university. Alumni specifically might come on campus to recruit you to their companies, knowing that you already have shared experiences.

» Smaller Alumni Specialty Groups

Your school might also have smaller alumni organizations, which might be independent or part of the alumni office. These organizations, such as the Business Alumni Association and the Law Alumni Association, concentrate more within career and major fields. This can be a gold mine for you. Like the usual alumni association, these specialty groups can have their own meetings, workshops, lectures, and networking events, as well as lists of past graduates. If you're in a particular field, make sure you ask the main alumni office or the head of your department if such an alumni group is active at your school. Or, naturally, go to good ole' Google and search for that information.

{ Kat's Tales from the Real World } I'm a member of the Mount Saint Mary's University MBA Alumni Group, which is reserved for those who finished the graduate business program. We have local meet-ups, attend events to talk to and mentor current students, and sponsor lectures and enrichment events. We have also been known to bring donuts the first day or last day of classes for the current graduate business students. We're on social media, have a growing list of our own, and truly seek to help current students succeed.

Use Alumni Network after You Graduate

Universities often offer special discounts, offers, and even insurance to their alumni. Some universities offer medical or life insurance to alumni while you're searching for work after you graduate or to help you between jobs or if you fall on hard times. A lot of graduates don't realize they may still have access to their college's career center, as well as networking opportunities with other alumni. Many universities have alumni chapters all over the United States or the world that meet occasionally to allow past graduates to reminisce about their past college days—and also to help each other in the present or for the future.

Again, lots of students don't take advantage of the fact that they're a part of the alumni network for life. Put your college to work for you even after you've finished that last final, walked across the stage, and driven away.

» Start Immediately

College shouldn't end the moment you have your diploma in hand. Make sure you leave a forwarding address at your school and know the benefits that will come with being part of the alumni network. When you move, contact or search for your local alumni chapter and start going to meetings and events. If you're in a new town, this is a great way to meet people who are already willing to help you because of your common connection. When you go to events and meet fellow alumni, make sure you follow up so that you can start building genuine relationships.

» Learn What Benefits Are Available

Your alumni center usually offers a variety of services for members beyond networking opportunities. You'll want to check with your alumni center to see what your school offers, but here's a sampling.

More classes! Okay, so you might be tired of classes and need to take a break. The good news is that when you're ready to come back, your college might offer discounted tuition on post-graduate classes and certifications. If your school offers specialty lectures or workshops, even webinars, you'll most likely be given an alumni discount. You might also be able to audit classes for free or at a discount if you need a refresher or need to keep updated in your field of study.

Career services. Yes, you can probably still take advantage of your university's career center after you graduate. Like current students, you can search job postings and inquire about companies that are closely tied with the university in order to get leads on new positions that become available. You may also be able to utilize the career center for career counseling, job searching, workshops, and events that might exclusively be for alumni. Increasingly, career centers are offering webinars on various career-related topics, making it easy for people across the country.

If you're looking to hire people for your company, you will probably be given concierge service at your alma matter because they would be delighted if you hire current students. Your school might offer you a place to post jobs, an invitation to career fairs, or other opportunities for recruiting events. This is a chance for you to be on the other side of the events that we just discussed!

Financial Services. Various campuses offer disability, long-term care, travel, and even pet insurance to alumni at discounted rates. They might also offer short-term health insurance until you can be covered by your employer or can afford an individual plan. Your alumni center might also offer car and homeowner's insurance at a group rate, so check on that—every bit of savings you can get as a graduate counts.

Discounts. Your alumni center might offer discounts and perks on various services just like your school did when you were on campus. If you stick around in the same area as your alma matter, you might be able to score discounts at local restaurants and the ever-coveted student price on movie tickets. You'll most likely always get a discount at your student bookstore or for tickets for campus concerts, shows, sporting events, and other events. These discounts might also extend to local/national banks, and perhaps even a university credit union. If you need a line of credit or don't want to pay fees on a checking account, your university credit union might be able to help you out. Yale actually has its own credit card. Mount Saint Mary's offers me discounted theme park tickets occasionally.

Travel. Every spring and fall, I receive a fat envelope inviting me to take a ten-day trip to a different part of the world. The invitation comes from my alumni center and offers a discounted rate including flight, hotel, and travel expenses for a trip somewhere that sounds exciting. While I haven't taken them up on it yet, I plan to some day.

Think of these alumni trips as mini-study-abroad programs. They usually are led by professors who can enhance your trip by providing historical or cultural information. The best part is the fact that your school does all the hard work and you get to show up and enjoy!

Campus perks. Even after you graduate, you will probably retain access to the library through the alumni center. You might even have free access to the gym. Once you've graduated, you're likely always welcome on campus. Just make sure you don't get a parking ticket.

Check into getting an alumni email account, too. I made a huge mistake by failing to do this; once I graduated, I lost the contacts I had in my campus email address book. Make sure that you transfer your contacts or find some way to forward email and contacts to your personal email account.

» Keep Networking with Alumni

Networking with alumni doesn't end when you graduate. Most colleges produce an alumni newsletter or magazine that will be sent to you. That newsletter or magazine is a great way to keep current with major news from other alumni.

Why would you want to keep up with other alumni? Well, it's another great way to network. For example, let's say you're a new graduate with a psychology degree who is interested in hypnosis and its effects on long-term behavior and you see in the alumni magazine that an alumnus has just completed a book on that exact subject. Reach out to him! You can probably do so through the alumni office or—since we're in the information age—you could probably reach out online.

14

Specialized Institutes

Another resource that your university may have placed at
your fingertips is a specialized institute or research center. These
subsets of departments (or multiple departments working together)
are often funded through grants or through the university for
faculty members to conduct a specific type of research regarding a
particular topic.

Institutes may employ researchers who just conduct research on
that topic and don't teach for the university—it all depends on the
university itself. Specialty institutes often have their own libraries
or other facilities and equipment, such as high-tech science labs or
film-making equipment.

What does this mean for you? It means that if you play your cards
right you might get a chance to work with a groundbreaking
professor, a leading researcher in your field, or with the latest high-
tech equipment—all on your college campus.

The University of California system has a variety of different
institutes. UC San Diego in particular has the Institute on Global
Conflict and Cooperation (the IGCC), which generates research
on international conflict and cooperation. (More information
can be found on the IGCC website: http://www-igcc.ucsd.edu/
index.htm.) Several branches of research are conducted through
this institute, including terrorism, conflict and development;
technology, innovation, security; environment and health; regional
diplomacy; weapons of mass destruction; and security at home.
The institute builds research teams from all of the UC campuses,

conducts operations at Lawrence Livermore and Los Alamos Laboratories in California, and holds numerous workshops and lectures in various locations. Fellowships are also awarded for graduate students, meaning that they give graduate students a stipend (an amount of money) to conduct field work and research.

Why Should I Get Involved?

You might be saying to yourself: I don't need that! I'm not a political science major, and I don't even have time to look into that, let alone time to conduct research or be someone's research assistant. What does it even mean to be a research assistant as an undergrad? Will I be fetching coffee?

OK, calm down. While you might have to fetch the occasional cup of coffee (*mmmm*, Starbucks) if you get involved in one of these positions, you should actively seek out opportunities to volunteer or get involved with specialty institutes like the IGCC.

First and foremost, it's great for your résumé. Saying that you've done research with an institute and worked with leaders in your field goes a long way, especially if you're planning on going to graduate school. Working side-by-side with a famous faculty member is not only a great way to learn from an expert, but also to develop a good, professional relationship for future networking and references.

If you're planning on going to graduate school and know your specialty—especially if you want to be one of the graduate students working for this institute in the future—this is the best way to get your foot in the door. Think about it: if you're at the workshops, at the lectures, you're involved with these professors doing the research, volunteering, being a resource to them, it's definitely going to help your cause if you decide to apply to a fellowship or if you need a letter of recommendation.

Networking is, again, paramount to your success no matter what your field (see Chapter 21), and working for specialty institutes is a great way to network within your field of study and to further investigate that field. Furthermore, you will be building vital contacts within your future industry, which will be useful when you start looking for that all-important entry-level position.

How Do I Get Involved?

While most opportunities for research are reserved for graduate students, that doesn't mean that undergraduates are going to be completely shut out. There are almost always volunteer positions and research assistant opportunities available. Even if you don't land one of those, you can always attend workshops and lectures to get involved.

Also, don't make assumptions. When reading about the IGCC, did you think to yourself it isn't in your field of study because you aren't a political science major? Look again at the list of its research interests. You might see now that there are also opportunities for computer science majors and health majors.

Most specialty institutes have websites, and that should be your first point of research. If you're not sure whether your university has any institutes, visit your university's main website or do a bit of Google research by typing in "Your University's Name" and "Institute." Usually even small colleges will have some specialty institute or another that revolves around their mission. I know Santa Clara had a variety of institutes centered around globalization and social justice, as that was the university's core mission.

TIPS AND TRICKS
● Here's a sample email you might send to ask about getting involved in a specialty institute.

Dear Dr. Expert,

I'm currently a computer science major at UC San Diego, and I am interested in learning more about volunteering or perhaps research assistant positions open at the IGCC. I'm particularly interested in cyber security. Is there an application process I could use? Or another way I could I get involved?

Best,
Kim Possible

The institute's website will usually include information on how to volunteer and what research positions are available to undergraduate students. If not, get in touch with the contact person listed and ask about opportunities.

The institute might have workshops or lectures throughout the school year that are open to students. Frequently, these lectures will include famous guest speakers or specialty topics. Go to those events and learn more about the research being conducted.

At the very least, it's a great way to network and to be involved in something a little bit bigger than yourself. You might even learn something or find a new perspective. Going to a lecture about global conflict and cooperation could make for an interesting Thursday or Friday night. These types of events will probably cost you actual money in the future, so take advantage of your student status while you can.

15

Job Shadowing and Informational Interviews

If I had ever actually watched an engineer at work or spent more than an hour assisting a veterinarian during high school or my early college years, I probably would have realized those professions weren't for me—*before* I invested a lot of time and energy into them. I could have saved myself time, money, and grief if someone had just told me about job shadowing or informational interviews.

Maybe you've chosen to follow in your father's footsteps and be a lawyer. Or perhaps you've spent every summer since sixth grade volunteering and working part-time in the field you're majoring in. You know exactly what an electrical engineer does all day or how many nights a week a journalist has to work. If you're one of those types, you can skip this chapter.

But if you're like most high school or college students, you're just beginning to realize that you're going to have to work if you want to eat for the rest of your life. You've pretty much given up your dream of becoming a professional video gamer, but you have no idea what kind of job you could possibly do all day every day that won't drive you crazy.

Job Shadowing

So what if I told you that there are ways you can really get a feel for what other people do for a living—*before* you spend years of your life and thousands of dollars getting a degree that prepares you for a job you hate? That you don't have to do anything formal to see what a doctor *really* does every day? Or an engineer? What if you could sit with a few bond traders, observe what they do, and see if that job still excites you? You can.

It's a little not-quite-secret technique called *job shadowing.*

Yup, job shadowing. It can be extremely formal, or it can be extremely informal—either way it will give you an excellent sense of what a specific career looks like on a daily basis. I think this is the best move you can make to determine whether to pursue a specific career or not.

Spending a day—or better yet, a few days—shadowing someone in the career you're considering can give you a much better picture than you'll get from filling out a "What Job Should I Do" questionnaire online. You can see the mundane and the exciting, get a peek into an everyday environment, and have a clearer idea about whether it would be a good fit for you. You can ask the person you're shadowing questions about what they do from day to day, what they like about their job, what they don't—it's very similar to interning, but with a lot less commitment for either of you.

» Becoming a Shadow

So, how do you get started? This is where advocating for yourself and putting your college resources to work become important. Reach out to a current engineer in your network. A doctor. A teacher. Reach out by phone or email and ask them if it's possible to shadow them for a day.

If you're not sure you know anyone in the field you're interested in, reach out to your college's career center, career counselors, or even the alumni network. Some companies have formal job shadowing programs, but many others are just happy to have a bright young college student hanging around for the day.

» Being a Good Shadow

Do some research on the company you're visiting so you can make the most of your time. Come prepared with questions and bring a little money for lunch. After your experience, send a thank-you note to the company and the person you shadowed. Keep in contact with the person you shadowed.

Seeing one engineer at work doesn't mean you've seen them all, so don't be afraid to look for additional job-shadowing opportunities within the career field you're considering. You want to get a broad, solid idea of what this career is like on a day-to-day basis. Companies differ greatly, and if you had a bad experience, it might have been because of the company culture and not the career itself.

TIPS AND TRICKS

● Don't be afraid of trying new things and investigating. We're taught in school to be the best and do the best, and it can be terrifying to chart a course into unseen territory.

Maybe you're wasting your time; maybe you're not. The thing is, you're never going to know what you like and don't like if you don't investigate, explore, and experience life a little.

An Informational Interview

There's another way to get more information from a person in a career you're considering that doesn't involve spending a day sitting beside someone watching them fill out spreadsheets. It's called an "informational interview."

An informational interview probably won't give you the "feel" of a work environment like a job-shadowing experience will. But you can interview multiple people in less time, and thanks to modern technology they don't need to be in the same town—or even the same country.

Setting up an informational interview starts in much the same way as setting up a job shadow. Think about careers you're interested in; then think about people in those careers who you could talk to.

Start in your college career center or your network—your friends, your parents' friends, your friends' parents, your relatives, your relatives' friends. Let everyone know that you're looking to learn more about publishing, engineering, or whatever field you're considering. Post something on Twitter or Facebook asking for recommendations or introductions to people you could talk to about this field.

Socialized Shadowing

You can use social media and email to look for job-shadowing experiences or informational interviews. A Facebook post might look like this:

I've been considering studying to be a mechanical engineer. Does anyone know someone (or know someone who might know someone) that I can talk to about the field? I'm looking to interview a few people who are mechanical engineers to take a closer look at the industry. I could Skype, talk over the phone, or talk in person. Any help is appreciated.

If you have a LinkedIn account, you can search for people in the field you're interested in and message them. (Learn more about using LinkedIn in Chapter 24.) Ask if you can sit down with them for a few minutes and interview them about their job. That message might look like this:

Hello, Bob. Your profile mentions that you're a mechanical engineer in Los Angeles. I've been considering majoring in engineering. I'd love to interview you to gain some insight into a day in the life of a mechanical engineer. Would you be interested in sitting down with me? Any time you could spare would be appreciated. Thank you!

Or, if you're more comfortable starting with an email exchange, you could write:

Good morning, Bob,
I saw in the local paper that you are a mechanical engineer for ABC Company downtown and were recently interviewed about college preparedness for engineers. As a local student/graduate, I'm considering going into the field and would love to gain some insight into a day in the life of an engineer to expand on the tips you gave in the interview.

I'm available weekdays after 4 p.m. and on the weekends, but I'd love to meet any time that you're available. Would you be willing to schedule a time to sit down and talk?

Thank you again,
Future Engineer

» Getting Started

Contacting someone you don't know to ask them questions about their career is, naturally, nerve-wracking. You're nervous because you've never talked to this person before and calling or writing to someone out of the blue is not easy or comfortable. Still, it's important that you reach out. Most of your classmates won't, so you'll already have an advantage.

When you reach out to someone you don't know to ask for a job shadow or informational interview, it's important that you tell them how you found out about them, what you're hoping to gain from the experience, and when you'd like to meet or call. I've found that providing preferred hours cuts down on the back-and-forth scheduling emails. Remember, however, that your schedule can bend. The career person you've contacted is taking time to talk with you, so make sure you accommodate their schedule first.

» Let's Start Talking

Before you call someone, it's best to write down a few points so you don't bumble or ramble when someone answers the phone or you get a chance to leave a voice-mail message. Those call points might look like this:

> Greet her and mention that your mutual friend Susie Q has given you her phone number
> Tell her what you're doing and why
> Ask her if she'd be willing to sit down and talk
> Propose a time/place/day
> Thank her

» Preparing for an Interview

An informational interview will be a bit different from interviewing for a job or internship because you will be the one asking most of the questions. So you're going to have to act like a reporter here, and that means you're going to need to do your homework. Remember that this person could be the gateway to your future career—if you determine this is the career path you want to pursue.

If you make a good impression, it's entirely possible that this person could later hire you for an internship or a job or recommend you to someone they know. So treat this opportunity seriously and make the best first impression possible.

Do your research. At the very least, Google the person that you're going to be interviewing. Most likely they'll pop up in some format, be it Facebook, Twitter, or LinkedIn, and if they're really big, you'll find articles about them or by them. Read these. Look at their profiles. What projects are they working on? What are they passionate about? Is their style formal or more laid back? Just this alone will give you tons of information about the person you're going to be talking to before you even sit down to talk.

TIPS AND TRICKS
● Here are some ideas for questions you might ask in an informational interview or in a job-shadowing experience.

- What do you enjoy the most about your job?
- What do you enjoy the least?
- What is the most important skill to have to do this job well? What other skills must a person have to be successful in this position?
- What would you do over again, if you were in my position and had the chance?
- Do you see any major changes coming in this industry in the future? How can I be prepared for that?
- What's the best way to market yourself in this industry? What do you do to get your name out there?
- What can I do to be the best candidate for this type of work?
- What types of skills should I have that aren't directly related to this type of work?
- Are there any opportunities for students in this field in terms of internships or non-profit work?
- How easy is it to gain more responsibility or continue learning in this field?

Let's face it, you're going be nervous. So having predetermined questions in your hands can be a lifesaver. After you've done your research, write down everything that you'd like to ask that person. Write down everything that you want to know. Then start editing, combining, and arranging questions so they flow a little bit. You don't want to jump awkwardly from one topic to the other.

If you're especially nervous, write down a few notes for what you should say when you first meet the person to help you ease into your questions.

Something along the lines of:

> Thank you for meeting with me today
> Let me tell you a little bit about me
> Here's what I'm hoping to achieve from this interview

Then start with your questions. Focus on questions that are specific to the job or career you're investigating.

» Taking Notes

Personally, I lose a lot of information when I try to write everything down while someone is speaking, so I prefer to record the interview either on my phone or computer.

WARNING: You need permission to record anyone. Some will allow it and some will not, depending on their preferences and company policies. Ask ahead of time, or come prepared with a back-up plan and your notebook and pen ready. If you're conducting the interview over Skype, you can record it with various apps, but again, obtain permission first. You don't want to get into legal trouble.

Although the job-shadowing experience or informational interview is a little different than an interview for a job or internship, you still want to look professional and polished. See Chapter 23 for tips on acing an interview.

» Following Up

Thank-you cards, while old-fashioned, go a long way today. Recipients are impressed that you took the time to sit down and handwrite a note to thank the person you interviewed or followed for a day. Grab a pack at OfficeMax or Target that fits your personality, sit down, and write something nice, thanking the person for their time.

For example:

Dear Tony Stark,
Thank you so much for taking the time to speak with me about your journey from child prodigy to national hero. I will definitely take your advice when applying to MIT and determining a major.

I would love to be a part of any projects or internships you have available, as you mentioned. Please keep me in mind.

Thank you again.

Best,
Future Superhero

Mail it to the office of the person you interviewed with—even if you only talked by email or Skype. People still love getting mail when it's positive news and not junk or bills.

Trust me: a handwritten, thoughtful, thank-you note equals instant brownie points.

The Finale

So you've reached out to a few people in the industry you're interested in, you've conducted some interviews, shadowed a couple of people, sent your thank-you notes. Now what?

Take time to think about all the things you've learned. Go back over the recordings and/or notes you took. Write down the points that are really important to you.

Do you think you've got enough information to make an informed decision? If not, start the process over again and interview more people.

Maybe you LOVED what you saw. So charge full-speed ahead into that major. Look into applying for internships at the company where you job-shadowed or with the person you interviewed.

Maybe you HATED what you saw. So consider adjusting your plans for college or changing your major.

Make changes based on what you learned and consider the advice you got from the people you talked to. Follow up on any organizations or leads they might have given you; think about getting any training they mentioned.

Finally, remember to keep those channels of communication open. If you've followed through with some advice, email them to give them an idea of your progress. Everyone loves to feel like they've helped shape the future of a bright young college student.

16

Internships

I remember the first time I heard about an internship while I was in college. I was sitting in class when one of my professors mentioned an internship at the local San Jose news station, where interns would operate the cameras for the sports update section of the news broadcast. They were looking for general interns, and there were rumors that you could gain full employment if you nabbed one of the spots.

The two teaching assistants in our class piped in to say that they had done internships at that station and were happy—busy, but happy. They loved it, they were offered incredible opportunities and learned more on the job, as it were, than they had learned in class. Our professor applauded their insight and encouraged everyone to apply for the three internships being offered that year. Naturally, the consensus among most of my classmates, myself included, was that we couldn't possibly have time for such a thing. Driving off campus to an internship every day on top of classes? I was balancing three part-time jobs and classes, so the thought of adding an internship seemed like too much.

Little did I know this was a big mistake. Who knows where that internship could have led me? Perhaps I would have discovered that broadcast wasn't the career for me; better yet, I might have discovered it was another passion. I could have expanded my network and maybe landed my first official job at that San Jose station. Instead I brushed it off.

Like I've said before: I don't want you to make the same mistakes that I made! So we're going to examine the ins and outs of internships—how to find them, how to get them, how to put them to work for you.

{ Kat's Tales from the Real World } Although I missed the boat on the San Jose TV station internship, I later had a few internships in Los Angeles that gave me insight into an industry that I found I didn't want to be part of. One was a production coordinator internship at a commercial agency, where I learned that organization is key to success. It took me only two months to realize that the entire two-person agency lacked organization and strategy. I learned a lot about the casting process, project management, and the pitfalls and struggles of having a start-up. All in the span of two months.

The next internship I held was for an independent film company that needed me to do odd jobs. The first day I arrived, the head of the company couldn't tell me exactly what he needed help with. He pointed out a few organizational jobs, a few filing tasks that needed to be done, but nothing specific other than that. So I ended up finding things to do until I was hired somewhere else.

My last internship was for a legitimate film company where I worked for a prominent producer and his assistant. My job was to read scripts and provide a one- or two-page synopsis. While some of them were more interesting than others, I learned a lot about the production process, including what it takes to get a film off the ground, what producers do, who is in charge of what task, and about the business side of film. I learned more in that internship than I did in any other. A few years later, I was watching a movie and experienced that incredible sense of déjà vu. That's when I realized I'd read the script years earlier. How cool is that?

No, not every internship is going to have you reading scripts. But even in the internships where I didn't have very interesting assignments, I broadened my network, gained valuable experience (I know you hear that a lot but it's true), and I got a great look at how businesses are run. If I had wanted to continue in the film industry, I would have a lot to talk about, a wealth of knowledge, and a few great references to pull from if I needed recommendations.

What I truly learned, however, was that the entertainment industry wasn't for me. After all those internships, I knew I didn't want a career there, even though it had provided some great experiences and I'd learned so much. In the long run, these internships saved me a lot of time, heartache, and money, even though they were unpaid.

The Elusive Internship

The best place to start is to define what an internship actually is. An internship can be either a paid or unpaid position that gives you a basic level of experience to better prepare you for a job. Think of it as the kindergarten of working in an industry. It may be a few hours a week during the school year or a summer-long, full-time position.

Your next question is probably along the lines of "Why do I need one?," to which I'm going to respond that it's the best way to get experience in the industry you're looking at pursuing. Like we've discussed before, I don't want you to make my mistakes and dive into a major or a career field without knowing exactly what you're getting into. You can learn a lot about a particular career through an informational interview or job-shadowing experience. (See Chapter 15 for more about that.) You will learn even more during an internship, which will last longer and give you a better idea of what people *actually* do.

TIPS AND TRICKS

● To get the best internships, you're going to need to do more than simply apply. Remember how competitive college admissions were? Well, welcome to the competitive world of internships. You're probably going to need to prove that you have some relevant experience even to land an internship.

This is where all your hours of volunteer work and community service (more about that in Chapter 17) come in. Don't forget to mention all those high school and college activities you've been involved with, including clubs, athletics, food drives, and service trips. All of this is going to help you land that first internship. Most recruiters or companies hiring interns are looking for more than competence. Obviously you're in college, so you must have some basic level of knowledge and the ability to follow directions (or at least one would hope). Turn to Chapter 23 for more tips on acing an interview, which can mean the difference between a great summer internship and flipping burgers—again.

Now, I'm not going to ignore the fact that there are companies out there that don't treat student interns very well. They promise you that if you work really hard in this thankless, unpaid position, you might be able to go from an intern to a temporary position to a permanent position—and then don't deliver on their end of the deal. And I'm not going to say that every internship is exciting or action-packed. However, this is one of the best ways to put college to work for you because internships will allow you to gain experience, build up your résumé, and get a good look at a particular career all at once.

Interning and the Economy

You think it's difficult to prove you have enough experience to get an internship? Well, proving you have enough experience to get a job after graduation is even harder.

Doing well in school and getting good grades is an important part of getting a good job. However, in today's job market, you're likely to find yourself in an interview where your potential boss will glance at the line on your résumé with your degree and GPA, nod, and then ask, "Okay, what else have you done?"

While your heart recovers a little from the shock, resist the urge to scream, "What do you mean?! Completing that much was a whole bunch of work! What do you mean what else was I doing? I was studying of course!"

Unfortunately, just like college admissions, finding a job is a highly competitive process. You know you had to put in a lot of extra work on top of your classes in high school to get into a selective college, but a lot of those activities don't count past college. You're going to need to put in more work in college to get in line for the best jobs *after* college.

The good news is, because you are reading this book, you're already putting in more work than your peers. And you're learning how to put opportunities you'll find in college to work for you. So pat yourself on the back for that.

Getting a good internship can be key to getting a good job after graduation. But getting a good internship is not always an easy process. The best ones are competitive, but that doesn't mean you should count yourself out immediately. It simply means you're going to have to put in extra work to get attention and earn them. If you're not sure you have the time to do that, check out the tips in Chapter 3 again for some time management help.

What's in It for the Company?

We've all heard the jokes about interns fetching coffee and babysitting the boss's kids. But most companies know that having interns around is a great benefit for both the intern and the company. You're learning more about the industry and being trained for a future position (hopefully at that same company). The company is getting help with smaller or seasonal tasks that their employees aren't able or available to cover. Basically, it's a win-win for both of you.

Internships can be full-time, part-time, or for a very short period, like winter break or over the summer. Most are doable even if you have a full class schedule. I know you're already very busy, but this should be a priority in your schedule. And the time management skills you learn will be helpful long after you leave college.

Start Freshman Year

Looking for internships your freshman year is ideal. Truly, the sooner you start, the better. You do not—DO NOT—want to wait to start with internships your senior year, if you can help it. Smaller, lower-level internships that will help you gain experience in an office or corporate environment are perfect for freshman year. Furthermore, the more internships you can complete during college, the more experience you'll have to reference—not only on your résumé—but also in interviews and for general knowledge later in your career.

Again, do you remember how terrified you were senior year in high school when you were worried about applying to college and whether or not you'd be accepted? You had to do a lot of extra work knowing that there were hundreds, if not thousands, of other students out there like you with the same grades and test scores. You used activities and specializations to help yourself stand out from the crowd.

Internships are no different. You're going to have to do some research and figure out a way to further stand out from your classmates. The sooner you start this, the better. I recognize that knowing where to intern and what you're interested in doing can be hard your first year of college. Just do your research and apply for an internship in an area of interest, even if you're not sure you want to pursue it as a career. No matter what, even in the dullest internships, you're going to gain some incredible experience and learn a lot about yourself, your specializations, and your future.

Yes, I know this all sounds overwhelming. The good news is that if you've done all the exercises from Chapter 2, you already have an idea where to start because you recognize your skills, weaknesses, passions, values, and interests. You know what your brand is and how you're portraying yourself. (If you don't, then go back and read Chapter 4.) Knowing yourself is the hardest part of determining where you want to go, so you've already done the hardest work.

» Get Experience to Get Experience

While internships are the kindergarten of the work world, you're not going to get the best ones with no experience. Does that sound like a catch-22? It doesn't have to. As we'll discuss in Chapter 17, not all experiences have to be paid or official. You're going to want to have experience in campus clubs and other extracurricular activities in order to stand out when you're applying to internships. The best candidates for internships have previous experience, have been leaders in some capacity, and are able to relate their experience back to the position they're seeking. See Chapter 17 for more advice about this as you enter your freshman year.

Don't forget that paying jobs—whether they are on-campus or off-campus—can help you get an internship you want, which can in turn help you get the job you want when you graduate. Although it might not sound glamorous, an on-campus job can solve two problems for you: experience and money.

Saying that you worked through college is always a plus when you're interviewing for an internship or a job, especially when you can relate the skills you sharpened through that job to the career you're pursuing. Having an on-campus job proves that you're already vetted—meaning, someone hired you. This goes a long way in terms of setting you apart from someone who has perfect grades but has never worked a day in his life.

{ Kat's Tales from the Real World } While I would love to say that I worked on campus for the work experience, I actually worked out of financial necessity. While my tuition and room and board were taken care of from the savings my parents had gathered during my life (along with a few scholarships and student loans), any expenses on top of that—like gas, books, and food—were up to me. Because of this, I worked during college in a variety of jobs—many at the same time.

My first job was in media services, back when you had to transport televisions, DVD players, and projectors to each classroom, set them up, and tear them down after the class session. Naturally, this was before most colleges put such equipment in each classroom.

I spent my time learning the school's program for scheduling, entering requests into the computer, and making sure that the schedule was ready each new day. I also checked in videos and DVDs that professors used in their classes and refiled each in the library. Since the video library happened to be downstairs in a creepy part of the old observatory, that trip was always made only once a week and as quickly as possible, so I wouldn't turn into the college student in a bad horror movie.

The great part about that job was learning the scheduling system and looking ahead for possible snags, like other student workers who might call in sick or orders that got mixed. While it was a minimum-wage job, my boss was awesome (*Dan, if you're reading this, you're amazing*) and would let me work on my homework when I was finished with my duties for the day.

Another campus job I had was acting as a teaching assistant for the video production department. I would help students in the beginning and intermediate production classes with their labs and projects and also help with the lectures. I'd also inventory our camera equipment each Friday and Monday, to make sure that it all was in good working order and had been returned after a weekend of shooting.

My last job on campus was proctoring the law finals at the Santa Clara law school. That was the sweetest job I've ever had. After passing out the exam and reading the instructions to the law students, I sat for four-hour stints with a book or my laptop, making sure people didn't cheat or leave the room. That was it. Seriously, it was one of the most amazing jobs of my life, and I read most of the fun books I'd ever wanted to read during those two years. Yes, I finished all of the Harry Potter books (well, the four that were available then) while proctoring exams.

The best part wasn't the fact that I was being paid for sitting for four hours; the best part was that I was being paid $2 more an hour than my regular on-campus jobs. And since the law school was on the semester system and not the quarter system, my finals were all finished by the time I started proctoring. I would spend the full week proctoring exams in the morning, afternoon, and evening, banking about $500 each semester. It was glorious.

Where to Start

If you're convinced that you need an internship but don't know what field to consider, go back to Chapter 2. Read the advice and take the related assessments (if you haven't already) in the Resources section. Or go talk to someone in your school's career center about possible internship positions; read Chapter 12 for more tips on using your career center.

Once you have an idea about your interests, skills, values, and personality, spend some time doing the kind of research shown in the section below. This kind of research will not only help you figure out where you might want to intern, but will later help you determine what kind of job you want to look for.

You can also download worksheets and bonus material at www. mymarchconsulting.com/PutCollegeToWork to help you figure this out.

» Do Your Research

Which field interests you? Which industry? Are you interested in journalism? Engineering? Business? What about teaching history or working in a museum? Being a psychologist or working in environmental science? After you've done the exercises from Chapter 2, you should have narrowed your ideas down to a few careers or industries. Now begin researching the industries you've selected.

The next step is to research which publishing companies offer internships and decide which ones you would be interested in working for. See the section on Job Fairs in Chapter 20 for more information about researching companies.

TIPS AND TRICKS

● Let's say you're an English major who is interested in writing and want to consider internships that relate to your major and your interests. Create an exercise like this one.

Major: English
Career path: Undecided, but leaning toward being a writer or an editor
Industries to study: Publishing

Why publishing? Well, think about it. If you're an English major wanting to be either an author/editor or working in that field, working for a publishing house is going to give you a lot of insight into both types of jobs. You'll also learn about how books are published, what goes into that process, how you can work at the corporate end or as an independent writer, if you're looking for freedom.

How do you get to this conclusion? Well, you can talk to your career counselor, to your professors, other students, and networking contacts. Your English department should be able to help you. You can also do some research online. A quick Google search can reveal more information about an industry than you think, especially if you're interested in salary, job security, mobility—all of those types of juicy details.

Since you're starting early, the things you'll learn about publishing can help you throughout your college years. You'll realize that you should consider a few creative writing classes and maybe a few publicity/marketing classes because you'll understand that publishing is a business that requires writers *and* people with promotion and marketing skills.

Build a list of the companies that have internships you're most interested in pursuing. Outline your research and generate a few questions. Know what you're looking for.

» Get Specific

It's not a bad idea to outline what you're looking for in an internship. I mean, what do you want out of this experience? Take a few days to think about that. The more specific you can be, the better.

For example, we all know that you want an internship for experience so that you can eventually get into the career you're pursing., That much is obvious. But if you approach a company and say that's what you want, they're going to shrug their shoulders and think, "So?" Any student can say that.

But you're not any student.

Instead, approach this internship as another step in your career. What do you truly want to get out of it? Do you want to learn more about a particular career? Industry? See how that industry functions and get deeper into the nitty gritty of how a particular company fits into it?

What if you can approach a company hiring manager and say you want an internship so that you can tailor your education to be of greater service to this industry? That response will make them much more interested in you as an intern. Get specific—as specific as possible. It will make a huge difference.

How to Get an Internship

Now that you've done your research and know what kind of internship you want and why, how do you find that internship? And how do you stand out amongst the throngs of other students applying? Well, these tips are all going to sound familiar because they're going to be the same ones you'll use to get a job. See Section 4 of this book to find much more about each of these steps.

» Network

Use your school, contacts, alumni, and even friends and family members to help you make connections with the companies where you want to intern. See Chapter 21 for more on networking.

» Career Center

Your school's career center should be your first stop for establishing contacts. A lot of times, local companies and companies who donate money to the school will contact the career center and provide information about internships. This is where having that top-notch relationship with your career counselor can benefit you. They might have additional insight into internships available at particular companies and/or the application process itself.

Career centers work with recruiters all the time and know what they're looking for. They can help you get into contact with that company and might have insight into other internships students have done in the past. See Chapter 12 for more tips on how to put your college's career center to work.

» Alumni

As we saw in Chapter 13, alumni can be one of your richest sources of contacts for internships, jobs, and more. Your alumni network includes thousands of graduates from your major who have landed in your dream industry and probably would be more than willing to help you land an internship (or give you tips to help you stand out and land one). Find more details in Chapter 13 about making your alumni network for you.

» Your Professors

Remember all that stuff in Chapter 7 about developing good relationships with your professors? They're going to know about internships in their industry and have suggestions or leads for you to follow. If your favorite instructors are adjunct professors— meaning they're working part-time for your university—that might be a benefit to you if they're working for other universities or colleges. They might have insight into internships your career center doesn't know about. They're also likely to have consulting jobs or other independent projects with companies on the side.

» Résumé and Cover Letter

To get a good internship, you're going to need a well-crafted résumé and cover letter. The cover letter itself is generally what most employers or recruiters will see first, so you need to put some thought into it. See Chapter 22 for lots more information about how to make your résumé and cover letter work for you.

» All-Important Interview

Ahh, it's happened! Your hard work has paid off and you've been called in for an interview. Panic ensues! The nerves start! You start wondering what you're doing with your life and whether or not a prime internship means you've made it. You also start questioning whether you're ready for this huge step and whether this makes you an official adult. Eep!

Let me reiterate one point: your hard work so far has paid off. This isn't a time to start slacking. All of the research that you've done for this particular company will come in handy. In fact, you're going to want to dive in a little deeper, finding all you can about this company so you have something to talk about.

The best thing you can do at this point is to turn to Chapter 23 and find out how to ace any interview you get!

Follow Through

If you need to fill out paperwork, turn in a personal essay, or submit your résumé to have a chance for an internship, do it! Don't wait until the last day either; that's not going to help you in any way.

If you need letters of recommendation, ask for those first, as you'll have to give the person time to write one. Professors or counselors hate to be asked to write a recommendation and then told that it's due the next day. I have a hard time providing a well-worded, awesome recommendation when I'm rushed.

Know what's required. Don't submit a partial application (again, use common sense here) and know the hiring process. If you don't know, ask when you pick up the application. Know (if possible) how interns will be chosen and when you will be informed.

If you end up interviewing, make sure to promptly write a thank-you note to your interviewer. If you don't get an internship that you interview for, don't be shy to ask why. Take any criticism with a grain of salt and try again next semester, summer, or year.

And of course, if you're selected for any internship, do a good job!

Treat the internship like any regular job—even if you're not getting paid—because you never know what other opportunities will jump up at you from this one.

17

Volunteering

I began community service in high school for two reasons: it was mandatory for my grade, and apparently you couldn't get into a good college without it. So I dragged myself down to one organization after another and put in some hours here and there, obviously for selfish reasons. What I didn't realize is that community service doesn't have to equal picking up cans by the highway.

Because I spent much of my time in competitive equestrianism, I had already been mentoring younger students and volunteering massive amounts of time for the United States Pony Club (yes, it sounds cheesy, but think of it like Girl Scouts or Boy Scouts for those who ride horses). Unfortunately, when it came time for college applications, I didn't think any of this volunteer work "counted." So I didn't include it—but I certainly should have.

The good news is that even though I didn't get "credit" on my college applications for all of that volunteer work, the hours I put in taught me a lot about different careers, organizations, and the way politics could make or break an activity/organization/group of people.

The catch-22 that snares most recent college graduates is that you're expected to have three to five years of work or industry experience before you even apply to most entry-level jobs. How are you supposed to get a job if you are required to already have experience? Are these companies crazy? You get caught in the circle of: I can't get a job because I don't have experience, and I can't get experience without a job. Frustrating!

There's a beautiful way to get around this circle of doom: volunteer work.

What, you say? How on earth do I get industry experience from volunteer work? Doesn't being a volunteer mean I'm not going to get paid? Yes, that's exactly what it means. But—although you might not get paid—you're gaining invaluable experience because you will probably have a lot more stake in your volunteer project than most students would ever get in a corporate entry-level job. This is paramount. College students will find many opportunities to get involved in nonprofit and community organizations that genuinely interest them. Take advantage of those opportunities, and you might find that your volunteer leadership role in an organization you love can help you get your foot in the door at the company of your dreams.

Put your volunteer opportunities to work for you—gain experience and expose yourself to different situations and opportunities. The more you do, the more you will have to emphasize on your résumé and in future job interviews.

{ Kat's Tales from the Real World } After a car accident when I was a teenager left me unable to ride horses as I had done for years, I left the equestrian world and found a new home in the arts—my other love.

I had always wanted to be involved in theater but hadn't been able to join in on the fun because I was spending most of my time at the barn. My one theater experience in high school was as the principal flute player in the pit orchestra for our high school's production of *West Side Story*.

During my freshman and sophomore year at community college, theater took over most of my schedule. It became like breathing. When I transferred to Santa Clara, I no longer had time for theater, although I used it occasionally in my film and television classes for my major. I picked up sewing (my grandmother had taught me when I was a kid) as a hobby to satisfy my need for art—countless bad dresses and doll clothes abounded. When I moved back to my hometown after college and some time in Los Angeles, I decided to go back to my theater roots.

Having picked up a job at a local costume shop, I wanted to explore the idea of becoming a costume designer. The local theaters were mostly nonprofits that did shows for the community and I attended a few performances, recognizing and reconnecting with old friends from my original local theater days. The more shows I saw, the more I noticed that most theaters had no one to help with costumes.

I was working at a local costume shop and thought it was important to expand my horizons a little bit and try to costume an actual show. Over coffee, I mentioned my desire to a friend, and he asked me to costume an upcoming local production of *Amadeus* (which is a telling of the life of Mozart). It would be the first show I designed, constructed, and fully costumed.

Before accepting this role, I had costumed a few shows with the assistance of my boss at the costume shop, who encouraged me to break out on my own. However, everything that we'd previously used had been premade or outfitted from the shop I worked for. *Amadeus,* on the other hand, was the first show where I was fully in charge of costumes. I composed a budget, selected and purchased materials, designed each outfit, and constructed each and every one, with the help of my friends.

It was a transformative experience. I gained a lot of insight into the world of costume design—especially when problems arose that I had to solve—and into working with different personalities in the theater world. It was a great experience, although most of it was done on a volunteer basis. I did get a small payment—which probably came to about two cents per hour, given how many hours I put in on the project.

But this one experience turned into multiple opportunities for me to design costumes for other theaters, allowing me to carve out a niche for myself in town as a costume designer. This one confession during an afternoon coffee meeting eventually led to employment at a local college as a costume designer. Plus, the more involved I became (particularly with one theater), the more I learned about how a nonprofit board operates, how a business is run, how decisions are made, what strategic plans look like, and how actions fall into the mission, vision, and values of an organization.

As I volunteered more at the theater, I eventually was helping run fundraisers, suggesting ideas to bring in audiences, and mentoring others who wanted to develop a career in costuming.

Had I approached a major theater and asked to costume one of their shows, they would have laughed because I had no experience. Now, I have a portfolio ready, and I have been complimented by a professional costume designer who saw my work in a show she attended. Plus, I understand more about running a business—especially a nonprofit—from every angle based on my volunteer experience.

Nonprofits

Nonprofit organizations exist not to make money (profit) but to make the world better in some way, whether that be finding housing for the homeless, caring for hungry children, bringing theater to local communities, or a million other causes. The options for nonprofit missions are endless—almost any and every industry has some sort of nonprofit. Corporations and universities can have nonprofits in the way of private foundations or groups that advocate for them politically.

Nonprofits don't do business for profit; that doesn't mean, however, that they never hire anyone. Usually a well-run nonprofit requires a number of staff members and volunteers to keep the organization moving forward, and staff positions can be paid. You may want to consider working for various nonprofit organizations when you graduate—all the more reason to volunteer while you're in college.

» Volunteering at Nonprofits

No matter how many staff members are on the payroll, nonprofits almost always need volunteers. At most nonprofits, a lot of things get done by volunteers or they don't get done at all. Nonprofits, unfortunately, rely on money from donors and often don't have the resources to hire extra help nor to do half of what they would like to achieve in the world.

Volunteering at a nonprofit, naturally, helps out the organization. But it can also help you because you can sharpen your skills and learn more about yourself while giving back to your community. While your primary motives in volunteering should not be selfish ones, volunteer work can reveal things about yourself as you give your time and talent back to your community.

It also gives you a chance to take theories from your university classes and apply them to real-world situations while gaining the experience that employers are going to look for when you start applying for jobs. When you volunteer for particular roles, you can be in charge of projects similar to ones you won't be allowed to oversee in a corporate office until you have a few years of working under your belt. Why not get a head start now?

Think about it. Had I walked into a Hollywood studio before my community theater experience (see Kat's Tales from the Real World in this chapter) and said, "I want to be your costume designer," they probably would've laughed at me. I might have been allowed to start out as an unpaid intern learning the ropes. Now, however, if I were to apply for a costume design position, I could demonstrate that I know much more about the process. I know about collaborating, and I can build on that experience while I prove myself.

So when you're putting a résumé together, remember to include all of your volunteer work, and don't forget to mention the projects you've done when you're interviewing. If you put your volunteer activities to work for you, you're going to stand out. Stand WAY out.

Define What You Want To Do

How do you find a volunteer position that you're interested in AND can help you find a job in a few years? Return once again to your skills, goals, passions, values, purpose, and mission—the ones you mapped out while reading Chapter 2. Look back at the Resources exercises you completed and remember what you're passionate about. (This might not be a bad time to start thinking about causes that you would be interested in contributing money to as well as working for.) What are you truly passionate about, in terms of improving the world?

Now, consider what skills you think you will need for your dream job. Next, volunteer for positions that will allow you to develop the skills you need. You can do this for on-campus organizations, such as fraternities or sororities, honor societies, clubs, service groups, or more. Or you can look beyond campus to community organizations and groups.

TIPS AND TRICKS

● You can use job postings for the industry you're interested in to help you think about what volunteer positions you might look for. For example, here's a sample job posting:

Multimedia Marketing Specialist
Company A is seeking a creative and multitalented multimedia specialist. This individual should have the needed skill set as well as a portfolio of previous work. As the title suggests, this position encompasses the latest technological methods of marketing, and you'll be expected to become the master of your domain working with a team or on your own.

You must possess experience in the following:
* *Video production & editing*
* *Green screen experience*
* *Web & landing page creation*
* *Graphic design & layout*
* *Email marketing*
* *Writing & blogging*

If you are a hard working, multi-tasking individual with attention to detail, people skills, and excellent time management skills with at least 1-2 years of experience, please submit your cover letter and résumé. All applications will need to provide a copy or link to their portfolio. Company A provides salary, full benefits, retirement, and paid sick and vacation time.

Take a look at the required skills and highlight the things you're not sure yet how to do or haven't done. Then look at 20-30 similar job postings. Write down the skills that come up again and again. Those are the skills you want to start developing.

The next step is looking for ways you can develop those skills. Because most nonprofits are understaffed and underfunded, they generally welcome any help they can get. So start looking for places where you can volunteer to take on tasks that will help you develop the skills employers are looking for.

Let's say you want to develop your email marketing skills. Head for your career center or volunteer center on campus to find out what campus or local organizations need help. Do your research on the organizations that speak to you. Go to their websites, look at their most recent events or classes. Go to their *About* page and read about their mission, their values, their vision for the world.

When you have chosen a few organizations you think you would like to work with, do some research about the people on their board. See who's in charge and reach out to them. A sample call might sound like this:

Good morning! I'm a student at Random State University, and I am interested in learning more about your organization and how I might be able to help. Is there a good time to set up an appointment to call or come by for a visit?

» Offering Your Help

When you meet with someone from an organization, take notice of ways you could use your skills to improve a certain area they need help with. Don't go in there with guns blazing, describing how you know everything and can do anything. Listen. Tell them why this particular organization speaks to you and why you want to give back to them. Ask questions about how you can help.

If you're really interested in email marketing, you want to get a feel for the organization's marketing campaigns. Remember that they might have a separate person responsible for that, so don't get frustrated if they brush you off

TIPS AND TRICKS

● If you're feeling a little stumped, here are some sample questions to ask when you meet with a nonprofit representative, particularly if you're wanting to build your marketing skills for the job we discussed:

- How do you do most of your marketing?
- Do you hire a company to do your marketing?
- What's your main goal when people come through the door?
- How do you engage with your donors?
- What are the best ways you've found to get the word out about your events?
- What areas do you wish you had help with?
- I saw that you have a Facebook account. What do you use Facebook for, primarily?
- Do you have a team that works on marketing? Have you considered forming a team?

at first and say, "Oh, Carol does that. You'll have to talk to her." Naturally your next question would be about setting up a meeting with Carol.

Ask questions as the conversation goes along. Ask for a tour of the facilities and ask about the classes or programs they offer. Finally, if someone else is in charge of an area you want to help with, ask for a meeting or an introduction. At the very least, get a card or a way to contact that person. Then do it. Here's a sample email for the infamous Carol in charge of marketing:

Good morning Carol,
I was talking with Cynthia yesterday about the theater and the marketing the theater puts out for children's programs. I'm in the process of gaining experience in college to help me develop a marketing career and would love to volunteer to take on a few projects. I would love to sit down and discuss how I might be able to help.

I'm out of class early on Tuesday and Thursday afternoons after 1 p.m. Is it possible we could grab coffee, or could I meet you somewhere convenient to talk about volunteering?

I'm really looking forward to meeting with you!

Best,
Future Super Hero

Again, remember that you're making *suggestions* on how you might be able to help. Don't criticize anything the organization is doing or point out things that are being done wrong. You're going to pitch your expertise and ideas as suggestions, like you're working together for the good of the theater. Remember that marketing might be her passion, or it might be something that was thrust upon her. Either way, treat Carol with the utmost respect.

If you do see a gaping hole in an organization's efforts—such as their use of social media—you can put together a small, TACTFUL proposal and call the person in charge to pitch your services. The conversation might go like this:

Good morning, Carol,
I saw a show the other night at the theater, having been invited
by a friend. The show was incredible, and I think that everyone
in town should know about it. I noticed that your Facebook
page hasn't been updated in a while and that most of your
audience was tweeting good things about the show afterward,
but it doesn't seem the theater has a Twitter account. I'm
looking to gain more experience in marketing and would love
to volunteer to help with your social media presence. In fact,
I've included a proposal (no charge!) on how you might better
leverage social media to reach out to your audience to sell
more tickets.

I hope this is useful. I'd love to help out.

Best,
Future Super Hero

» Being Dedicated

The key to really making your volunteer activities work for you
is that you have to treat your volunteering as a job—because
essentially, it is. This is the chance to prove you can do anything.
And it will happen while you're networking, developing future
references and contacts, and demonstrating that you can take a
project and make it into something amazing, even with little to no
help.

Like any college student, you're going to ask questions when
you're unsure and seek out help from others who have done what
you're attempting. But be sure to make this *your* project. Take
responsibility for it; be accountable. Show up and have a plan.
That's going to be eighty percent of the battle.

Volunteering as Networking

Volunteering for an organization or a cause you're passionate
about does more than demonstrate that you're going beyond
simply attending class and getting good grades. It's also an
excellent way to make new connections in the surrounding

community that isn't connected to campus. Most nonprofits have a relatively flat structure locally—meaning that the person in charge is probably in your community, not light years away in some corporate office—so you can be recognized for doing a good job by those who are running the organization.

Other successful members of the community will most likely show up at fundraisers and events hosted by your nonprofit. Those people can be very helpful future acquaintances and contacts for you down the road. After all, you both share the value of hard work for a cause you both believe in.

Finding Organizations To Get Started

This might be the easy or the hard part, depending on what you're interested in contributing to. Here are a few ideas to get you started.

» On-Campus Organizations and Clubs

This is probably going to be the easiest way for you to get volunteer experience. While it sounds like extra work (which it is), it's also a great way to network and get to know other students at your school who have similar passions. If you're interested in engineering, you'd better be joining the engineering club or the engineering honor society. They're probably entering in competitions, doing special projects, and bringing in guest speakers from that particular industry. Any experience you get with that club is perfect to outline when looking for internships or jobs.

Just like when you were in high school, starting a club shows major initiative. If your university doesn't have a club or organization in the field you're interested in, start one. You get to design what it looks like. I know a few students who have done this, designing the organization specifically to give themselves and other students opportunities to be more employable after graduation. Don't be afraid to create your own organization where you can volunteer if needed.

» Rotary

Nearly every area has a Rotary Club. Your school might even have the younger version of Rotary—Rotaract—which can get you into contact with the nearest Rotary Club. This was the biggest life-changer for me, I have to confess. Not only is it a service club that believes in giving back to the community in a variety of different ways, but it also gives at the district and international level. Have you ever seen the eradication of polio movement with the big cog-wheel in the background? Rotary is behind that entire movement.

Rotary is more than a service club. You'll meet the best, brightest, and most friendly local professionals in Rotary who simply want to get together every week, have a little fun, and give back. They pride themselves on honesty and ethics, professionalism, and fun. Definitely check them out. While officially you're not allowed to be a member until you're 30 years old, some clubs have bent that rule a little. Or you can join Rotaract, where you can be a sort of junior Rotarian and yet have access to all the regular members to start building lasting professional and friendly relationships.

If you go to their meetings, prepare for a little bit of ceremony, some inside jokes, and a presentation of some kind. You'll definitely be introduced, but make sure that you contact the president ahead of time before attending the meeting. You can Google "Rotary" and the name of your town to get results. You can also visit the Rotary.org website and search. Most (if not all) presidents have

TIPS AND TRICKS

● Once you've picked out an organization you might like to volunteer with, make a phone call or send an email to ask about attending an event or meeting. Here's a sample cheat sheet you might find helpful:

Hello, Mr. Thor,

I'm a college student/young professional who is looking to give back to our local community as well as internationally. I've heard great things about (name of the organization), and I would love to visit a meeting and see what your group is all about.

I see that you meet each week on Thursday at noon at the country club. Would this Thursday be the best meeting to visit? If not, is there a better time?

I look forward to meeting you.

Best,
Future Super Hero

some way to contact the club. They have some wild social events, parties, community service events, and international conferences that you would love to be a part of.

» Boys & Girls Clubs of America

The Boys & Girls Clubs of America is an amazing organization that provides after-school and weekend programs for kids across the nation. They specialize in providing programs that foster leadership and life skills, enhance education, encourage sports and the arts, and offering other specialized programs for their members. Its mission is to "provide a safe place for all children to learn and grow, develop ongoing relationships with caring, adult professionals, provide life-enhancing programs and character development experiences, and to provide hope and opportunity to all."

As such, the Boys & Girls Clubs always need volunteers, professionals, and skilled role models for their club members. Connect with your local club chapter and see where it needs help. Ask about volunteering. There are great opportunities for you to not only enrich the lives of future generations, but to demonstrate your skills as well.

You could volunteer to start a program or teach a class on your specialty. Are you a history major? See if you can make history come alive for a small group of kids at the club. Are you interested in theater? Ask the club if you can teach interested kids the joy of acting or how to write a screenplay. Maybe your specialty is computers—see if you can teach coding or something equally valuable. The possibilities are endless, and there are more than enough willing minds who are interested in what you're interested in doing.

» The Arts

Budget cuts and economic woes have hit the arts hard in recent years. Nonprofits like theaters, music programs, art programs, and the like were cut drastically at the school levels and throughout communities, forcing many to shut down. This is an area that really needs all the expertise it can get through volunteers.

Now before you stop reading this section (I'm looking at you business majors, pre-law, STEM fields, and the like), there are plenty of non-art-related skills needed to run an art-centered nonprofit.

For example, most nonprofits still need to operate like a business in order to create programs for their specific organizations. This is where business acumen can be helpful, as well as skills in marketing, accounting, and engineering. Yes, engineering. Can you design ways to build sets for a show or cases to display art? There are tons of opportunities for you to utilize your skill set and contribute.

Don't Be a Jerk

Here's a final warning: remember that you're a volunteer. If you want to join the board of an organization or get more involved, I encourage you to do that! But remember that nonprofits have politics, people in charge, and ways of doing things just like any organization. You don't want to barge in and declare that what they're doing is wrong and you have the answer.

If you see problems, assess them silently to yourself first. The more you volunteer, the more projects or solutions might present themselves. If they do, then suggest them in a professional manner. Be an asset, not a liability.

18

Conferences, Competitions, and More

As I grew older, I discovered the importance of going to conferences, trade shows, and events in my community and surrounding areas. That's something I wish I'd known in college!

{ Kat's Tales from the Real World } It all got started because of audiobooks. I had a data entry job that was so tedious that I started listening to audiobooks during the day so I could have a sense of accomplishment—feeding my brain so I wouldn't feel like a paper-stacking monkey. Since picking up a novel at work was frowned upon, I started downloading audiobooks. It started with an obsession with fiction—a lot of fiction. I admit it, I listened to *Twilight*.

Later, I started listening to personal finance books, so I could join in on the conversation intelligently when co-workers talked about their 401(k)s and budgets. Personal finance interests spread to finance itself, which forced me into the business section, especially women in business. The more I listened, the more empowered I became.

While now it seems almost cliché, listening to the likes of Suze Orman, Dave Ramsey, Donald Trump, and Kim Kiyosaki, made me realize that I could be in control of my choices, my decisions, and my direction in life. The topic of personal growth surfaced a lot in all of their books, as did creating your own opportunities through networking and developing your skills.

Many of them mentioned the value of attending conferences, workshops, and seminars to hone skills and expand your network.

Having never been to a conference before, I decided to buckle down and do it. I started looking for different conferences in my area and eventually registered for the annual Women's Business Conference in my city. I thought it would be a great way to get out of my comfort zone and out of the house, networking and meeting other women like me who were looking for the same sort of enrichment.

A thousand thoughts and doubts floated into my head leading up to the event, including the thought that I wasn't technically a "woman in business." I was simply an employee who was *aspiring* to be in business. Still, I forced myself to take the day off and attend the conference.

It was life-changing. The first keynote speaker talked about life outside of your comfort zone. She spoke right to me, describing how nothing was ever going to change unless I took a risk and took the leap outside of what I felt was comfortable—which at the time, also felt like it was strangling me. The next two breakout sessions inspired me to start learning about marketing online and building a brand on social media. At lunch, Joan Lunden, a prominent news personality formerly on *Good Morning America,* talked about how she took a chance and said yes to an opportunity that ultimately led her to *Good Morning America*—and not in ideal circumstances. Taking a call at three in the morning, she headed down to the station tired, bags under her eyes, not looking or feeling her best. But she arrived regardless, put on a smile, and proved to herself and the world that she could be a dynamic, on-air personality.

For me, the Woman's Business Conference was the start of a new direction in my life. It inspired me to start looking at blogs of people who were similar to me. I looked at the news and began to follow a robust list of people and sites. I compiled a huge list of events and workshops that I wanted to attend, and I slowly but surely got to them all, learning something new and meeting a whole new group of people at the same time.

It has changed my life!

I know that you're thinking the last thing you want to do is to make room in your schedule for another event or to sacrifice a whole weekend hanging out with your friends to attend an event with a few hundred strangers where you have to be "on" all the time, networking. But, that's really not the case with conferences.

While it's true that you need to come to a conference prepared, they can be a fantastic way for you to expand your skills, network with people who may have a job to offer you in a couple of years, and to learn something new about yourself.

Almost every profession has some sort of national or regional association. Since no one wants to work in a vacuum, most professionals are members of a number of organizations (whether by choice or requirement) where they network with other professionals in their fields and keep informed on changing trends in their industries.

What does this mean for you? As a student, you can join in on the fun, meet professionals in the field you want to go into, and learn more about your future career. And here's a big benefit to attending a few conferences while you're still in college: most every organization offers student discounts.

Not many college students will take advantage of these opportunities, so this is another way you can put your college years to work for you so that you will really stand out from your classmates.

Conferences

You might be surprised to find out that you will be able to pick up a few new networking contacts, a few self-development tips, or a whole class on a certification requirement at a single conference— but you can. There are a variety of different conferences available in every region throughout the year.

The best-known conferences might be in major cities, but even if you're going to college in an area that's off the beaten track, there most likely will be some kind of gathering close to you. I encourage you to search out a few different conferences that focus on the things that you're particularly interested in.

Conference Structure

Let's take a look at a typical conference. No matter the industry or the theme of the conference, they all have a common format. Once you've registered online (or through the mail, though few do this now), you'll receive confirmation that tells you the location, hours, and sometimes a tentative schedule or breakout session list. Parking passes or parking instructions might be included as well.

When you arrive at the event, you'll register at a front table and receive a badge and some sort of swag (a welcome packet or a bag of goodies, depending on the conference). The schedule for the day will be in that packet, showing you when and where the main keynote speakers will be and the breakout session offerings and room numbers.

> **TIPS AND TRICKS**
> ● Say, for example, you are a business student interested in entrepreneurship. There are thousands of conferences every year that cater specifically to entrepreneurs, addressing topics from marketing, to sales, to setting up your business, to Facebook hack-a-thons, and all different kinds of opportunities. Since you're looking to start your own business someday, you've found a conference that focuses on just that topic.
>
> You take a weekend off homework to attend and pick up some great practical tips on how to start your business. You go to a couple of breakout sessions, get fired up by a couple of keynote speeches, and meet other people who are interested in becoming entrepreneurs. It's a great experience for you. Conferences like this usually last a day or two, and if you can get a student rate, there's no reason for you not to go.

» Keynote Speakers

A keynote speaker is usually someone the conference has paid to come to the event, someone who is famous in that field or has inspiring words to share with the audience. He or she will spend anywhere from 30 minutes to an hour inspiring you and talking about their experiences. Getting a chance to hear a notable keynote speaker gives you an opportunity to listen to someone that you've been following—or should be following—in your industry. Sometimes the topic they cover is important for you or your industry, depending on the conference itself.

The key is to not skip the keynote, even if you think you'll be running late or it won't be relevant to you. These sessions can pack a punch and may even offer life-changing insights.

» Breakout Sessions

In most conference schedules, there is a keynote speaker to start the day; after that comes something called breakout sessions. They're mini-workshops that other specialists give about specific topics. There are often multiple sessions at the same time, so you get to choose which ones you want to attend.

Breakout sessions generally last anywhere from 50 to 90 minutes, and often they're themed. At the conference for entrepreneurs, you would have the opportunity to go to a breakout session on marketing so you can learn from people who have been successful in marketing or are marketing coaches. This is where you can gather tips, gain another resource, or learn more about a particular topic.

There are often two or three breakout sessions before lunch followed by another two or three sessions in the afternoon. Check your schedule carefully.

» Lunch and Two More Keynotes

Lunch often is part of the conference and features another keynote speaker to listen to while you eat, or you might break for lunch and then get another keynote speaker after you return. The afternoon is filled with a few more breakout sessions, and then there's a closing ceremony of sorts. The last keynote is the one many people are tempted to bail on, but don't! Conference organizers might save the best for last.

» Networking Events and Exhibition Halls

Some conferences might also include a networking breakfast, networking cocktail hour, or a networking lunch, so pay attention to those as well. Most conferences have sponsors and booths in some sort of exhibitors' hall. This is a great way to make contacts in companies you'd like to work for or contacts just in general, so walk around and get an idea about what's going on in the industry.

Subscribe to newsletters or magazines. Get contact information for vendors, suppliers, and industry leaders. This is a great way for you to wander around and do some research away from your computer.

Competitions

Competitions provide another avenue for you to explore your industry and network with others. Keep in mind that competitions between industries vary—for example, engineering majors have a number of competitions, from robotics to design competitions, while a history-related field may have knowledge-based competitions. If you're entering the gaming industry, there are a number of gaming competitions and conferences you can attend. If you're a communications major, you might be involved in a film festival, journalism competition, or debate tournament.

TIPS AND TRICKS

● Don't head to a conference, competition, or lecture without creating a game plan. Prepare your materials before you go. I would have a spare résumé on hand just in case. Definitely have your business card, and have your smartphone ready to take pictures or notes.

You can't go to a conference or similar event without knowing why you're attending. Of course you're going there to learn, but you should also know your other objectives as well. Are you mainly interested in making more contacts? Are you there to learn more about the industry to see whether you would be interested in entering it? Are you there to scope out potential future employers? Are you there to look at suppliers for your new business?

To put your conference to work for you, you're going to have goals and a plan to achieve those goals. Be prepared to talk to people. This is the scariest part about going to a conference, but this is also a great opportunity for you to meet people who are interested in the exact same things you are interested in. Make sure that you talk to people—every time you sit down for a keynote or a breakout session. Strike up a conversation by telling them how you're a student and excited to learn. Talk to people at lunch, talk to people in the booths, talk to people in the halls.

You're going to have to reach outside your comfort zone and make some contacts. Collect business cards from everyone you talk to, and then follow up with all these people after the conference. Few people take the time to follow up, and it's a gold mine. Follow up, remind them what you talked about, and ask the local ones out for coffee or something of that nature. This is your opportunity to network outside the walls of your university, so take full advantage of that.

Like everything else I've mentioned, going to competitions can provide a great environment for talking to future employers or networking and actually meeting professionals in your field. Competitions of this nature are usually sponsored by companies (hopefully a company you want to work for), and you can learn a lot about the company, current employees, and what it offers students just by attending.

Even if you're not competing, I encourage you to go to these events. Sometimes they'll have some sort of learning session or workshop, but even witnessing the competition can give you an idea of the projects being created in your field. It's a great way to network and get outside of your comfort zone a little. Even if you're a shy person like I am, showing up and having your face seen and talking to one or two people is going to be better for you in the long run than staying in your dorm room.

Attending competitions is also a way for you to discover what works and what doesn't work (say for a design competition) and understand why as you see each of the teams go by and try out their new experiment or talk about their project. It's also a way for you to find out what's developing in your industry, what's new, what folks are talking about and speculating about—so keep your ears open.

Lectures

While attending more lectures on top of the lectures you already have five days a week might seem like the worst idea ever, going to lectures offered by a professional organization not affiliated with your university is yet another way to your network and explore topics within your field of study. For example, the AIAA, the American Institute for Aeronautics and Astronautics, has lectures a couple times a year for specialized topics in the aeronautics industry.

Lectures are a great way to learn more about a specific area within the industry that you're studying while meeting other people who are also interested in these specializations. It's a great way to meet potential mentors, people at other companies, and to gain knowledge of the industry so you have something to say when you go to a job fair or an interview.

Being aware of what's going on in your industry, as I mentioned before, is going to put you ahead of your peers. When you're at a job fair and can mention that you heard Dr. Smith talk about space travel and the likelihood of a space elevator to NASA, you're going to appear far more prepared and eager—and thus more desired—as a potential hire.

Professional Associations

We can't talk about going to association conventions and lectures without talking about joining an association. Yup, this is another aspect of being a student that most don't take advantage of. Instead of paying the normal fees, which can be hundreds of dollars, to join an association of professionals in your career field, you can join as a student and get a huge discount; most of the time it's a pittance in comparison. It's worth checking out.

Once you're an association member, you can add this to your LinkedIn profile and your résumé. You will also be invited to their conferences, workshops, lectures, local meetings, etc. You'll probably receive a monthly newsletter, magazine, or something similar that keeps you updated in the field you're studying. Go to the events, make yourself known, and take full advantage of this membership.

TIPS AND TRICKS
● How do you find these professional associations, you ask? Google, of course! Start Googling associations in your industry. From there, you should be able to navigate from their homepage to the membership section, where it will describe the different types of membership, including student members.

If you don't see a student rate listed, don't be afraid to contact the association and ask for one. Usually, a membership should be anywhere from $25 to $50 for the year. Considering a lot of these professional organizations cost anywhere from $200 to $400 for professionals, it's a great deal for you as a student. Take advantage of it!

19

Graduate School

Most of this book is geared toward helping you get a job when you graduate college. But what if you haven't decided whether you want to get a job or go to grad school? Well, here's a chapter just for you.

The first thing I'm going to tell you is that if you decide to go to grad school, it's extremely important to know *why*. Make a pact with yourself that you're going to investigate the schools, the programs, and your own motives before you start filling out a single application.

{ Kat's Tales from the Real World } **Grad School Path, Part 1:** As an educational consultant, I probably shouldn't tell you that I tried for graduate school three separate times. Instead, I'm probably supposed to tell you that I am this amazing, Ivy League graduate who has kno wn from the moment I started middle school exactly what I was going to do the rest of my life.

However, that would be a lie. One huge, fat lie.

I started graduate school concurrently with my senior year of college at Santa Clara. The summer of my junior year, I applied for and was accepted into the graduate education program because I thought I was going to be a teacher. I took graduate classes while also finishing the remainder of my undergraduate senior coursework.

It was extremely challenging, I'm not going to lie. I can't tell you how I got through three quarters of graduate school while also being an undergrad communications major with an emphasis in video and film. Seriously, making a film in ten weeks and/or doing studio work while surviving my classes was insane. There aren't enough hours in the day for that, so I don't think I slept much.

But come spring, there I was, all set to finish college with one year of graduate school under my belt. I would finish out the last year of that program, move to Colorado with my then-boyfriend, start teaching at the school district near his hometown, get married, and settle down. Done! Perfect life? Check.

However, things didn't turn out that way. My boyfriend and I broke up. And, right before graduation, my roommate and I decided that we were going to use our communication degrees. After about three hours of decision-making—where I weighed how much I actually wanted to teach, my philosophies on the new No Child Left Behind law, and how much I wanted to move and start over—I decided to jump ship and start new.

I abandoned my graduate studies and moved to Los Angeles with my roommate to pursue a career as a technician in the entertainment industry, planning to become a cinematographer. I loved the *idea* of becoming a cinematographer and was sure it would be an amazing job that I would love. Sad to report that that didn't happen; partly because I found that I wasn't as interested in the job so much as I was the job title.

That was my first bout with graduate school. My parents were very disappointed, but *c'est la vie.* A couple of years later, lost again, I decided I was going to go back to teaching—only this time, I was going to teach college. Because I'd always been interested in history, I decided to look at the requirements for admissions into graduate history programs. I found that I could either concentrate in medieval history, which I loved, or the classics, which I almost had a double major in (I was one class shy of my double major in classics when I left Santa Clara). Looking at the graduate program requirements, I found I needed Latin, Greek, and either medieval French or German. Since I had only taken Greek and French in college, I decided to ask my local university if they had Latin and either medieval French or German, which they did not.

However, after doing a little networking, I discovered that the head of the history department at my local university knew Latin, and the head of the language department knew enough of medieval French to help me along, and the head of the science department was German. Thinking that I was definitely going to grad school in history, I invested in a semester of all three classes at the same time, all of them independent study. I hobbled through those courses and applied to five graduate schools, not knowing really what I wanted to study, other than the classics or medieval history.

My admission essay didn't clear anything up. I couldn't really explain why I wanted to pursue what I wanted to pursue or what I was going to do with my advanced degree. I was a communications major applying for a history graduate degree; even though I was a classics minor, I never addressed that in my essay whatsoever. Ugh. Being the naive person I was back then, I was quite surprised when all five universities inevitably said, "Thanks, but no thanks." Granted, I had applied to five of the most prestigious history programs in the United States, because *why not?* I had good grades. And I was passionate—kinda!

I have to give New York University love for taking my convoluted, odd essay and recommending that I pursue interdisciplinary studies instead and accepting me to their masters program in interdisciplinary studies. So thank you, NYU, for that little ego boost.

Once I got my rejection letters, I took a good honest look at myself and did an assessment. I realized I wasn't really sure why I wanted a graduate degree in history other than I wanted a master's degree. I was convinced the universe might be trying to tell me something, with all of these rejection letters. History professor? Are you *sure* you want to be a history professor, Kat? Anyway, I ended up in what I considered a dead-end career in project management.

So now I was in corporate life, but I soon realized that this—and apparently everything else I had ever done in my life—wasn't right for me. That's when I started getting interested in finance and business topics (see my audiobooks story in Chapter 18). So I started investigating grad school for the third time.

But this time was completely different from the way I had done it the first two times. See the "rest of the story" later in this chapter.

Weigh Benefits and Costs

First and foremost, you want to make sure that going to grad school will be beneficial for you. You don't want to go to graduate school if it's going to put you in immense debt and not help with your career advancement. A lot of people did this during the most recent recession because there were no jobs to be had. So, when they got their undergraduate degree, they went directly to graduate school in the hopes that the job market would improve. While not ideal, I can understand that choice since we were weathering a huge recession.

However, realize that unless you get a fellowship or a grant, you're adding two, possibly three more years of debt to your name with student loans. You're also delaying obtaining real-world work experience if you go to graduate school right after college (or at all). Now, there are professions where going straight to graduate school is the best idea. Medical professions, students absolutely sure they want to pursue law, and engineering majors should not hesitate. With these professions, if you decide to take what's called a gap year (a year off from school), make sure that you're working or volunteering somewhere related to your grad study field.

If you're going to spend the blood, sweat, tears, and money to go to graduate school, know the benefits and costs of doing so. Be as sure as you can be that this is the field that you want to go into, hands down. After reading this book, you should have a head start on understanding your strengths and values, networking, job shadowing, and internships—put all of those resources to work when trying to make a decision about grad school.

Don't go into graduate school for a piece of paper. Know *why* you're getting that piece of paper and what you're going to do with it afterward.

TIPS AND TRICKS

● Gaining your master's degree or PhD could be a faster path to a higher salary, but there is also a caveat—it could hinder hiring as well. In terms of being an elementary or high school teacher, having your teaching credential is almost required, but a master's degree is not. If you have a master's degree, you might be guaranteed a higher starting salary, but some schools might be *less* likely to hire you because they would have to pay you more than other candidates.

Talk to people in the field you're considering, your undergraduate professors, and professors in the graduate department about the best plan for your goals. Research the career you're considering and learn whether or not a graduate degree is required or desired.

{ Kat's Tales from the Real World } **Grad School Path, Part 2:**
When I decided to try for graduate school the third time, I made a pact with myself that I would research business—my expected grad school path—for an entire year. No complaints, no grand schemes. I would simply learn as much as I could for free before investing time and money into a graduate business degree. At the end of the year of research, I would evaluate whether or not graduate business school was needed—and whether or not I was still interested in the business path.

I made my pact on New Year's Day and started on January 2. I listened to podcasts, I went to conferences, I read books and blogs, I subscribed and religiously read the *Wall Street Journal.* I gathered as much information as I could about business in general, entrepreneurship, personal finance, and finance related to the stock market.

The effort paid off. I spent the entire year getting more engrossed in business, and I realized I loved it; I really loved it. At the end of that year I decided it was time to try for graduate school again, this time for all the right reasons.

I had decided I wanted to help students not make the same mistakes I did. I wanted them to think about themselves as a business, not as a pawn to be pushed around wherever best suited other people. I wanted to try out this entrepreneur idea of mine, and I wanted to learn more about the structure of business in order to make my business as successful as possible. I was hooked.

Now when I made this decision, I did a cost-benefit analysis on how much it would actually cost me and what I would gain in wages afterward. In doing so, I decided that spending $120,000 on an MBA was not a good investment. I already had a house and a mortgage, I was married, and the thought of taking on a second student loan equal to the size of a mortgage in my little town didn't fly. Also the thought of quitting my job to become a full-time student wasn't an option at the time because I was the provider of health insurance for my family unit.

So I started searching universities and colleges for programs that were smaller, that fit my schedule, and that would allow me to develop strong relationships with my classmates and my professors. I looked for programs that weren't extremely expensive, and I looked for programs that had a concentration in entrepreneurship, because that's what I really wanted to study. I made a list of what I wanted to learn and why. I wanted a graduate school that would teach me what it takes to start and grow my own business, how to interact with and properly approach other businesses, and how to network. In addition, because of the field I was going into, I knew graduate school was very important for the sake of my credibility.

In my search for a program that would fit my needs and goals, I found the perfect program for me at Mount Saint Mary's University in Los Angeles. It provided a weekend executive MBA program that had classes all day Saturday and Sunday with a small cohort of students and professors who had experience in entrepreneurship and the corporate world as well as academia. It was also a small private school that reminded me of Santa Clara.

My visit sold me completely; I was home. The two-hour drive to and from Los Angeles from my home was the biggest roadblock for me. I could have completed my MBA at my local university, but at the time, budget cuts to the public university system made me wonder if a reduction in classes would make it harder for me to get what I needed in order to complete the program in a timely manner.

So I applied only to Mount Saint Mary's, although I do not recommend applying to only one school. Apply to at least three to four programs that provide a range of chances to get accepted. Do yourself a favor and don't put all of your eggs in one basket.

But for me, at the time, it wasn't completely dire that I be accepted immediately, and so I decided to let the cards fall as they may. I submitted my application and wrote my essay, and this time my essay was specific about what I wanted, my goals, and how they matched with the goals of the university. I was called in for an interview with the head of the department who asked me why I wanted my MBA— and I was able to supply a list of in-depth reasons. Lo and behold, I was accepted; I started graduate work immediately and finished two short years later.

Evaluate Your Choices

There are a lot more options out there than there used to be for graduate school, so keep in mind what the best path is for you. You could go straight from undergraduate work to graduate work, take a gap year (or two) where you gain life experience while recovering mentally a little from four strenuous years of college work. You could work for years and then go back to school, which is what I did.

You could commute (as I did) to a weekend program and work during the week. You could take night classes while continuing to work, or you could get your degree online or in a program that presents some combination of online and in-person classes. You could take one class at a time or attend as a full-time student, like you did for undergraduate studies. Programs exist where you can teach at the university while you're doing your graduate work, and there are programs that don't offer that option at all.

Do you want to work and try grad school at the same time? Yes, the money's great, but the workload can be daunting: trying to get your assignments done and all the reading completed is a lot more challenging when you're working full-time, so keep that in mind.

Do you want the prestige of a degree from a well-known school? Are you looking for a solid alumni network? Do you want something hands-on? Or theoretical?

Consider all the options and then investigate any program you're considering. What do graduates do when they finish? What companies do they work for? These are some basic questions you should consider when selecting a program.

Requirements

Be prepared to meet the requirements of admission at the program you choose. Some programs—like a select variety of business programs—are going to require work experience because they want to see you have developed a few years of your career before you take your education to a higher level. This is not only to establish that you can leverage your education to achieve a higher position, but also to assure the program that you have real-world experience that you can relate to all of the situations and knowledge that's presented.

Standardized testing scores might be required. For medical school, you're required to take the MCAT. For other programs, it might be the GRE; for business school, it's the GMAT. If you're looking at law school, you're facing the dreaded LSAT. If you want to go to grad school as soon as you graduate, you're going to have to study for these tests your junior and senior year of college just as you did for college entrance tests during high school.

So set out a study plan for your graduate test prep; you can do some online prep, get a book, study with friends. Many universities offer free test prep for their undergrads, especially if they have graduate programs.

Interviews or a portfolio might be required as well. Each program has different requirements. Make sure you evaluate each one, what fits you best, and what you have time to do.

Wash, Rinse, Repeat

All the advice I've been giving you in this book about how to put college to work for you? The stuff about networking, conferences, institutes, research positions, internships, and alumni connections? It all applies to grad school too—and it's even more important that you be proactive about getting the most from your grad programs.

The good news is that you're a master of these steps now, so they won't require as much sweat equity. You've already started building your platform and establishing your personal brand; now you're simply going to have to make it grow and continue to work for you.

Expect graduate school to be different from your undergraduate years. You're not going to have the same experience. You might not have the high-impact social life, or have time to go to university games, and you're probably not going to be living in dorms. You'll be spending a lot of your time studying; your professors aren't going to lead you through as much, and you'll have to be self-motivated.

The biggest difference I found was that in undergraduate work, you're analyzing work from other people and determining how ideas and concepts relate to each other. In graduate school, you're asked more about your own research, or your own analysis or your own opinion on data. That was the most shocking change, in my opinion.

PART 4

Having a Particular Set of Skills

> But what I do have are a very particular set of skills–
> skills I have acquired over a very long career.
> *–Liam Neeson's character in the movie* Taken

It's all about the skills.

If you've read even a couple of the previous chapters, you know there are certain skills you need to develop so you can truly put college to work for you. Whether you want to go to grad school, get a job, find an internship, or arrange a job-shadowing experience, you need to figure out how to write a résumé and cultivate the right network.

If you can further develop your skills and cultivate the opportunities that you create, you'll be unstoppable.

You can find lots of opportunities at job fairs—but you'll have much more success if you know a few tricks before you get there. If you can ace an interview, you can talk to anyone, anywhere, anytime—and that's a skill you'll still be using when your college days are just distant memories. Social media can help you get a job—or hurt you in ways you might never understand.

But you will understand all this once you've finished this section. Because this section is all about the skills. Those skills are going to turn into jobs, opportunities, and money. Ultimately? Happiness. But that all hinges on if you know how to use the skills. How to leverage them to your advantage. How to ultimately create a career for yourself. Not a job—a career. A lifetime of work that you can be happy with, that will lead you to new opportunities, salaries, and interests. Onward, fearless reader.

20

Rocking Your Job Fair

If you've been through all the exercises in Section 1 and checked out all the resources in Sections 2 and 3, you know that I've mentioned "job fairs" in quite a few of those chapters. Job fairs can be one of your best tools for finding your dream job or internship while you're in college. Or they can be a total waste of time—it all depends on how you approach them.

If you're new to the college scene, you may not be totally clear on the concept of a job fair. Most colleges hold at least one job fair per year, inviting representatives from all sorts of companies, businesses, and industries to show up and check out the up-and-coming workforce. While the reps are looking at you and your fellow students, you will be sizing up the companies the reps represent. Be sure to keep tabs on your career center as discussed in Chapter 12 to get the best information about upcoming job fairs.

I've seen students rock their college job fairs, and I've seen students completely and utterly bomb them. Unfortunately, job fairs can sometimes appear to be a throng of desperate students all clamoring for jobs they're not sure they want at companies they know nothing about. But you're not going to be one of those students.

Do Your Homework

In order to make job fairs worth your while, you can't just stumble in, look at each company's booths, take some preprinted brochures, and leave. You're going to have to do some research and planning and approach the job fair booth like it's your first interview at a particular company instead of an information session. That's because—essentially—this *is* an interview. Or it will be if you've done your homework and come properly prepared.

TIPS AND TRICKS

● If all you're planning to do at the job fair is collect some brochures, just skip it. You can look up a company online to get that kind of information without standing in line or rubbing elbows with your germy classmates (unless you *really* want that cheap coozie or stress ball, of course). You can get so much more than cheap giveaway gifts and slick brochures from a job fair—but only if you're ready to do the gritty prep work.

Start with your career center (again), which should have a list of all the companies expected to be at the job fair. Ask for the list. This is the first step. With that list in hand, go online and look at the website of any company that even slightly interests you. Pay careful attention to the "About Page" and read about the company's mission, vision, and values. Browse around on the site itself and see if you can glean more information about what it does and why, and what it's been up to lately.

For more information on how to conduct research on a person or company you encounter at a job fair, turn to Exercise 20.1 in the Resources section.

Be Prepared

Okay, you've done your research and you show up to the job fair and impress me so much that I want to hire you on the spot. Or at least enough for me to ask for your résumé. Do you have a copy with you? How about a business card?

If you aren't ready to hand something to these companies, you are missing a prime opportunity. In fact, if you really want to be prepared, you might want to tailor your résumé and cover letter to present to each company. Yes, lots of companies now want you to submit everything online, but having a paper version is always a good idea. These reps will be talking to a few hundred students at every job fair—you need to go the extra mile if you want to make an impression on them. See Chapter 22 for more details about how to create memorable résumés and cover letters.

» Business Card

I know that money can be tight as a college student. A business card is a necessity, though, for job fairs and other networking events. Your business card can be very simple; it just needs your name, phone number, email address, and a job title of "Student" or "Future Engineer." VistaPrint and others offer free and low-price card offers. Or you can pick up pre-cut business card paper at your office supply store and print your own cards. Microsoft Word has dozens of templates for you to use. So even if you forget this detail until the night before the job fair, you can still have cards ready.

» A Nice Folder

It's always awkward for you and the person at the booth when you're digging past last night's granola bar wrapper, a half-finished bottle of Powerade, dirty gym shorts, and whatever else you have in your backpack or purse to locate a copy of your résumé. So leave all that at home. Put your ID, cash, and keys in your pocket. Find a nice portfolio or leather folder where you can keep your résumés, cover letters, and any material you pick up at the job fair.

You'll use the folder later in job interviews and anywhere else you want to look professional. Your college bookstore should have one with a school logo on it, or you can grab one from Amazon or an office supply store. It doesn't have to be expensive, just something basic that looks nice. I'd recommend a neutral color too, like brown or black; that way you don't walk into a Fortune 500 company later and have to explain why you have a neon pink folder.

» Thank-You Notes

While you're at the office supply store (or your bookstore), pick up a package of thank-you notes. You're going to need them immediately after the fair ends. If possible, get ones that represent your personal brand. However, if your brand screams leopard print, hot pink, and sparkles, you might want to tone it down a bit and simply get a pack of thank-you cards that are black with white or pink writing. Again, consider your audience: your potential employer.

Be Organized

Put your cover letter and résumés together, paperclip them, and find a way to keep them neat, clean, and tidy in your folder. Include business cards in a holder in your pocket, or in a pocket in your folder or portfolio. Carry a nice pen and put a notepad in your folder so you can take notes. Type up and print out the notes you made about each company during your research. Carry those with you in case you want to brush up as you go. Trust me; after you've talked to a half-dozen company reps, you're going to forget some of the details you so carefully researched.

Create a Plan

Know what you're trying to achieve at the fair, have specific goals in mind, and create a game plan for how you're going to achieve them.

» Your Elevator Pitch

See Chapter 21 for a deeper discussion of an "elevator pitch." Just know that you have to be ready to talk to the reps at the job fair. You're going to introduce yourself, tell them what you're majoring and minoring in, and what makes you different. Focus on the

---

TIPS AND TRICKS

● A job fair elevator pitch (in its entirety) might look like this:

Recently I saw that your company has made large strides to become more environmentally conscious and is launching an environmental initiative in your industry. Since I'm passionate about what you're doing, I would love to contribute.

I'm Katniss Everdeen. I'm majoring in politics with a specialization in political theory and am pursuing a minor in environmental studies. I want to work within the political system to make our society more sustainable and equitable, and I also have a passion for environmental sustainability and thought my minor would prepare me to work in that arm of the government.

I'm a member of the environmental research team here at the university and serve as the chairman of the human rights committee on campus, helping to organize protests and provide support to families affected by political upheaval.

research you've done about the company, the interest you have in what they're achieving, and how you can contribute.

Remember to practice your spiel beforehand, so it flows off your tongue and seems (and feels) natural. Don't try to do it all in one breath; make it conversational. You might comment about the company and a little of your research first and then offer your hand to introduce yourself. At that point, the person in the booth will ask what you're majoring in and the second part of your elevator pitch will happen naturally.

If they then ask about your experience, you follow up with the third part of your pitch. Give it time and practice. You don't want to sound like an eager kid at a birthday party, trying to recite everything you've done that day. Keep it relaxed and try not to be nervous. Remember, you're pitching your personal brand.

» Treat It Like an Interview

Although you're probably standing on the campus quad with hundreds of other people streaming by, you should treat this job fair encounter as a type of less-formal interview. After all, this is your first person–to-person contact with this company, so be prepared for whatever they might ask.

At the very least, be prepared to explain why you've come to visit a particular booth at the job fair. Think of your long-terms goals again in relation to your short-term goals. Then match them to the reasons you are going to this job fair. Are you looking for potential opportunities or just trying to gain more information about different industries? Perhaps you're evaluating the differences between entering the petroleum engineering field as opposed to aerospace engineering and you know that both industries will be represented at the job fair.

Include that as part of your conversation, maybe even as part of your elevator pitch: *I'm looking for an internship that will help me learn more about the petroleum engineering industry. I am interested in both petroleum and aerospace engineering, and I'm hoping for an internship that will give me practical experience so I can make an informed decision about which professional path to choose.*

Look at Chapter 23 for more information about preparing for an interview before you head to the job fair. If you skip this section, you may find yourself tongue-tied and sweating when the company rep shows a real interest in you.

» Ask Questions

Prepare a few of your own questions to ask recruiters. Don't be afraid to ask questions about next steps for an interview, the application process, or how an employee can grow when they're working for the company. You're interviewing this company just as much—and actually probably more—than they're interviewing you.

Make sure that you ask questions about the company culture, what the recruiters love about the company, what projects you might be working on, the management structure, and any training it might offer entry-level employees. If you're looking for an internship, ask about the likelihood of being hired full-time at the company after an internship has been completed.

» Take Notes

You're going to follow up with the recruiters and hiring managers that you meet at the job fair, so be sure to take notes. Jot down names and little things that made an impression. Take notes on the answers they give to your questions about the hiring process, or any other tidbits of information that they give you. Remember to note which company goes with which recruiter and get their cards, tucking them safely away for later.

If you think you're going to remember everyone and everything that was said the day after the job fair, you're wrong. Sorry, but you're going to be talking with a lot of people, and you're going to be tired at the end of it all. Do yourself a favor and take notes.

Look the Part

Make sure you dress professionally. Do you have to be in a full suit? Maybe not, depending on who will be attending and the climate of your university. Personally, I'd much rather be overdressed than underdressed; however, use your best judgment. At the very least put on a nice blouse and skirt or a button-down shirt and trousers. And look clean.

You're being evaluated in the same way that everyone else around you is being evaluated, and your goal is to stand out in the best way. Most recruiters want to know that you're making an honest effort and that you'd represent their company well in the future.

TIPS AND TRICKS

● Remember that recruiters or hiring managers are most likely older than you and may have different standards of dress. While your generation might view an untucked shirt as casual, a recruiter might see this as sloppy and disrespectful. Keep in mind your audience and how you're presenting yourself.

Try to wear comfortable, supportive shoes since you'll probably be on your feet for a few hours. Girls, leave the really tall heels at home; guys, don't wear flip-flops or basketball shoes, unless the company you're trying to impress encourages such footwear.

Be the Part

Business etiquette is important. When you shake someone's hand, make sure that it's firm and not wimpy. Firm = confident. Make sure that you are using your best manners, and start out by calling people Mr./Ms. until (unless) they ask you to call them by their first name. Make eye contact with anyone you're talking to and try not to touch your face or play with your hair while you're talking.

Stand on both feet or sit up straight. Remember proper hygiene (this should be the easiest part) and don't wear cologne or perfume at the risk of overpowering someone's nose in close quarters. Also, if you have any piercings or tattoos, it's best to take them out or hide them the best you can. Remember you need the most professional appearance you can muster.

You also want to do your best to be positive and cheerful at the job fair. Everyone knows someone who enters a conversation and is instantly negative about everything. They seem to suck the energy right out of you with their negative comments. Don't be that person. Try to be cheerful no matter what the day has brought, put a smile on your face, and ask people you meet how they are feeling. You'll be amazed at the small difference this makes.

Follow Up

Ah, perhaps the most important (and sometimes the hardest) part of anything: doing the follow-up. But it's the way you will make yourself stand out from the hundreds of students a recruiter meets who won't take the time to reach out.

The thank-you notes you bought at the office supply store are going to get used immediately when you get back to your dorm or apartment. It's very important that you get your note out within the first 24 hours. It shows that you follow up, are grateful for the time they spent (even at a job fair), and that you're on top of things—a real go-getter.

> Want to know a secret? People go gaga over handwritten thank-you notes that are sent by mail—yes, snail mail.

Besides making you look good, sending thank-you notes gives you a chance to mention something you forgot in your short interview, to remind the recruiter who you are, and to reiterate why you might be a good choice for the opening you heard would be coming up soon.

If you haven't heard back within two weeks of the job fair, you can write a follow-up email or letter. You want to stay fresh in that recruiter's or hiring manager's mind. Hopefully, a follow-up communication will move your application further up in the pile.

Make it interesting and tailor it to the company and the hiring manager you're speaking with. This is your chance to remind them who you are and why you're a perfect fit for their company.

Don't be too discouraged if you don't hear back right away; many times recruiters or hiring managers travel extensively for a few weeks—visiting job fairs all over the country. Just don't let them forget you before they get back to their company. Even if you don't hear back, go ahead and submit your application. Be realistic and know that you're not going to land every internship or job you apply for. But don't let that stop you from applying!

TIPS AND TRICKS
● Here's a sample thank-you note you might write after a job fair.

Dear Mr. Smith,

Thank you so much for the conversation and the advice you gave yesterday at the university job fair. I'm excited to apply for your upcoming internship. As I mentioned, I have been conducting research and writing reports that are similar to what you're asking for in your internship position.

Thank you again for your time and consideration. I look forward to hearing from you.

Best,
Jarvis Wheeley

21

Networking Effectively

Networking. People are always trying to convince you of the "best" or "proper" way to network, but—honestly—no one's even sure what the word really means.

In the business world, "networkers" are too often thought of as the people who shove their business cards into your hands or interrupt conversations to tell you how proficient they are at a task you've never much thought about. Don't turn into one of "those people."

Instead, let's look at a few ways to *network* that will generate meaningful connections with people who can help you get a job or an internship or an introduction to someone who can help you get a job or an internship. Let's start by changing the mental image you have of your network.

Picture the living room in your house full of people, all of whom you know well. Everyone in that room would help you if you needed it. Congratulations, that's *your network.*

You continue to grow your network by inviting more people into that room. And you really cultivate your network so you can put it to work for you by allowing some people access to more rooms of your house. The better you get to know a person, the further into your house they get to go (such as your best friend, who has complete access to your house and knows where you keep your cups and the best ice cream in your freezer).

{ Kat's Tales from the Real World } I was horrible in math during my undergrad years. Dismal. It took a mountain of effort—including tutoring and appealing to the professor—to pull a B average in my math classes. One day, I was talking with a friend of mine who happened to be an engineering major and math whiz, and I complained that I didn't understand one of the concepts in my precalculus class. He commiserated by talking about how awful he was in his English classes. He wasn't a native English speaker and, although he was fluent in English, he struggled to communicate his ideas.

After a bit of discussion, we decided to trade expertise: I would help him with his English papers, and he would help me with my math class. We worked closely all semester and both ended up doing well in our classes. Our success was based on the idea that I was in his network and he was in mine. It may have been accidental, but the results were the same.

Why Is Networking Important?

Networking is pretty much the path to a job these days. Yes, let me say that again: if you want a job, you'd better have a pretty solid network. Unfortunately, the old adage that it's not *what* you know but *who* you know applies more now than it ever did. Gone are the days that you could show up with a résumé and ask for a job; gone are the days that you could get hired right after graduation just because you excelled in college.

Networking is PARAMOUNT to getting the position you're looking for. Knowing someone in an organization is the only way you can guarantee your résumé is even going to be read, let alone lead to an interview. In fact, there is someone waiting to take most of the positions that you're applying for out of college—someone that the hiring manager already knows personally or through a friend or co-worker. All of the best positions I've ever had were discovered through networking.

You can't successfully put college to work for you without learning how to cultivate a network, so don't skip this chapter.

I bet you're familiar with the stereotype of the trust fund kid who becomes the vice president of a company straight out of college because his father is the president or pulled stings with his connections to get him there. Look at the key word there: *connections.* That's what you want to cultivate within your network. You want to start making connections to get you where you want to go.

I know you're already thinking to yourself: *I don't have to do this. I'm independent. I have plenty of friends. We have the Internet and email, right? Do I really need to go out and meet more people?*

It's true that you can make great contacts in many places—the supermarket, your intramural basketball team, your fraternity's alumni event (see the story in this chapter about my grandfather). But don't skip all of the "traditional networking events." These can give you a leg up because you'll meet many people at one time in a place where the playing field is pretty level: everyone is there to meet others. And if you learn how to network effectively at these events, you can use your skills to network wherever you go.

As someone who doesn't revel in the thought of meeting new people, I had to force myself to go to events at first. I would go to a "networking" event, spend most of the time trying to figure out how to talk to someone, fail miserably, and go home.

TIPS AND TRICKS

● Before we go further, I want to make sure you recognize that there's a difference between using your connections and being part of a healthy network. You can't meet people and expect them to immediately start doing favors for you—that's not how it works. But you also can't expect to take years to build the kind of relationships you want in your network. This is not about becoming bosom buddies—this is about making "professional" friends. This is about being able to recognize when someone in your network needs something, offering what help you can, and expecting that your network will give you a hand when you're the one in need. That's a healthy network.

You want to have a healthy network so that when you're ready to start looking for a position, or to open a business, or to make a career change, you have people in different industries you can ask for advice or help. If you're looking for a job, you can ask if they know of anyone who is hiring. If you're looking to start a business, you can ask about business processes. You get the idea.

The thing was, I had no plan. No goals, no practice, no research to lean on. I would show up and expect things to happen. That's not going to happen to you because I'm going to show you how to avoid my mistakes. You need to be prepared, and you need to know some basic networking event etiquette in order to feel comfortable when you walk into the room.

Do Your Homework—Again

It's important for you to make some preparations before you start showing up at events so they won't be a waste of your time. Remember all the stuff you learned in Chapter 20 about preparing for a job fair? Most of it applies to networking events, too, although you may not know exactly who will be at an event before you show up.

Even so, you should be able to get some ideas about which companies will be represented, so do your research about those companies. Get an idea of who you would most like to meet at the event before you even show up. Think of some questions you can ask about certain companies or particular topics.

Your Elevator Pitch

At any networking event, the most important topic you should be prepared to talk about is—*you*. For most people, that's not easy to do, so here's some more homework for you. I want you to create what in many types of business is called an *elevator pitch*.

Basically, an elevator pitch means you need to be able to convey your most important message in the time it takes to ride a couple of floors on an elevator. Traditionally, this has been a salesman's pitch about the product or service he's selling.

In the networking world, you are selling you, so that's what your elevator pitch must be about. It's important that you be able to introduce yourself and provide a new acquaintance with the most relevant facts about yourself in one or two smooth, compact sentences.

How do you do that? First and foremost, you're going to tell them WHO you are; next, you're going to tell them WHAT you do and WHERE—for a student that would be your major or your classification at your college. Finally, you're going to tell them the WHY, which will hopefully spark conversation about HOW the person might be able to help.

For example:

Hi, I'm Kat Clowes,

I'm a communications major at Santa Clara University.

I'm looking into broadcast media and am in the process of applying for internships.

» Perfect Pitching

So, does your little pitch sound a bit awkward? Then practice it in the mirror AT LEAST twenty times. This could be awkward if you're in your dorm with your roommate, but maybe you could get your roommate to practice with you (they could seriously use the help too). Once it flows off of your tongue easily, you've got it.

Now comes the hardest part—using it.

This little pitch is perfect for when you're introducing yourself to people at a table or introductory activity. You don't have to recite all of it every time you're introduced to someone—but it will be easier for you to chat when you know the pieces and how they might fit in a conversation.

For example:

Professional #1: Great event. Are you a member of the Chamber of Commerce?

You: No, not yet. I'm a communications major at Santa Clara University.

Professional #1: A student, that's great! What do you think you're going to do with your degree?

You: Well, right now I'm looking into broadcast media. I want to investigate more opportunities there and get my feet wet, so I'm in the process of applying for internships.

Professional #1: Broadcast? You know, I have a friend who works for the local news station. I'm Bruce, by the way. Bruce Stark.

You: I would love to talk to your friend. I'm Kat Clowes. Nice to meet you.

Professional #1: Nice to meet you too. Let me see if I can introduce you.

See? Once you know what you're going to say, conversation is much easier. In a simple conversation, you were able to tell that professional who you were, what you were looking for, and your name. It flowed, it was natural, and you were confident in what you said.

Remember that people are generally open to helping students. Remember this especially when you feel shy and don't want to talk to anyone. Everyone you come into contact with was your age at one point in their lives and knows how hard it can be. This is where you can really put your student status to work for you. Ask for help. As long as you're courteous and respectful, most people will be glad to oblige.

Those who aren't? Forget them.

» A Card-Carrying Event

We talked about branding yourself in Chapter 4 and discussed how important it is for you to have your business card ready at a job fair in Chapter 20. Make sure you also bring them to any networking event! There's nothing more annoying than meeting someone you would like to follow up with but finding out they don't have a business card.

I don't care how archaic business cards might seem; having a card is still serious contact currency. It's also a rite of passage, so make sure you don't forget this valuable little nugget. Oh yes, and take it out of your fancy new business card holder before you try to hand it to someone.

{ Kat's Tales from the Real World } I wasted a lot of time.

I attended countless events just because I thought merely showing up was going to do something for me. I'm not going to lie—once in a while I would randomly meet someone incredible, but let me tell you, that was too rare.

I can't pretend that I don't get a little nervous every time I enter a new room with lots of strangers. So why do it? Because I've finally learned the lesson my grandfather was trying to teach me years ago.

My grandfather used to be known by everyone in town. He would talk to everyone and anyone to the point that we would tease him, saying he was "politic-king." As a shy little girl, I was terrified when he'd start talking to someone; I guess I thought they might lash out if you said a word to them. I was a huge rule-follower back then and would never say anything without raising my hand and being called on first. But my grandfather developed amazing relationships with strangers. Never would he leave a conversation without a new friend.

And every new friend benefited him. He always knew where to go for advice, how to connect people who needed each other, who to ask for what, and what was going on around town in different industries. Whenever someone was looking for a job, he knew at least four people who would hire that person and would actively connect them.

When I was in college, he'd constantly encourage me to call this friend or that friend to interview them or just to have a conversation. I would quietly agree and then never make the call. Do I regret that now? You betcha.

My grandfather was the king of networking. He didn't constantly go to networking events looking for contacts—instead he would make friends wherever he went and stay in contact with them. Even though the world changed during his lifetime, he was successful for many years because he always cared for people. He listened and was genuinely interested in what people had to say.

That's the key to networking: take an interest in people. Listen to their story and find a way to help them.

Networking with Manners

One thing to remember about networking events: they are not honest meetings; *everyone* there will have an agenda. You need to be aware, as you begin to build relationships with people you meet on these occasions, that diligence counts. Be smart and do your homework and you'll discover that networking events can be filled with opportunities for you to meet like-minded people and develop meaningful relationships.

But you also need to be ready to behave in socially acceptable ways in a room full of strangers. The better your manners, the better people will remember you, so let's discuss a few basic network etiquette rules here.

» Don't Be a Jerk

We all know that, ultimately, when you take the time to show up at a networking event, you're wondering what's in it for you. You've done your homework, so you know which people should be here that you *really* want to meet. You want to introduce yourself to the president of the organization or you want to connect with people who could potentially hire you.

However, if you go in with that attitude and concentrate just on those people, you're doing yourself a disservice. Everyone at the event has different backgrounds, points of view, and groups of friends, and you never know when you might meet someone who can introduce you to someone who might be your next employer.

This should be common sense, but you want to make sure that when you're talking to someone you're not looking over their shoulder, trying to find someone better. Give your full attention to the person you're talking with at the moment—there's nothing worse than feeling like the person you just met thinks you're insignificant. But if you give that person your full attention, chances are, no matter what happens, they'll remember you and think about you positively. Although this should be common sense, unfortunately it isn't always practiced.

Act like every person you meet could be the President of the United States someday. A good attitude and good manners go a long way, even if the other person is acting like a jerk. People will remember how poised and professional you were during the situation.

» Drinks and Snacks

The key here is knowing why you're at this event. As a college student, you're going to see more delicacies at big networking events than you will in your school cafeteria or dining hall. However, you must remember this: *you're not there to eat.*

Repeat after me: you're not there to eat.

You don't want to be stuffing your face and balancing a plate and drink cup when you're trying to shake hands and talk to people. Think about that for a moment. It's awkward. Instead, grab a plate after the event—or not at all. You should also always eat before you go, so you're not starving. You'll thank yourself when you get there.

As for drinks—don't. While I understand you might be nervous and think a drink or two could take the edge off, there's nothing worse than trying to have a conversation with someone who has wine breath or is flat tipsy. If you're worried because it looks like everyone else is drinking—or you're under age—ask for a soda water or a Sprite with a lime in it and a small straw. That can make it look like you are drinking a gin and tonic while leaving you fresh and ready for good conversation.

Real-World Advice

- Set a networking goal. Know why you're networking— more specifically, know what help are you asking for.

- Make it a win-win. Know how you can help the person you want to network with and offer to help them. Then ask for whatever help you need from them.

- Follow up. Know to follow up with a memorable note about your encounter, a reminder of how you plan to help them, and a reminder of what they offered to do for you.

—Lolita Taub, Global Female Millennial Entrepreneur Champion and Spokesperson; TV host, writer, producer of the *F Show*

If you have a drink in your hand while you're introducing yourself, make sure to keep it in your left hand and shake with your right. Don't continually take it on or off the table or leave it somewhere and forget the drink entirely.

» Shaking Hands

Practice a good, firm handshake, which demonstrates that you're confident and mean business. There's nothing worse than a limp, fish-like handshake. Your handshake should be strong, firm, and palm to palm. If you're just offering your fingertips, it conveys an odd message: either you're worried you'll get the plague from this person or you're uncomfortable and you don't know what to do with your hands.

Make eye contact when you shake someone's hand, which also conveys confidence and proves that you're paying attention to the person you're meeting. Instant credibility points. Practice your handshake/eye contact with a friend or roommate.

» Treat Other Business Cards with Respect

Would you want someone to glance at your card and shove it into a stack with a bunch of others? Or haphazardly throw it into a book or a bag? No, you'd want someone to take it, look at it, and treat it like something they're actually going to use. Give that same courtesy to someone else.

When someone hands you a card, look it over and feel free to comment on how cool it is. Then—while your new acquaintance is watching you—put it somewhere safe, like your card case. Treat it with respect.

» Don't Throw Your Cards at Everyone

Did you just get a picture of someone flinging their card at you? Believe it or not, people do that ALL THE TIME. It's annoying. They don't take time to get to know me, or to talk to me; they just assume I want their business card and shove it at me—and everyone else in sight, in the hopes that a few people might call at one point.

This is NOT the way to put your business cards to work for you. Instead, start a conversation; after some actual meaningful conversation, you can ask if the other person would like your card or if they can give you a card so you can make contact later.

Where to Find Networking Events

Now that you know how important networking events are and how to behave at networking events, how do you find an event where you can start practicing your skills? Professional organizations, local chapter meetings, service clubs, and events in town are a perfect place to start. Your college probably offers free lectures or alumni events (alumni events are a GREAT place to network—see Chapter 13 for more tips); your department might offer industry events or presentations.

These are all wonderful networking opportunities—attend as many of them as you can while you're in college. Naturally, you won't want to do this if you have an exam the next day, but sprinkling a few such events through your semester (or quarter) is a great idea. Hiding in your dorm room is not.

Here are a few suggestions that can apply to any major.

» Your Professors

Most of your professors are going to have some ties to their subject matter or industry. This is the most basic way for you to initially engage with the industry. Develop good professional relationships with your professors and ask them questions about the "real world." Ask about events they attend and get suggestions. You'll find your professors are a treasure trove of information.

» Google

I can't stress this enough. If you want to know your industry, start researching. Google should be your first stop. Seriously, I just Googled "aerospace engineering careers," and NASA was the first search result. Try out different terms, do a little digging. "Aerospace engineering conference" got me to the IEEE Aerospace

Conference. While this one seems to be closed to students, it is sponsored by two organizations that include student membership. (For more information on how valuable student memberships can be, see Chapter 18.) You're going to have to do some research if you really want to get ahead.

» Join Organizations

Organizations that have conferences or competitions—and student memberships—are especially valuable. See Chapter 18 for more information on how to find these groups and how to take advantage of everything they offer. Organizations will link you to conferences, trade shows, and lectures and guess who is going to be at all these cool events? That's right, not only superstars in the field, but potential employers to network with.

Local chapters of big organizations often meet periodically to have coffee, discuss events in their fields, or to network. Can you imagine the wealth of knowledge that one group might have? Go forth, my friend. Go forth and network.

» Online Networking

Online networking—although less traditional—is also possible. I suggest joining groups that you're interested in. Some have email discussion lists or forums or even Skype meetings. Where do you find these groups? Look for them through Google, Facebook, LinkedIn, etc. See Chapter 24 for more details on using social media.

» Family and Friends

Don't forget good ol' Uncle Bob who works for the city! Although you might not be interested in following your Uncle Bob's career path, it's likely that Uncle Bob knows someone in your industry. Or knows someone who knows someone. Your friends and family members can sometimes be the best extension of your own personal network. Don't be afraid to ask them if they know about events at a particular company or in the industry you're pursuing. Ask your friend's parents, members of your church, or other such organizations. You'll be amazed at how small the world is when you start asking for help.

Network Your Network

Have you ever heard of the theory of six degrees of separation? Otherwise known as the Kevin Bacon rule? Well, there's a silly game you can play that says any actor can be related back to Kevin Back in no more than six steps: one actor worked on a film with another actor who worked in a restaurant with another actor who worked . . . you get the idea. The same applies to your network. You're six degrees away from anyone you want to meet. You simply have to ask for the connection.

Since you're putting your college to work, you know to start early to develop your network. You do not want to wait until the month before graduation to begin desperately flinging yourself at people like the one student without a prom date the night of prom. You're *building* relationships.

Don't aim solely at getting introductions to the biggest players in your dream company. You never know who might have a valuable piece of information for you, or who might know someone (like the hiring manager) at the company you're looking at.

Don't ask for an introduction on your first meeting; instead, get to know the person first. Offer *them* some value. Then ask if they might know someone in the industry you're looking to get into. Once again, solidify your relationship first.

That's how you build—and cultivate—effective networks.

22

Crafting Killer Résumés and Cover Letters

I know, I know, if you hear one more time that you have to create or polish your résumé and cover letter, you're going to puke. Truly though, your résumé is the representation of all you've done and how you're different from every other college student out there. And your cover letter is going to tell a potential employer how you are the best candidate for a particular position. This is the time to really shine and show off all of that hard work you've put in.

If you're completely clueless about how to put together a résumé, I suggest you make a trip to your career center, that helpful place we discussed in Chapter 12. You can gain a lot of insight there about how to draft your résumé, what items to include, and how to describe all your best features.

But if you need a quick résumé to take to tomorrow's job fair or want to have something in hand before you walk into the career center, you can find the basics here in this chapter.

Résumé

Most résumés should be arranged something like this:

> Your name
> Your contact information
> Your education

> Your experience
> Your skills
> Your honors/awards

How to Make Your Résumé Pop

Of course, you know it isn't that simple. To make your résumé really stand out, you need to tailor it to the description of the job, internship, research associate, or volunteer position you're applying for. You have to highlight your skills and experience to show why you're the perfect fit for the position and for the company.

TIPS AND TRICKS
● Here's a sample résumé. The formatting will depend on your own style and the preferred style of the business or industry you're applying to. Your career center can probably supply you with some format templates so that you can choose the one you like best. But most résumés include the information shown here.

Buffy Summers
4116 Seaside Lane, Sunnydale, CA 92716
555-555-5555 // Buffy.Summers@gmail.com

Education
Sunnydale High School, 1996-2000
University of California, Sunnydale, 2000-2004
Major: Engineering

Experience
Engineering Society, President
Team Captain for the State Robotics Competition
Organized and instituted an engineering program that visits local elementary schools once a month
Researched, invited industry speakers to monthly meetings

Skills
C++, Java, Robotics, Customer Service
Fluent in Spanish

Honors/Awards
1st Place, State Robotics Competition
Engineering Honors Society
Phi Beta Kappa Honors Society

You've learned how to research people and companies in the chapters on job fairs and networking, and you've looked at Exercise 20.1 in the Resources section. You should also do a little of that kind of research before you write a résumé in response to a job ad. Then put the information you glean to work in your résumé. What does this company say it's looking for in employees? How has what you've done fit into that model?

» Tailor to Your Strengths

This is where your personal branding (see Chapter 4) comes in. Remember, what you offer is a product (*you*), and you're marketing your product to this employer through your résumé and cover letter. So take the time to highlight certain qualities and experiences you think this employer is seeking for this particular position.

Employers or overworked volunteer coordinators shouldn't have to ferret out why you're the best candidate; that should pop out from your résumé at them immediately. Don't make them work for it and don't be generic. Here's how.

You have the description of the position you're applying for in front of you, right? Now, on a piece of paper, I want you answer the following questions.

> What have I done that matches with the description?
> What skills do I have that can be highlighted to fit the job requirement?
> Of all of my experiences, which ones relate the most to this experience?

> **TIPS AND TRICKS**
> ● You may see online or on old résumé tip sheets that you should include an "Objectives" section in your résumé. This is an outdated notion that is no longer required. You used to have to state the objective of sending your résumé, which usually read that you were interested in a particular job. It's considered redundant now, so cut out the "Objectives" section, if you have it.

Take your responses and start drafting your résumé to answer those questions. Ideally, you will tailor your résumé for each position, but if you're applying for jobs or internships in the same industry, they should be similar enough that you don't have to start from scratch each time. But be prepared to spend a little time on the first résumé you create for a specific type of position.

Don't be afraid to move sections around. If your experience speaks the most about why you're perfect for the position, list that first, followed by your education. If you're applying for a teaching assistant position or want to be an adjunct professor, you should probably list your education first.

» Describe the Action

Last (but not least), you don't want to simply list your job duties under each experience. One of the best tidbits I learned in graduate school was to create an action-oriented résumé—meaning one that describes what you accomplished while you were in a position. For example, instead of:

Office Assistant
> *Answered phones*
> *Filed records*
> *Managed boss's calendar*

Try this:

Office Assistant
> *Organized and created a filing system for client records*
> *Developed a system for ordering office supplies that cut expenses by 30%*
> *Prioritized meetings and tasks for management*

» Do It Early

You also want to create your résumé in time to have a few people look it over, or to take it to the ever-helpful folks at the career center (Chapter 12). Once you've read over your résumé a few times, it's easy to miss grammar and spelling issues. Also, others might have pointers about how to strengthen your résumé even further.

» Tailor to Job Listing

If you've ever been to a workshop or read any advice online about writing your résumé, you've probably heard about tailoring your résumé to get past the software that looks for specific keywords. If a résumé doesn't contain whatever keywords the software is looking for, you won't even be advanced to the next step in the hiring process.

This keyword search is used mainly to hire for positions with an online submission process, which allows a company to collect applications from all over the nation—or even the world. The best

Hypothetically Speaking

Are you a little confused about how to tailor your résumé to a specific job description? Let's look at this example, starting with a hypothetical internship posting.

Company: Student Vogue

Internship: Trends Intern

Description: Student Vogue is looking for an intern to create a daily blog series during the summer months that highlights the summer and fall's latest trends. Candidate must show an interest in fashion, have great communication skills, and demonstrate an interest in blogging or writing. A portfolio of past work is recommended.

An internship blogging about fashion? It's your dream come true, right? And, oh man, Student Vogue? They work with some of the biggest stars in Hollywood! So, how can you tailor your résumé to this position? Let's see how a hypothetical student named Kevin hypothetically created a résumé in response to this internship posting.

Kevin has dreamed of entering the world of fashion and aspires to be a fashion journalist. He has a small portfolio, mostly from writing little press releases for a local theater and covering a few of its fundraising events. He also writes his own small blog that's updated weekly. He's a fashion major with a minor in journalism who founded the fashion club at his university. Lately, he just picked up a job in the theater department on campus, helping repair and maintain the costumes in the costume shop. Let's see how Kevin could best present himself for this internship.

Kevin Paulson
1234 University Lane, University City, CA 93586
555-555-5555 / Kevin.Paulson@myuniversity.edu

Qualifications
Maintain and create original content for my own fashion blog (www.
   thatsmyblog.com) that's updated weekly, highlighting fashion news and
   updates in the industry
Wrote press releases for and reported on fundraising events for the
   University Community Theater, many of which were printed in the local
   newspaper
Majoring in fashion and minoring in journalism
Created the University Fashion Club, which supports fellow fashion majors in
   the development and marketing of their collections through collaboration

> > >

way to submit a résumé, however, is always through a personal contact; take a look at the previous chapters on networking, alumni, career center, and job fairs to get some ideas about how to make those kinds of contacts.

> > >

Education
University of Everywhere, 2012-(expected graduation, 2016)
Major: Fashion
Minor: Journalism
GPA: 3.8

Experience
Marketing Volunteer, University Community Theater, 2012-14
Created press releases for each of the theater's upcoming shows for media outlets, many of which were published
Interviewed and reported for theater fundraising events, submitting articles for the local newspaper
Pitched, created, and maintained a blog for the theater highlighting trends in the theater community and upcoming news
Provided office assistance and organization, wherever necessary

Wardrobe Assistant, Generic University, 2014
Organized and maintained current theater costume collection
Repair of current costume collection
Developed a system for photographing and cataloging costumes for inventory purposes

President & Founder, Generic University Fashion Club, 2012-14
Organize events and monthly meetings to help fellow fashion majors collaborate to market and create their fashion lines
Organize and arrange for industry leaders to attend quarterly club events

Skills
Blogging, basic web design, HTML, CSS, proficient in Microsoft Office, excellent communication skills, photography, journalism.

Honors/Awards
1st Place, Generic University Fashion Competition—Most On-Trend Fashion Line
Most Valuable Volunteer, 2014—University Community Theater

See? It's that easy.

But when you *do* have to submit an application or résumé online, be sure your résumé repeats some of the same keywords seen in the posting for the job or internship. For example, if the job announcement seeks an intern to write blog posts, use the words "writing" and "blog" in your résumé if possible. *Don't* say: "have posted weekly online articles in theater newsletter." *Do* say: "have written weekly blog posts for theater newsletter." Although you're describing the same activity, a software program may not recognize that the first description fits the blog requirement and might kick out your perfectly qualified résumé before a human ever sees it.

» Make It Look Professional

If you're going to be hand-delivering your résumé, such as when you attend a job fair or networking event, you need to print it on nice paper. Spend ten bucks or so at an office supply place like Office Max to buy a supply of premium or linen paper. Print your résumés on this paper in dark ink with your printer set at the highest quality setting.

It's a little extra time and money, but the results will make your résumé stand out from the pack and show that you've put thought and effort into the process.

Cover Letter

Good cover letters outline why you're a good fit for a company and/or a particular position. But the best cover letters describe how you can solve some of the problems a company is facing, making it obvious why they should call you in for an interview. So, let's look at some ways to make your cover letter one of the best.

» Don't Be Generic

There's nothing worse than a generic cover letter. Think about the Christmas cards that you get from companies that say "Happy Holidays," signed Company X, with all of the words printed on the card. How many of these did they send out, you wonder? Does it make you feel special? Nope.

Think of your cover letter in the same way. As an employer, I don't want a *Dear Sir/Madam, you're great, I'm great, let's be great together because I'm submitting this stupid letter to 100 companies and hoping someone will pick me* kind of letter. I want to feel special as an employer or recruiter. I want to get a sense that you've looked into my company, that you have an idea about the position and know what you're getting into, and that you can tell me exactly how you're the ideal candidate for the job—beyond being a go-getter, motivated, or a real hard worker.

How do you write a letter like that? Well, first you're going to have to do some research. We've talked about researching companies in other chapters, such as Chapter 20 on networking. If you haven't read it already (or you've read it but forgotten it), turn to Exercise 20.1 in the Resources section for an in-depth discussion of how to conduct research so you can dig up the nuggets of personalized treasure you're going to include in your cover letter.

» Filling a Need

If you do your research, you'll probably be aware of a few situations a company is facing before you apply for a particular position. For example, if you looked up my company, March Consulting, you might notice that we're growing or that we're starting to offer career services for high school students.

So, use a little logic when you write your cover letter and see if you can come up with a way to address a problem you imagine March Consulting might be facing. Perhaps you have experience with career counseling or with high school students. Did you do any youth leadership in college? High school? Do you work well with mentoring high school students? Perhaps you spent a lot of time working for the career center when you were in college. Or, because you know March Consulting is growing, you can assume that it needs people who can take a project and run with it without being told what to do. If you're that kind of person, then tell me that in your cover letter!

Yes, you're going to have to think outside of the box here, but it's no different from your college applications essays. Remember those? (Groan, I know.) Remember when your college asked something along the lines of, "Why this university?" Remember trying to answer that question? I hope that before you answered that question, you wrote down what you were looking for in a college in one column and what the college offered in the other. Then you made them fit together in a basic love letter to the university.

Real-World Advice
Liz Ryan, a former senior VP of human resources for a Fortune 500 company, gives further examples of this concept in what she calls a "pain letter." While designed for professionals with significant work experience, her pain letter format can be easily adapted for students like you. For more information, refer to the Resources section for links to her articles.

A cover letter is no different. You're going to represent your personal brand by describing what you offer and explaining how you would work to solve the company's problems. Remember that it's all about this potential employer. They are not in business to give you a job just because you need a job. They are in business to serve their own customers, so how can you help the company do that?

While it's difficult to draft distinct cover letters for every job you apply to, it's the best way to tell each potential employer how you could be a great fit for them. Your personal brand can really help you out here, which is why it's important to develop one (see Chapter 4). Now fit your brand in with your research on the company. Bingo! Instant cover letter.

{ Kat's Tales from the Real World } I'm going to be honest: I used to hate writing cover letters. It wasn't until I finished graduate school that I felt like I understood what to say in them. When I became an employer, I really learned what you should and shouldn't do with your cover letter.

» What NOT To Write

For clarity, here's an example of a generic, cardboard cover letter written by a hypothetical student for a hypothetical job in the fashion industry:

Dear Sir or Madam (or even worse, To Whom It May Concern):

I'm writing you in reference to your internship. You see, I would love to work in your industry, it would be great for my career. You see, I'm a dedicated worker who is studying hard to become a fashion journalist and your company is a leader in fashion. You'll see in my attached résumé that I'm in college, have a little work experience, and am a hard worker. I would be an asset to your company.

Sincerely,
Student

Imagine you're a recruiter or hiring manager and you get 500 different versions of this letter. Yes, I know the internship would be good for your career. You say that you would be an asset to my company in the most generic way possible. How? You haven't demonstrated to me why you'd be a good fit or that you know anything about me, so how can you say that you'd be an asset? As far as I know, you're applying to each and every fashion company in the world.

» An Eye-Catching Letter

Your cover letter should be as specific as possible and make me want to read more. Again, your career center (Chapter 12) can help you draft your cover letter, giving you specific pointers. In the meantime, here's an example of a cover letter that would catch an employer's eye.

Dear Ms. Clowes,
Your mission to provide high end fashion to the middle class on a tight budget is what I have been trying to encourage young women to follow with my small university fashion blog. I'm a junior at Generic University and am working toward being a fashion journalist. You're looking for an intern who

has great communication skills and an interest in blogging. In addition to my weekly blog that highlights affordable fashion, I have also volunteered for a local community theater and have been creating press releases and reporting on fundraising events, many of which have been published by local media. I also started a fashion club at my university in the hopes of encouraging other fashion designers to collaborate and market their fashion lines.

With a passion for fashion and journalism, I am thrilled at the possibility of creating a daily blog highlighting trends in the way that High End Fashions sees the role of clothing in the lives of its readers. I would love to meet with you and discuss the value that I might bring as an intern. I appreciate your consideration and look forward to hearing from you.

Best,
Student

Do you see the difference? In this example, the student knew who he was writing to, was able to identify something unique about my company, and talked about how he might fit into that picture. Furthermore, he highlighted his experiences in a way that made me want to take a look at his résumé.

Each of your cover letters should be like this: as specific and respectful as possible. Trust me, it will make you stand out in the sea of generic résumés and cover letters. If you want more information and further reading on how to tailor your résumé and cover letters, check out the Resources section.

23

Acing an Interview

Congratulations! You got an interview!

That means someone—or more likely a majority of people on the hiring committee—were intrigued by your résumé and cover letter and want to talk with you. This is a big step toward that job or internship or research position you want. You've worked hard to get to this point—but there's more work to do. Now is not the time to slack off and hope for the best!

Prep Time

It's research time again. Review the notes you originally took before you applied for this position. Look at what the company is doing, its mission, vision, and values. Exercise 20.1 in the Resources section gives you more details about how to research a company or individual.

Since you will probably be interviewing for a specific position, try to get as much information as possible about that job. Also try to get as much information as possible about anyone who may be involved in your interview and learn as much about them as you can without becoming a stalker.

You're going to try to figure out how you fit in at that company— just like you did when you wrote your résumé and cover letter. What can you offer this company? How can you help them?

Find out who in your network might have contacts in this company and ask if they have any information to share. You might pick up a tidbit from a networking contact that this company likes to promote from within and wants to hire entry-level applicants with some leadership skills in the hopes that they'll progress to management quickly. That little piece of information is interview gold: now you know to mention the leadership experience you have and how you hope to move up within the company someday.

» Create Your Questions

Using all your research results, prepare a list of questions you can ask your interviewer. You might wonder why on earth you're getting ready to ask questions; aren't they the ones who are supposed to be asking you questions? The truth is, most interviewers want you to ask questions. It's another chance for you to stand out, show off your research, and make sure this is a place that you want to work.

Interviewing is a two-way street. You are interviewing them as much as they are interviewing you because you need to make sure this company fits in with your vision, your values, your goals. You want to know if it's a work environment you'll enjoy and whether you're going to fit in with the company culture.

Here are some questions you might want to ask during your interview:

> What is your company culture?
> Does everyone seem to get along?
> Is this a highly competitive organization?
> What do you specifically like about the company?
> What would you change about the company?
> What do you like about being here?

TIPS AND TRICKS
● *Company culture* is used to talk about the type of work environment you'll find in an organization. Is it fun? Research-oriented? Is everyone working alone in a cubicle, or do people share desks and workspace and collaborate all the time? Is it a start-up company or long-established corporation? These are important factors, and you want to find a place where you will be comfortable and productive.

> What don't you like about being here?
> Am I going to be working a lot with other team members?
> Am I going to receive any training for this position?
> What opportunities are there for growth in this company?

Don't be afraid to ask a little about the interviewer. They obviously picked this company for a reason, so you can ask questions about that—just remember not to get too personal.

Type up your questions, leaving space so you can take notes on the answers, and take them with you to the interview.

» Get Your Stuff Together

Make sure that your materials are ready. Review your résumé and cover letter to ensure they're tailored for the position you're interviewing for. Reread the job description and your résumé to confirm you're drawing clear parallels.

Remember that portfolio you took to the job fair (see Chapter 20)? Pull it out again and pack your questions and several copies of your résumé you can hand out in your interview. Be prepared for the possibility of meeting with more than one interviewer—you might be talking to a committee or sitting in front of four people. I don't say this to scare you, but to prepare you. Have ample copies of your résumé to hand out to anyone who doesn't seem to have a copy in front of them when you walk into the room.

Print up your questions and résumés well in advance, not the night before. Printers can smell fear and desperation and they will refuse to cooperate when you need them the most. Also, map out the interview location ahead of time, if you're meeting in person. Find out where you're going to park (plus an alternative if you're in a city that has limited space), what office you're going to, and how you're going to get there. Print these directions out too, in case your phone decides to run out of battery or die on your drive. Phones also smell desperation when you're running late.

Remember that technology will always fail when you are counting on it. If you're Skyping, make sure everything runs smoothly a few days before. Don't wait until five minutes before your interview to discover that things aren't working or that you didn't download the most recent version/update/random notification.

» Dress to Impress

You've updated your résumé, cover letter, and questions, printed them out, and packed your portfolio. Now to prepare what you're going to wear to the interview. While you want to dress according to the company culture, I feel that it's always better to be overdressed than underdressed.

In Silicon Valley, this might be a little bit different, but for the rest of the working world, men will want to wear a traditional suit and tie, shirt tucked in, that sort of thing. Ladies, you're going to want to wear a skirt or pantsuit. If you don't have nice business clothes, there are a lot of options, including picking some up at your local second-hand shop for pennies on the dollar. You can also borrow something from a friend or relative.

You want to look as neat and tidy as possible. Hair styled. Ladies, wear makeup. Your nails need to be neatly manicured. No overwhelming cologne—tone down the Axe body spray and Clinique Happy. Keep in mind that you want to project professionalism while also expressing your personal brand (see Chapter 4).

Practice, Practice, and—uh— More Practice?

Going into an interview cold is never a good idea. You're not sure what they're going to ask, not sure how to talk about yourself, and you don't want to blow your interview because you're not prepared. The good news is that your career center (see Chapter 12) should have tips on interviewing, and you may even be able to sit down with a career counselor and practice your interview skills.

If you're down to the wire, get your roommate to ask you a few questions about yourself. You should be able to talk about yourself and define some personal goals and aspirations without stumbling too much. Keep the *ums* and *uhs* to a minimum (learning to avoid the *ums* and *uhs* will make you a better public speaker, interviewer, and communicator in general).

» Anticipate Their Questions

Of course, you will be asked specific questions about the position you're applying for, but most interviews will contain some traditional interview questions like: *tell us your greatest weakness or strength* or *describe a situation where you were a leader.* The more you field these types of questions, the easier it will get to talk about yourself, so make sure that you practice any way that you can. Practice makes perfect.

When answering these types of questions, think about all the experiences you've had, and how that would relate to the position itself. If you're applying for a research position, you'll need to give examples of when you were a leader, self-starter, and when you worked on your own research or research for others. If you're applying for an office position, be prepared to give examples of work you've done in an office or show off your office skills with your answers.

If you don't have specific experience, try to describe your skills and relate them to the position you're applying for. Rely on your brand, your mission, vision, values, and passions to help you when you get stuck in answering. Keep in mind that you've already done most of the work—now you just need to answer questions about what you've done.

Don't be surprised if the interviewers throw you an odd question or two. Questions like *Do you know Section 2 of the safety code?* or *If you were a fish, what kind of fish would you be and why?* could be your worst nightmare. The worst thing you can do, of course, is lie. If you don't know Section 2 of the safety code, say so. But if you know other parts of the code specifically, say that you do, or explain how you're aware of the code itself but not the specifics. Never lie. Trust yourself to give an answer and don't be afraid to take a moment to gather your thoughts before you reply.

Last but not least, remember to outline a few big accomplishments of your own. Especially if you don't have work experience, mention leadership roles you've taken on or big projects you've helped with. This is where your volunteer work, leadership roles in clubs, or other such experiences can help set you apart from your classmates. Think about the role you played in each experience, the skills required to be successful, and how that relates to the position you're looking at or the company that you're applying for. Try to make as many parallels as you can.

> **TIPS AND TRICKS**
> ● You can prepare for typical interview questions by reviewing your personal brand and your goals, values, and passions. (See Chapters 2 and 4 if you need a refresher.) Here are a few sample questions you are likely to encounter in an interview:
>   • Tell me about yourself.
>   • Have you had any internships?
>   • What have you been doing outside of the classroom?
>   • Have you been working on research projects?
>   • What can you bring to our company?
>   • What brings you here today?

The Night Before

Make sure you eat, don't drink alcohol, and get a good night's sleep before your interview. Before you go to bed, set out your clothes, your bag with your questions and résumés, and everything else you might need, and set a few alarms to make sure you don't oversleep or miss your appointment.

Put gas in your car if you're driving or make sure you have money or a pass for public transit. Always have a back-up plan in case something goes wrong. You don't want to be stranded if your car won't start in the morning. Remember that in most towns and cities, there are always last-resort taxis.

Practice introducing yourself a few times so it sounds smooth. You don't have to do this in front of a mirror, but make sure the words leave your lips, even if you're talking to yourself in the shower. Also practice the start of the interview, in case you get nervous. You'll be less likely to get nervous if you know what you're going to say.

The Interview

For the interview itself, arrive fifteen minutes early and wait patiently. Smile.

Before you even go into the building, when you're driving or walking up, I want you to think about the happiest moment you've ever had and get really excited about it, and I want you to keep that mindset as you're walking through the building to your interview. Forget the nerves, forget about everything else; I want you to picture yourself as the most happy, confident person you've ever been. This is going to radiate off of you and overshadow your nervousness.

Remember to be extraordinarily polite to everyone you see. When you talk to the person at the front desk and let them know you're here for your interview, ask them how their day is going. Be personable, be nice. Trust me, it goes a long way. Keep in mind that anyone you come into contact with might have something to say about your candidacy. Even a comment from a secretary like, "Man, that guy was really nice; he seemed really happy," could tip the scales in your favor.

Greet everyone you meet with a strong, proper handshake. Make sure you thank your interviewers at the start and end of the conversation. Remember that time is money, and they've invested in you. When you sit down for your interview, don't slouch. Sit up straight, don't talk too much with your hands, but don't keep them between your legs the whole time.

Make eye contact, have confident body language, and don't shrivel up into a little ball and stare at your fingernails the entire time. Appear confident and relaxed, but not cocky. One of the worst mistakes interviewees make is to immediately ask questions of their interviewers, as in: "Okay, what do you guys do?" Let them take the lead and show them professionally and politely that you've done your research.

Be enthusiastic about the position; show excitement to be part of this position, this company. Don't say something like, "Oh yeah, my dad's forcing me to get a job," or "This'll be great as a stepping stone, I guess."

STAR Method of Responding

Making sure your responses are clear and you're not talking yourself in a circle can be hard when you're nervous or surprised by a question. Recently, the corporate world has been abuzz about using the STAR method of responding to questions: Situation, Task, Action, Result.

I have a tendency to go off on tangents when I'm answering questions because I get excited about the topic. So, when I'm being interviewed, I use the STAR method to keep myself from going on 50,000 random tangents that aren't relevant.

How does it work? To answer a question using the STAR method response, you would mention a certain *situation*, describe the *task* at hand and the *action* you took, and elaborate on the *results*. You don't have to keep to this exactly (unless your interviewer asks you to), but it's a good way to keep your mind and mouth on task when answering questions.

Situation: Give context here. Think who, when, where.

Task: What needed to be done? Why? What challenges did you face?

Action: What did you do? How did you do it? Why did you do it that way?

Result: What happened because of your actions?

For example, if the question is, "Give us an example of a time that you took a leadership role," this would be the STAR response:

(Situation) I was the president of my drama club, and we organized a fundraiser in the spring to raise money for the spring production.

(Task) We needed to raise at least $3,000 to meet our goal, and different ideas were brought forward for the fundraiser itself. The problem was that the previous couple years, the drama club's traditional fundraisers—car washes and bake sales—had not raised the minimum amount needed.

(Action) We decided to put on a variety show instead, showcasing the talent of faculty members and students from different departments at the university. We contacted the university activities department, put up posters, and had the cooperation of all of the department heads for the event. We were able to use the theater for our fundraiser and contacted sponsors to bring in food and award prizes.

(Result) The event was a hit. We had over 400 attendees and raised $8,000 for the drama club.

You might also add what you learned from the situation, arranging a large event and the challenges that arose from it, etc. It depends on the job that you're vying for and how your answer showcases your different skills.

> > >

> > >

Remember that this is your chance to showcase yourself. Brag a little. Show off your skills and make parallels between what you're talking about and the job description itself. In the above example, you might be applying for an entry-level position at a nonprofit for fundraising, so show off those fundraising skills.

Wrapping Up the Interview

When they ask you if you have any questions, take out your printed sheet, your pen, and start asking. Ask follow-up questions if you need to and don't be afraid to let the conversation happen organically.

Last but not least, don't be afraid to tell them that you really want the job, or the internship. You want to leave selling yourself, so make sure to tell them that this is what you want, you're really excited, that if there's anything else that you can provide, you're willing to provide it.

» Thank-You Notes and Following Up

After your interview, you're going to send a thank-you note within 24 hours, just like you did for the job fair. If at all possible, send a handwritten note. There are two reasons for a thank-you note:

> To show them that you can follow up, which is extremely important in the corporate world;
> To genuinely thank the interviewer and also remind them a little bit about you.

Be as specific and personable as you can. If you discussed something or found a common interest, point it out. Remind your interviewer of the connection you made.

Remember to get this in the mail within 24 hours of your interview. Since we're now working across generations (meaning your interviewer could be slightly older or significantly older than you), it might not be a bad idea to send an immediate email, followed by a handwritten note.

If you haven't heard from anyone for two weeks after you interviewed, don't be afraid to send another follow-up letter. You can express your continued interest in the position and let them know how to contact you if they have any other questions. The bottom line is to make sure you follow up after the interview.

TIPS AND TRICKS
● Here's an example of a post-interview thank-you note:

Dr. Banning,
Thank you so much for the interview. While I might not be as skilled a golfer, I can hold my own on the course and love talking to other golfers. Like I had mentioned, my love for golf and being president of my fraternity has given me a number of opportunities to talk with different types of people, getting to know their personalities and how to best serve them. That's why I think I'd be a great customer relationship manager at your company. Most business is done on the golf course, and I think it would be a fantastic way to bring in more customers.

Thank you again for your time.

Best,
Gordy DeGroote

Real-World Advice

Let's see, what could I say to potential interviewees? Treat it like one would treat an important exam: study. Study the company, study the job description, study the job. If you know someone that either works for the company or a similar industry, ask questions about what job-specific knowledge might help in an interview.

Get to know the industry that you're applying for. For instance, industrial industries and utilities are extremely safety conscious, something that's very important to know. Prepare for questions that will revolve around safety and ethics. If you study the company and the job, you should be well prepared for your interview.

Of course, some experience will only help your cause and separate you from those that do not have any experience. So, seek out internships in the industry in which you would like to pursue a career. The job landscape is very competitive; gain any advantage you can. Last, but not least, be confident and cordial but not long-winded. Pay attention to the question and answer the question. Stay on point and don't go off onto tangents.

—*Gabe Ruiz, Senior Engineering Estimator, Pacific Gas and Electric Company*

24

Using Social Media—Wisely

I'm not going to tell you what social media is. If you don't know what Facebook, Twitter, Instagram, Snapchat, Tumblr, and other social media sites are, then you need to get a bigger book because this one is not going to cut it.

There is no doubt that social media can help you get a job or internship. It can also ruin your chances for certain jobs or internships. Social media is great and all, but what a lot of students don't realize is that I can learn a lot about you (everything about you) online through social media—even when you think you've set up privacy controls. And if I can search you, so can future employers, networking contacts, and the like. It's becoming more and more important that you be portrayed in the best light possible in all of your social media accounts. You don't want a potential employer to find multiple pictures of you doing keg stands at last night's party.

Remember all our talk about personal branding in Chapter 4? Social media is an extension of your brand. You're putting yourself out there: your personality, pictures of yourself, responses to conversations, and other such demonstrations of what kind of person you are. Everyone knows someone who is always complaining in online forums or posting vague pictures in an attempt to attract attention. Even worse is the selfie queen who can't seem to put her phone down and can't seem to stop taking pictures of herself with every meal or new shopping find.

Now that you're in college—and thinking about life *after* college—you're going to have to look at social media in a more professional manner.

The Assessment

I want you to take a good look at all of the profiles you have online. That means your Instagram, Twitter feed, Facebook, Tumblr, LinkedIn, Snapchat, and any other social media account you might have. Take an honest look at your profiles. Look at the pictures you share, the things you say, and ask yourself: does this portray a positive, professional image of me? Sometimes this can be hard to evaluate, but here are a few questions to keep in mind.

> Do my pictures portray me in a professional, fun, or otherwise acceptable manner? Meaning—do you have pictures of yourself at parties? Drinking? Vomiting? Showing off body parts that wouldn't be allowed in a corporate arena?
> What do my online pictures say about me? Take a good look and think hard about this question. If you were hiring somebody to work for you, what would you say if their pictures looked like yours?
> What kinds of things are you posting? Is it all about drama? All about "poor me?" We all know a person on Facebook or Twitter who is constantly posting complaints about their awful boss and their awful life. Who wants to hire that person? Who wants to be around that person? Are your posts mostly positive? Are you inspiring people? Are you too political? Are you posting things about your industry? Are you posting things about Pokémon? Well, maybe not Pokémon, but you get the idea. I want you to look at what you're posting through the eyes of a potential employer.
> What are your friends posting on your page? Is it appropriate? Would you want an employer to see what your friends are saying about your latest party shenanigans?
> What kind of language are you using? When you post something or respond to comments, do you always write in text-speak, or do you use full, grammatically correct sentences? Do you swear a lot? You might want to curtail the swearing.

» Re-Branding

Now that you've done your assessment, what do you think? Are you finding things in your social media accounts that would worry an employer? Finding things that don't give off the best impression of you? Don't panic, you can always start fresh.

But what kind of fresh, you might ask? What should I be posting online? The truth is that it depends on your personal brand and your goals. The social media profile of a future fashion journalist should look completely different from the social media profile of a future financial planner or future engineer. Someone who is vying for that ever-competitive position at a start-up in Silicon Valley should have a different profile and be sharing different content than someone who wants a consulting position in New York.

{ Kat's Tales from the Real World } The top five qualities I want to convey through my social media are: classy, professional, informative, helpful, fun. Oooh, that last one doesn't seem to fit with the other four, does it? Funny thing is, being classy, professional, informative, and helpful doesn't have to mean stiff and boring. That's why it's also important for me to convey a fun persona.

If you look at my social media accounts, you'll find that I share a number of industry-related articles about college and career, updates that are positive in general, and occasional pictures that reveal something about my personal life in a positive manner. You'll also occasionally find mentions of my hobbies. In addition to my educational consulting, I am also a historical costumer, meaning I reproduce garments from museum copies and attend different events (think Comic Con for history buffs). You'll find references to those activities throughout my profiles as well, showing a different side of me.

Nothing that I post is negative. My picture is professional. My brand is reinforced through each of my profiles. If anything I posted ever happened to show up on the front page of the newspaper, I wouldn't be embarrassed because I know everything I post is a good representation of me and what I stand for.

Considering and mapping out your personal brand is vital for this section, so if you haven't done that yet, go do it now! See Chapter 4 and Exercises 4.1 and 4.2 in the Resources list. Those exercises will help you create master lists of the top positive qualities you want to convey to people and the negative qualities you never want to convey.

Now look at those lists and decide how you can use your social media profiles to evoke those qualities. The language and posts you use will vary a little bit depending on the platform, but the message you're trying to get across should be pretty uniform.

This is what you want for your profiles. If the *Wall Street Journal* or *Time* magazine (or your local newspaper, which your mother still reads) printed something you had posted, would you be embarrassed? Could it hurt your brand and hire-ability? Could it jeopardize your chance at a position down the line?

Cleaning Up Your Profiles

You don't necessarily have to delete your accounts and start fresh, though that is an option. Delete and clean up what you can. I know that might be hard if you have 17,000 tweets.

» Consider Your Friends and What They Post

Do you have friends who post explicit content? Are they constantly swearing and bringing up inappropriate references? It might be time to consider weeding those folks out of your friends list. If you catch any flack, just say you're cleaning up your profile in order to maximize your chances for a few job opportunities.

You don't want your friends posting inappropriate pictures to your wall, or commenting on your very appropriate posts with rude language, or even retweeting inappropriate content.

» Professional or G-Rated Pictures

Make sure that you edit out inappropriate pictures. Your profile picture should be a clear photo of you. By clear, I mean that I could recognize you at an event if I saw your face. While there's

nothing wrong with going to a party once in a while, make sure
the pictures you share online are appropriate. Pictures of you with
your friends, at the game, Instagram pictures of an amazing tree
or fantastic breakfast are perfectly all right. That's professional,
that makes you look human, that's fine. But if a stranger Googles
you, what kind of image will they get from the online pictures
you've posted? Will they think you are a hard-partying frat boy? A
community-minded activist? Someone with a dark view of life? A
positive person? And how does that image relate to the industry
that you're interested in?

Having appropriate pictures doesn't mean that you need to go to a
portrait studio for a profile pic or only post photos of puppies and
butterflies. But make sure that the pictures you have, again, are
G- or PG-rated. If you're trying to enter the corporate world and
most of your pictures show you drinking at parties, you need to
reevaluate what you're posting.

» Privacy Controls

If you want to leave up your favorite pictures from your over-the-
top Spring Break trip (which I highly recommend you NOT do),
make sure that your privacy controls are in place. These aren't
always easy to find, and they change all the time. And now with
Twitter, it's even harder to do, but keep it in mind. Spend some
time looking through ALL the screens of the privacy settings of
ALL your accounts. And try to keep up with the changing settings.

Your New Profiles

So, now you know what you DON'T want on your social media
profiles. But what should be there? Your new profile should now
reflect your brand. If you want to get specific and stand out from
the crowd, share interesting tidbits and articles about the industry
you're aspiring to and post positive career messages and positive
life-in-general messages along the way. Share uplifting quotes and
good news here and there. Selfies are all right as long as they're
not taken every day and littering your profiles.

Share how you're volunteering, going to community events, lectures, and things of that nature. Share pictures from the latest conference or trade show you attended, your self-enrichment activities, classes, or a new tidbit of information you learned today. Make your brand clear. If you love to learn and meet new people, share that on social media. If you're interested in the news and other serious issues, share that as well.

Most importantly? Share what you're doing and what you're studying. I want to see that you're putting in more work than just going to class every day. Let's look at some different social media platforms and how to put them to work for you.

TIPS AND TRICKS

● I told you to share what you're interested in, but this comes with a warning, like everything else. Unless you're a political science major with a hard stance on certain issues, stay away from hardcore religious views, political messages, and things of that nature. You never know who your next employer could be, and you don't want to offend anyone. With that said, if your career requires you to take a strong stance on a contentious topic, that should be taken into consideration as well. Use common sense.

LinkedIn

If you're like most contemporary college students, you know all you need to know about Facebook, Instagram, and Tumblr. But you may not be so familiar with LinkedIn, which is the one social media platform that can help you the most if you're looking for a job or internship. So let's take a long look at LinkedIn, which is one of the best ways to contact and form connections with business professionals and network online.

LinkedIn is a professional social media platform that allows you to create a profile and share your résumé, a summary (like a cover letter), a professional picture, your portfolio, recent projects, and recommendations. You can also join industry groups and connect with people in businesses you're interested in. LinkedIn is the greatest source of information for a student, as it also provides job postings, and companies are using it more and more to recruit and hire students.

For example, let's say that you're interested in working for Disney. You're not sure if you know anyone who works there, but you're set on being on stage as one of the Disney princesses. With LinkedIn, you can look for openings for Disney princesses on the Disney company LinkedIn page, research who serves as the hiring manager for Disney princesses, look to see if anyone in your network or your alumni group works at Disney, and get tips from Disney industry groups about how to impress at a job interview in the Disney princess world. Basically, you can find out almost everything you need to know in this one platform.

TIPS AND TRICKS

● LinkedIn actually makes it easy for you to connect with alumni from your school—and if you don't know why that's important, then go read Chapter 13. If you go to your university's LinkedIn page, you can easily see who lists your college as their alma matter. From there, you can ask to connect with some of these folks. If they're local, you may even want to ask if you can schedule time for coffee or a quick lunch. Don't ask immediately to tap into their network (no one wants to be *that* guy). Instead, get to know them, ask them about their industries and be honest about what you're looking for.

Recruiters are now using LinkedIn to qualify people (meaning sifting through candidates for possible positions). Think about that. Internships, jobs—there are thousands of them posted every single day. That gives you a huge opportunity for a head start. LinkedIn is a little more robust than Monster.com, or some of the other online job-search platforms because recruiters can see immediately if your profile matches their search.

» Your Profile

Setting up a LinkedIn profile is free; you can pay for a premium account plan, but I recommend that you stick with the free service unless you see the need to get a paid account. If you find that you're using LinkedIn to manage connections, network, learn about your industry, perform job searches, and want to reach out to recruiters, a paid account might be a good idea. But before you shell out the cash, make sure you're going to use the service, as paid accounts are a monthly charge.

To set up your profile, just fill in the boxes: put your first name, last name, e-mail, answer a few questions about yourself and—bam—you have a profile. It's really easy. LinkedIn walks you step by step to help you fill in your school affiliation, the classes you've taken, the skills that you have. You're going to fill in your résumé, projects you've been involved with, things like that.

LinkedIn allows you to post your résumé and everything and anything you want to share about yourself for future contacts, recruiters, or employers to find. Your profile is, naturally, one of the most important components of LinkedIn. To make the most of your LinkedIn profile, you need to pay attention to the following elements.

Your Profile Picture. First and foremost, make sure you have a clear profile picture that portrays you in a professional manner. If you're an artist, this can be true to your brand and more artistic. If you're looking for corporate work, you should be dressed professionally and be looking at the camera in a nice setting with good lighting. Remember that this picture will be the first impression that someone is going to get of you, so it shouldn't be a selfie, against a blank wall, or a bad party picture where people are around you.

Take some time and have your roommate or friend take a good picture of you outside in natural light. You can do this with your phone. Crop it well and use it as your profile picture. If you're confused about what good profile pics should look like, look at a few leaders on LinkedIn and check out their profile pictures. Does your picture look like it should be on the jacket of a book you authored? Good.

Remember your branding here too. If you're aiming for a tech position in Silicon Valley, there's a certain look to that sort of employee, as opposed to a finance manager or a corporate accountant. Keep that in mind when taking your picture. Make sure you're recognizable, looking straight at the camera, and not taking a selfie.

Your Headline. You're also required to have a headline. Oh no! A headline! Yes, a headline to describe yourself. Get creative here, depending on your brand. Your headline could read: "Kat Clowes, visionary and future rocket scientist" or "Kat Clowes, fashion designer, blogger." Your headline will depend on your brand, what you're trying to communicate to future contacts, and what your goals are. Currently, my LinkedIn profile reads: Kat Clowes, Founder, CEO—March Consulting, Educational Consultant, Author, Speaker, Entrepreneur. It expresses all that I want to get across on LinkedIn. I'm the founder and CEO of my company, an educational consultant, an author, a speaker, and an entrepreneur.

Get really specific about what you want and what you're looking for. Since LinkedIn is also a search engine of sorts, you want to make sure to use keywords in your headline. The headline communicates what you specialize in and what you're interested in doing within your industry.

Your Summary. Your summary is like your cover letter. It tells me why you're qualified to do what you're seeking to do, what experiences you've had, and what your goals are. Your summary

TIPS AND TRICKS

● When creating a headline for your LinkedIn profile, think about your personal brand and what you want to share. Are you looking for a job? Do you want to make alumni connections? Here are a few questions to consider in order to generate your ideal headline.

- What is your current major?
- What is your specialization?
- What are you looking for in a career?

A good headline: Future Aerospace Engineering Graduate specializing in aerodynamics. Interested in research and analysis.

A bad headline: Engineering graduate looking for employment in the industry.

A really bad headline: Dynamic team player looking for opportunities in the engineering industry.

Do you see why the bad headlines are bad? They don't tell me anything about you and they are essentially corporate-speak. While a little bit of corporate-speak can be good, too much is too much of a bad thing.

is perhaps the most pliant piece of your profile, in that you can make it whatever you want it to be. My summary, for example, tells a little about my story and how I've become passionate about what I do, along with how I can help and how you can contact me outside of LinkedIn. Since I'm no longer looking for a job, that's not the focus of my profile and summary.

You, on the other hand, have a different goal. A good LinkedIn summary gives me enough information that I'm inspired to look at your résumé and the rest of your profile. It should be tailored toward me and what I'm looking for in a candidate—*me* meaning whoever your target market is. Be specific about what you want.

You might find it easier to tell a story about yourself in your summary. If so, your story should be in first person and should be a small demonstration of how you moved from the beginning to where you are now and how you're hoping to continue.

Then, at the bottom of your summary, consider listing a few keywords. LinkedIn, after all, is a search engine for people with particular skills. When people search on LinkedIn for these qualities, you want your profile to show up in their results. Think about how you want to be found. Instead of listing keywords under the title "Keywords," consider listing them as specialties or special skills, like you would in a résumé.

> **TIPS AND TRICKS**
> ● Consider these questions when developing your LinkedIn summary.
> - How did you develop yourself from high school to college? You could mention relevant work experience, important/relevant extracurricular experiences.
> - How have you been strategic about where you're headed? This should focus on activities and events that you've been part of that support your specialization.
> - What skills have you developed during this journey?

Your Résumé. LinkedIn makes filling in your résumé rather easy. Fill in your paid work experiences as they prompt you to do. As a student, you're probably going to include all of your work experiences, as you might not have a very long list. But if you have been working the last ten years, list only relevant work experience that pertains to what you're trying to achieve in your career or that highlights your skills.

Instead of listing every duty you ever had for your LinkedIn résumé, try to highlight accomplishments. For example, if you

{ Kat's Tales from the Real World } Here's an example of my summary, complete with a specialties section where I list keywords based on who my audience is and how I want to be found.

When you're little and they ask you what you want to be when you grow up, I always had a million different answers, never being able to decide if I wanted to be an Olympic equestrian rider or an orthodontist. When I was introduced to thinking about college in junior high, I used to spend hours planning out different career routes, dreaming about the different majors that would lead me down different paths and what college could help me get there.

Encouraged after college to experience various industries, I pursued knowledge, attracted to positions where I could develop leadership, business, and facilitation skills, teach others, or mentor. Embracing my entrepreneurial passion, I teach what I have learned to students who have their whole careers ahead of them, setting them up for success. We no longer help students in high school prepare for the workforce; we prepare them for college and let them figure out the rest on their own, in a vacuum.

That's what I share with students. I'm creating the dialogue that equips students with the right questions to ask in planning their future while facilitating that plan in terms of college admissions guidance, career guidance, and taking advantage of the opportunities available to them during their college years.

I look forward to connecting with you.

Facebook—www.facebook.com/mymarchconsulting

Specialties: College admissions guidance, transfer admissions, early career strategic planning, educational consulting, project management, leadership, small business consulting

Your summary will look differently since you are still a student, but not by much. I want to learn something about you that keeps me reading, on a professional basis. Tell me something about yourself and make it interesting. Highlight special projects you were involved in, or a special effort that you led through a club or organization that sparked an interest. This is the place where you answer that infamous interview question: tell me a little bit about yourself.

were an office assistant, most people have a good idea of your general duties, which probably included answering phones, filing, organizing, etc. Instead of listing those duties, list what you achieved in your position.

Compare these two examples:

Green Screen Theatre, 2014–2015
Office Assistant
> *Answered phones*
> *Organized file system*
> *Printed out schedules to hand to crews*

Or

Green Screen Theatre, 2014–2015
> *Reorganized filing system to make file retrieval easier for the office*
> *Created a system for distributing work schedules to the crews*

When you make your résumé duties more action-oriented, they not only read better, but they tell me that you did more than the bare minimum. Now, there's an important caveat to this: *don't lie.* If you didn't achieve something new while working there, don't say that you did.

If you're currently working right now and you're not achieving something and making daily improvements, start being more proactive. See if there are ways you can make your work flow better or make things easier for your supervisor or boss. Then you can honestly list those achievements on your résumé.

List volunteer experience that you have in the same way under LinkedIn's volunteer experience section. It's very important that you list your experience volunteering, as it shows that you've been doing more than just school—especially if you're not working. If you are working *AND* going to school *AND* volunteering, it simply makes you look that much better.

Other Highlights in Your Profile. If you're a member of any professional organizations or have received any honors and awards, make sure those are all listed. Be sure you have listed your school and your intended major and concentration. If you've published anything—blog posts, articles in your university newspaper, research in professional journals—make sure to include those publications on your profile.

You can also list any projects you've been involved with. Think about larger projects that took a lot of time and energy that might support your skills and areas of study. Your senior thesis will definitely go here, but there might be other projects you've done or collaborated in that fit the bill too.

You can also list skills on your profile, which are different than your keyword skills in your summary (though not different, really). Other connections can endorse you for your skills, meaning they agree that you have those skills. Those endorsements, believe it or not, do help you as well. So endorse others and you'll get endorsements in return.

» Recommendations

Once you start making connections on LinkedIn, you're going to want to start providing recommendations to other people that you've worked with or know. Why? So you can build strong recommendations in return. Recommendations are LinkedIn's portable references tool. Recruiters will notice if someone you've worked with vouches for your skills.

Instead of *asking* for a batch of recommendations, try *giving* a batch of recommendations to people you've worked with, perhaps casually mentioning in a person-to-person conversation that you'd like to build up your own recommendation list. Only ask others who know you well or have worked with you, so they can give you a great reference.

Putting LinkedIn to Work for You

You have your LinkedIn profile all ready to go; everything is complete. Now what? Like I said before, LinkedIn is a robust system for everything about your career, but you have to know how to use it. Let's take a look at its tools, starting with your network.

» Connections

There is a certain way to go about connecting with people on LinkedIn. It's not like Facebook or Twitter, where you can simply send a friend request or start following someone. There's a right way and a wrong way to increase your connections on LinkedIn. When you open your account, you'll be asked to allow LinkedIn to

---

TIPS AND TRICKS

● To reach out through a current connection, you'll need to ask for an introduction. If you're an introvert like me, that can be daunting. After taking a few workshops on LinkedIn from Starr Hall, a LinkedIn guru, I had a few "stock" sample scripts to adapt when connecting with people.[1] They made a huge difference, as I no longer had an excuse *not* to connect with people.

Here's a sample script to get you started. Remember to be assertive but not pressure your connections.

Hello Amy,

As I mentioned the other night at dinner, I am looking for job shadowing opportunities and applying for internships. I saw that you're connected to Peter Gonzales at Disney. I've been looking at internships at Disney, and Peter works in the Imagineering department, right where I'm hoping to be after I graduate. I would love to speak with him about his day-to-day and what it takes to be an Imagineer at Disney. Would you mind introducing us?

If there's anyone in my network that I can connect you with, I would love to do it. I know that a good friend of mine, Katie Jones, is looking to volunteer at the Red Cross. Perhaps I could introduce the two of you? I know you've been looking to expand the volunteer efforts at the Kern Chapter of the Red Cross.

Best,
Kat

---

[1] If you're looking for formal training on LinkedIn, check out Starr on her website http://www.starrhall.com/.

go through your email contacts, asking them to connect with you. This is a great way to start with people that you know, requesting them as connections on LinkedIn automatically.

LinkedIn won't allow you to reach out to complete strangers and ask for a connection. That doesn't mean, however, that you can't connect with someone you're not friends with currently—there's simply a different way you have to go about it. You can ask current connections for an introduction to one of their connections. Or if you have a paid account, you can reach out through what's called InMail, a sort of direct messaging system that you can use to connect with those who aren't in your circles (people in your circles meaning people you already know). If you have a free account and try to connect with someone outside of your circles, you will be asked how you know that person, whether they're a friend, past co-worker, etc. If you can't identify some past connection, sometimes LinkedIn won't allow you to connect through your account.

It's important that you know the right and wrong way to connect with people, as it can be considered rude if not handled properly. This isn't meant to scare you, only to prepare you for the differences between LinkedIn and other social networks. In 2014, a job seeker was given quite a surprise when she requested a connection to Kelly Blazek, the founder and executive of a Job Bank in Cleveland.[2] Ms. Blazek wrote a scathing message back that not only was inappropriate, but created a social media storm that harmed her brand. The job seeker was issued an apology letter. Although Ms. Blazek's answer was inappropriate, her response emphasizes the importance of people stating who they are, how they know someone, and why they want to connect.

This is what I want you to focus on. When you ask for a connection, introduce yourself, mention how you know the person you're asking to connect with, and say why you want to connect.

---

[2] More information on what was said and not said can be found here: http://time.com/10860/linkedin-rant-apology-kelly-blazek/.

Don't simply use the old, standard LinkedIn script, which is: "I'd like to add you to my professional network on LinkedIn." Bleh, this doesn't tell me anything about you or why I should connect with you.

While it might seem intimidating, you'll get the hang of it. Like networking in person, you have to remember to emphasize what the other person will gain by connecting with you. Be polite and professional and don't be afraid to tell people why you admire them, or why you're a fan of theirs. Genuine flattery (not gushing) is usually welcomed.

TIPS AND TRICKS
● Here are examples of good connection scripts for LinkedIn.

Hello Kat, I'm Katie Smith. We met when you spoke at the NAPW meeting last week. I loved your points about using LinkedIn to search for jobs. I would love to connect with you and share tidbits as I start my journey.

***

Hello Kat, I'm Katie Smith. I came across your profile in the women's networking group and loved the points you brought to the discussion on branding. I would love. to connect with you.

» Influencers

As though it couldn't be more complicated, there are different types of connections on LinkedIn profiles. Those that are higher up, have a number of different connections (usually over 500), or are leaders in their industries are called LinkedIn Influencers. It's much harder to achieve direct connections with these influencers or to add them to your network.

But you can follow Influencers, which means that their updates (much like article-sharing or a blog) will post to your newsfeed. You can keep up with and comment on their updates, which is probably the first step to getting to know them. But don't expect an immediate response from these Influencers; like anyone with a huge following, they have many followers and people who want to connect.

» Companies

That's right, you can follow companies as well as people. With companies it's easier; you simply click the link that says you want to follow them. This is particularly useful when you want to keep up with news for a certain company, such as job openings and the like. I highly recommend that you follow a few companies that you're interested in, and keep up to date with them through LinkedIn, which will be especially helpful if you get an interview.

» Alumni and Your University

LinkedIn recently rolled out University pages. While this might sound lame, it's actually a useful tool to connect with alumni. (See Chapter 13 for more details about why you would want to do that.) Through your university page, you can see what industries alumni are working in, which companies they're working for, and which areas of the country (or world) that they're in. Once you click through those search terms, you can see the specific profiles of past alumni. Now, if you happen to see alumni at the company where you want to work or get an internship, LinkedIn provides a great way to introduce yourself and seek out a connection. This is probably the most valuable thing about your university page, so I highly recommend that you use it.

» Groups

Another valuable tool that LinkedIn provides are groups of all shapes and sizes. They can be classified according to industry, specialization, interest, area—you name it. Some require specifics for you to join (such as being a CEO), but others are open to all who are interested.

You can increase your network through LinkedIn groups by posting relevant articles, news tips, and commenting on posts made by others. Groups also allow you to gain more information about the industry you're looking to enter. This is a great research tool for you, and I highly recommend you take advantage of it. There's no limit to the number of groups you can join, but I would suggest quality over quantity. Also seek out groups that are more active than others.

» General Searching

LinkedIn will allow you to search profiles according to keywords, which is a great way to see the experiences and résumés of people in positions where you want to be someday. Searching also provides a way to connect with recruiters, alumni, and other valuable future connections.

» Job and Internship Searching

LinkedIn is a spectacular job searching tool. Specify "jobs" in the search field, then search by job title, by company, or by internship, and by your desired area. There are thousands of jobs posted each day on LinkedIn—internships too—so why not put your account to work for you? Reach out to recruiters and hiring managers and apply through LinkedIn for jobs that have been posted.

{ Kat's Tales from the Real World } Although you might think I'm getting a commission from LinkedIn (I'm not), I can't emphasize enough how great a tool it can be for you as a high school or college student. It takes a lot of the leg work out of networking, making connections, researching industries, and looking for future job opportunities. I highly recommend that you spend some time learning the platform and putting it to work for you while you're in college.

25

The End? Or Is It?

There you have it, everything you need to know about getting ahead before you graduate and putting those tuition dollars and years of study to work for you. The only ingredient that I can't add to make this work for you is ACTION. If you do nothing with what you've read, nothing's going to happen.

Stand out from the crowd by doing all of this work AS SOON AS POSSIBLE. Remember that the competition is fierce. Look at all the students JUST in your class. Your year. Your school. Now think of the hundreds of universities and colleges out there with college students just like you. Don't do the same old thing that everyone else is doing. Seize the day, seize your opportunity, and put all of this information to ACTION. If you follow this book step by step, you'll be miles ahead of the others.

Now get to work.

In case you're a little too busy to chart out a path yourself (or if you're like I once was and don't have a clue where to start), I've included a quick year-by-year synopsis of what you should be doing in college in addition to your classes. You can find it in the Resources section or download it at www.mymarchconsulting.com/PutCollegeToWorkTimeline.

I've included a number of worksheets and bonus materials on my website too, because I know you're awesome and super busy.

That's it! Get out there and make something happen for yourself! You deserve it! After all, it's just the rest of your life, right?

Resources

Put College to Work Timeline

Congrats! You made it to college. Now the work begins.

Fall of Freshman Year

- Familiarize yourself with the resources your particular school offers, including any extra opportunities (like study-abroad programs) you would want to take advantage of in the next four years.

- Complete your assessments, talk to your career counselors, and start figuring out which careers and fields you want to explore and WHY.

- Spend a lot of time evaluating your skill set and considering what fields would maximize your skills *and* make you HAPPY. Happiness is important.

- Make sure you know what the bigger picture is (i.e., your goals). Don't get too caught up in the name of your degree or major; instead, focus on how it's going to help you get where you want to go.

- Start volunteering at the alumni office.

- Explore nonprofit opportunities in the surrounding area that interest you.

- Join campus groups, clubs, and organizations that interest you and are related to your possible future career. Notice leadership in these groups and what they do right. Volunteer to help an organization/club/group and get involved in its events.

- Remember you can count all of the experience you get now on your résumé, which will help in a few years when you're applying for jobs that require three to five years of experience. So don't be afraid to build your skills.

Winter of Freshman Year

- Take the opportunity to start job shadowing and conducting informational interviews either during winter quarter or over winter break, when you will likely be close to family who can help you find opportunities.

- Write down what you thought of each experience and what you learned about each field.

- Do some investigative research on the career fields you're considering. Don't be afraid to use Google or ask social media contacts their thoughts on how to get ahead.
- Decide on at least two fields you want to learn more about.
- Research / ask the career center / ask your professors for any leads on internships in those fields.
- Prepare your first résumé and cover letter. Reach out to the career center for help, if needed.

Spring of Freshman Year

- Start applying for summer internships in late winter or early spring. Remember to tailor your résumé and cover letter to how you can help the place where you are applying instead of making yourself the focus of attention.
- Practice for interviews with your roommate, friends, or the career center. Be prepared for the format, typical questions, and be ready to talk about yourself.
- Conduct more interviews or do other research to further narrow down the career fields you're considering. Use the alumni office or your network to start learning more about those fields.
- Research professional organizations that you might join. Go to a conference or a lecture that they offer.
- Work on further building your network by getting yourself out there, even if it's only for a department BBQ at your school or a lecture at a specialty institute.

Summer of Freshman Year

- Internship time! Make yourself valuable and soak up as much information as possible. If you're invited to lunch or an event, make sure you go! Take advantage of these amazing networking opportunities.
- Even if you're not a journal person, try to jot down some notes each day at your internship so you can review at the end what you loved and hated about the job. This will help you make decisions later.

- Follow up at the end of your internship to thank the firm for the opportunity and keep in contact. You never know when you'll need that connection.

Fall of Sophomore Year

- If your internship was everything you thought it would be, continue to investigate that field. Conduct more informational interviews and start researching / following the industry online (news articles, etc.).

- If your internship showed you that you don't want a career in this field, make sure that you can define why. Start investigating other fields that you might find more interesting. If you had two fields starting freshman year, investigate the other one. Don't give up if you didn't enjoy where you worked this summer. It might take a number of tries before you find something that you enjoy. In the meantime, try to keep moving forward while you repeat the research and soul-searching that you did freshman year.

- Review your goals and how much progress you've made toward them. Adjust as needed, especially the short-term goals.

- Look at job boards in the fields you're considering. What skills are they looking for? What are you missing? Chart out the skills you'll need to develop and what steps you will take to get there.

- Meet with your career counselor again to share what you're thinking and ask how to further develop your skills or make any adjustments in your plan. Reaffirm your goals and discuss how your school can help you achieve them.

- Meet with your academic adviser and solidify your classes and academic plan. Make sure you seek out classes that will help you develop the skills you'll need to achieve your career goals.

- Map out the conferences and events you want to attend in the following year, including what you're hoping to learn and who you're hoping to meet at each.

- Continue to volunteer at the alumni office and events throughout the year. You never know who you might meet.

Winter of Sophomore Year

- Approach your department or professors about research positions or special opportunities in your field of interest. Do a little research and start keeping your eye out for summer opportunities.

- Investigate and narrow down a few volunteer organizations you would love to help. Try to figure out where you could be of the most help and reach out to those groups. Start making inroads with projects that will boost the skills you need (particularly the ones you identified after looking at job boards and considering your future goals).

- Continue contributing to on-campus clubs and organizations. Begin narrowing down your involvement to make room for volunteering in outside organizations. Pick groups that you're passionate about and that will help you in the long run, either through networking or skill development.

- Research organizations that you'd want to get involved with and work for over the summer. Start looking for internship opportunities.

- Update your résumé and start new cover letters.

- Make an appointment at the career center and talk with a career counselor about your résumé and summer opportunities.

- Practice for interviews with your roommate, friends, or the career center. Refine your answers to include experiences that you had during your previous summer position and explain how you're prepping to be an asset.

Spring of Sophomore Year

- Attend a job fair to get the lay of the land. Try to connect with a few companies you're interested in working with.

- Further refine your résumé and add in your volunteer experience, on-campus activities, and internships (if you haven't already).

- Apply for internships for the summer

- Don't forget those professional organizations. If you've settled on a field, join one of them as a student member. If not, keep visiting a few until you decide which one to join. Also consider joining Rotary or another professional organization where you can give back to the community, network, and be with people with similar goals and values.

- Consider whether you might want to apply for graduate school. If so, start gathering information and learn about what entrance exams you'll need to take. Start studying for the GRE/MCAT/GMAT/LSAT or whatever you need. Talk to your professors and / or career counselor about the benefits of attending graduate school in your field.

Summer of Sophomore Year

- Internship time (or study abroad)! Again, remember to make yourself valuable and learn all that you can in the time you're there. Also, try to picture yourself doing the sorts of things your managers are doing. Are you intrigued? Hate it? Make sure you get the entire picture before you leave.

- Keep your journal again to keep track of what you liked, didn't like, and what you learned.

- Make sure that you keep in contact with those that you interned with in this job as well as the one from your previous summer.

- Revisit your goals. If you're still not sure what you'll major in, spend the rest of the summer seriously investigating a few different fields. Revisit your assessments and ask others what they think you're good at doing. Consider fields that you already participate in and enjoy .

Fall of Junior Year

- Time to declare your major! You should have enough experience by this point to commit to a major. Remember not to get sucked in by the name of what you're majoring in. That's not as important as which skills you'll gain to get to your ultimate path.

- Revisit job boards and see what skills they're looking for in new hires. How can you build those skills in the next two years? Which leads to...

- If you haven't joined a professional organization yet, do it now. You'll need these contacts senior year.

- Recommit to volunteering at the alumni office. Don't be afraid to share with alumni what you've learned the last two years and where you're hoping to go.

- Meet with your career counselor again; revisit your goals and your path to see how the school might further help you.

- Meet with your academic adviser and solidify your classes and academic plan for the next two years.

- Consider the specialty institutes at your school or in the area and find out what it will take to land a position there, even if you're only volunteering.
- Attend a few more conferences or events where you can learn something outside of school. Attend a lecture or two at school and branch out from there.
- If you're looking at fields like finance, consulting, or business, this is when recruiters start considering candidates, so keep abreast of that information through your department, professors, or the career center.

Winter of Junior Year

- Update your cover letters and résumé.
- Attend job fairs and recruiting events for summer internships (the good ones are increasingly competitive, so you want to get your name in the hat early).
- Volunteer for leadership positions in your campus groups and clubs.
- Consider performing a special project at school or with your volunteer organization where you can test your skills.
- If you haven't already, apply for the research positions that are reserved for juniors and seniors.
- Update your profile on LinkedIn (work experience, skills, résumé) and join groups in your areas of interest. Start connecting with people who can offer advice and / or people you can help. Join LinkedIn groups to start making inroads with other professionals. Following the companies you think you'd like to work for so that you know when that company is in the news or posts information on their page.
- Select your electives wisely and take extra opportunities to gain more experience.
- Practice for interviews with your roommate, friends, or the career center. Refine your answers to include experiences that you had during the previous summer and your years in college.

Spring of Junior Year

- Keep applying for those internships! This is the time to gain the prime internship that might develop into a full-time position. Even if you don't grab your dream internship, you should look to get more experience and further develop your skills in any summer position. This also applies to research you might conduct with professors.

- If you're looking at graduate school, start gathering everything for applications now. Determine who you are going to ask for letters of recommendation; buckle down even more on studying for your graduate standardized testing.

- Attend another job fair and really target the companies you're considering.

- Revisit your goals and refine as needed. Consider what you want to do with your last year in college. What skills are you missing? Chart out how to beef those up. Do you need to try some new projects at the organizations and activities that you're participating in?

- Take a look at your network. By now it should be rather developed. Consider how you can contribute to your network (again, the best way to receive is to give). Are there connections you could make? Ways you could help someone else? Brainstorm and start tending to this network you've been developing.

- Ask the alumni office for a formal introduction to someone in the field you're considering. Take that person to lunch or start a discussion over the phone or by email. Ask for advice and information on how to best set yourself up for senior year in your field.

Summer of Junior Year

- The coveted internship you've been working for! Congrats! This internship should be specifically tailored to what field you want to go into and should offer opportunities for you to network in your field. Hopefully, this internship has the opportunity for full-time work next year or gives you the experience you need to gain full-time work elsewhere. Remember, it's all about the experience.

- Again, keep your journal.

- Really keep in contact with those you've worked for and met at this internship. Make sure you ask if there will be full-time openings next year. If they say no, don't be discouraged. You've been working on developing those three to five years of experience.

- Before you return to school, map out your entire senior year. What's the end goal by graduation? Start there and work backward, taking the rest of this timeline into consideration. What do you need to do in your field to get where you're going? More research? More work experience? More volunteering? Does your network need to be more robust?

- Plan to gain or supplement your skills through your volunteer work and participation in campus organizations. Still need web development experience? Project management? Now's the time to remedy that.
- Update your LinkedIn profile, adding in all of your experience, and change your headline, if need be.
- Practice for interviews with your roommate, friends, or the career center. Refine your answers to include experiences that you had during the summer, your skills, your leadership at the organizations that you're at, etc.

Fall of Senior Year

- Meet with your academic adviser to make sure you will fulfill all graduation requirements by the end of the school year. You don't want any surprises in the spring.
- Notify your network of the type of position you're looking for—unless you already have a full-time gig waiting for you from your last internship.
- Research, research, research. Look at where alumni on LinkedIn work after they graduate and research those organizations. If you haven't already, reach out to the alumni office to get a list or be paired up with someone who works at your dream organization. If you're going into grad school or starting a business, ask to be linked up with alumni who can help you.
- If you're applying to graduate school, gather all of your application materials, take your last standardized test, and get your recommendations in order. Submit your applications.
- Double down on those conferences and events where you might meet someone from the company you want to work for.
- Revisit your overall goals and the goals for this year. Where are you in your plans? Adjust as necessary (and don't procrastinate).

Winter of Senior Year

- Polish your résumé and cover letters. Adjust your cover letters to each place you apply to.
- Start searching for open positions and remind those in your network that you're looking for a position. Be specific about the types of skills you have and your goals.

- Look at job boards on LinkedIn and in the groups you've joined. Connect with others on LinkedIn who might have insights. Apply for jobs that you find on the job board. Don't be afraid to contact recruiters or hiring managers.
- Go to job fairs your school offers and put your best foot forward.
- Apply, apply, apply.
- Talk with your paired professional from the alumni office and get more advice. Don't be afraid to ask if their organization is looking for someone.

Spring of Senior Year

- Continue to hunt for open positions and apply. Develop a list of when they're due, what you have to get done, and make the applications a priority. If you need help, go to the career center and ask them to look over everything before you submit.
- Do the research on the companies so you know how you'd be an asset to them.
- Go to the alumni events that are held for seniors (and those that aren't). Don't forget your department BBQs, job fairs, and the like.
- Finish your capstone project/thesis and make sure you graduate!
- If you're not having any luck, start making small adjustments. Reach out to your network and get advice. Most importantly, keep trying. It's a rough world out there.

Summer after Senior Year

- Congrats! You made it! Remember that your job (whatever it might be) is a chance to learn and advance, and it will be what you make of it. As an entry-level employee, you have a lot to learn. Stay out of office politics and gossip, spend extra time learning from the experts, and don't be afraid to advocate for yourself, just like you did in college. Remember to never get stuck, to take opportunities, and to keep the adventure going.

Consider What You Hate

List at least 10 things that you hate doing that are related to work, school, or activities.

_____

_____

_____

_____

_____

_____

_____

_____

For each of the items you said you hate, write down at least one reason WHY you hate them.

_____

_____

_____

_____

_____

_____

_____

_____

_____

_____

Finally, if your dream job REQUIRED you to perform two of the activities that you hate, which two would you choose?

_____

_____

Examine Your Values

Circle the five values that resonate most with you from the list below. If there's a value that's really important to you that isn't on the list, write that in the blanks provided.

If there are terms in the list that you do NOT value at all, cross them out.

Accomplishment	Control	Fidelity
Accessibility	Contribution	Flexibility
Affluence	Cooperation	Focus
Assertiveness	Courage	Forgiveness
Accuracy	Creativity	Freedom
Acknowledgement	Curiosity	Friendship
Adventure	Determination	Fun
Ambition	Discipline	Generosity
Authenticity	Dependability	Gentleness
Balance	Directness	Growth
Beauty	Discovery	Happiness
Boldness	Diversity	Harmony
Bravery	Ease	Health
Calm	Effortlessness	Helpfulness
Celebrity	Empathy	Honesty
Challenge	Efficiency	Honor
Collaboration	Empowerment	Humor
Community	Enthusiasm	Idealism
Compassion	Excellence	Imagination
Comfort	Expertise	Impact
Comradeship	Faith	Independence
Confidence	Fairness	Intelligence
Connectedness	Fame	Innovation
Contentment	Family	Integrity

Intuition	Productivity	Tolerance
Joy	Punctuality	Tradition
Justice	Recognition	Trust
Kindness	Respect	Understanding
Knowledge	Reliability	Unity
Leadership	Resourcefulness	Vision
Learning	Romance	Vitality
Listening	Security	Wealth
Love	Self-Esteem	Winning
Loyalty	Service	Wisdom
Optimism	Significance	Zest
Originality	Simplicity	Zeal
Organization	Sincerity	
Participation	Speed	_____
Partnership	Spirituality	
Passion	Spontaneity	_____
Patience	Strength	
Peace	Sympathy	_____
Perfection	Tact	
Power	Teamwork	_____

Are your eyes crossed yet? Do you find yourself questioning what you really stand for? Nailing down what you stand for is no easy task, so don't get frustrated with yourself. Once you can identify your top five values, you're golden for the rest of this exercise.

But before we leave this section, I want you to think about the values that you crossed off. What made you cross them off? Why? Being mindful of what you value is important, but so is knowing what you don't value so that you won't accept projects or opportunities that are going to go against what you believe. Store that away in your mind for later.

Now on to the rest of the exercise.

Using your list from above, write your top five values here.

_____

_____

_____

_____

_____

You've identified your top five. Now you're going to define those words and explain what they mean to you. Write a sentence or two, draw a picture, or philosophize on what each word means to you. There has to be some reason you picked these terms; they obviously struck a chord on the inside in some way.

You want an example, you say? Well, why not?

Let's take the word *growth*. I value growth because it means that whatever I'm doing, I should be advancing—learning a new skill, honing an existing one, or opening my mind to new possibilities, points of view, etc. To someone else, *growth* might mean helping a company grow in a healthy and business-sustaining way. To others, *growth* might be defined as opportunities that allow advancement and expose them to new opportunities in one company.

These definitions are your definitions. I can't tell you what your values are because they are your values. Have fun with this process.

Using your list from above, define your top five values.

_____

_____

_____

_____

_____

Exercise 2.3

What Are Your Strengths?

List what you consider to be your strengths. These can include school-related items, like "math" or "writing," but you don't have to stop there. What other qualities might be considered strengths? Maybe you're a "good listener" or "attentive to details." Give this one some thought.

_____

_____

_____

_____

_____

The Opposite List

Sometimes it's easier to think about what you're *not* good at, like we did above with listing things that you hate to do. So take a few minutes to list what you consider to be your weaknesses.

_____

_____

_____

_____

_____

Consider Your Skills

List your skills. Include the ones that involve computers, outdoor activities, people, technology (Twitter, iPhone repair, etc.), education, and whatever else you can think of.

_____

_____

_____

_____

_____

_____

Now describe in a word or two how those skills relate to the strengths you listed in Exercise 2.3. For example, your skill at "designing websites" can be related to your strength of "seeing a project from start to finish."

_____

_____

_____

_____

_____

_____

Now think about how those skills and strengths can relate to particular jobs, and describe those connections in a few words. For example, "meeting deadlines" can be related to your strength of "punctuality" and it can be a real asset for jobs in "journalism, theatre, construction, small start-up companies."

_____

_____

_____

_____

_____

_____

Uncover Your Passions

List the activities you love. They could be hobbies, interests, or anything you do that seems to make life worth living.

_____

_____

_____

_____

_____

_____

Write a sentence or a few words about why you love doing those things. What is it about video games that you love so much? Or being at the beach?

I happen to love sewing, especially historical sewing involving costuming or museum copies. Here's where I'll start to think about why I like this particular part of sewing. Yes, I do love creating something, but it's more than that. I almost feel through my research and in wearing the garment that I'm connected with that historical era. So, under "sewing" on my list, I'll jot down that sewing feeds my need to be creative and make something out of nothing while also feeding my need to feel connected to the past through research and recreation.

Doesn't that sound easy? It is, but it's going to take a lot of thinking, so be patient with yourself. Maybe one of your favorite activities is researching the newest Apple product or software. In that case, you should write that you love learning and embracing new technology. Think outside of the box with this one and keep asking yourself *why*.

Write your reasons for why you love your activities in the spaces below.

_____

_____

_____

_____

_____

_____

Your Long-Term Goals

Consider where you want to be twenty years from now. When you have a general idea in your head, start jotting down ideas. Build a picture of yourself in terms of money, where you're living, what you're doing, and who you're helping. While you're doing this, consider your values and your passions. Do you see ways you can meld your passions into your purpose? Perhaps you paint your own paintings on the weekends to escape the boredom of city and corporate life. Or maybe you're working in an art gallery, selling the work of other artists.

Describe where you are living in 20 years (big city, small town, house, apartment?)

_____

_____

_____

How much money are you making? (comfortable, millionaire, starving)

_____

_____

_____

What do you do with your spare time?

_____

_____

_____

What kind of environment do you work in?

_____

_____

_____

What significant things do you do at work each day?

_____

_____

_____

Who do you help each day?

_____

_____

_____

What are you doing each week that fulfills your passions?

_____

_____

_____

What kind of people do you spend your time with?

_____

_____

_____

What are you known for?

_____

_____

_____

Have you received any awards or recognition?

_____

_____

_____

What part do you play in your group of friends / co-workers / community?

_____

_____

_____

Your Bucket List

List all of the major things you want to accomplish in your lifetime. Try to be as detailed as possible.

_____

_____

_____

_____

_____

_____

Your Short-Term Goals

Beginning with your long-term goals in mind will help you see what short-term goals you need to set. For example, let's say your first milestone goal is to be a CEO at a gaming company. The steps to get to that milestone fall below it.

CEO at a Gaming Company
> Getting into management at a gaming company
> Getting hired at a gaming company
> Meeting people at gaming companies
> Doing well in classes that will build skills for working at a gaming company
> Going to gaming conventions to find out what classes and major I should consider

A good general start will show you how to get where you want to go.

Milestone 1

_____

_____

Steps I need to take to get there

_____

_____

_____

_____

_____

Milestone 2

_____

_____

Steps I need to take to get there

_____

_____

_____

_____

_____

Milestone 3

_____

_____

Steps I need to take to get there

_____

_____

_____

_____

_____

Milestone 4

_____

_____

Steps I need to take to get there

_____

_____

_____

_____

_____

Milestone 5

_____

_____

Steps I need to take to get there

_____

_____

_____

_____

_____

Your Purpose in Life

What's the one thing that you can imagine yourself doing that is going to make you feel good about yourself? Fill your soul? Make things worthwhile? If you get stumped, think of things you've already accomplished in your life. Which ones make you feel like you've lived your purpose in life? What does that look like?

Brainstorm here

Now, try to list two things here, or put them into a sentence: "My purpose is to be able to be happy and share that happiness with others." Or "My purpose is to give back to other kids the same way that my mentor gave time and energy to me." Or "My purpose is to be successful, so I can serve my clients in the best way I'm able."

You can spend a lifetime trying to identify your purpose, so don't get too down on yourself if you find this exercise is the hardest. Most people do. The secret is to be aware that you're searching, because then you will be more likely to eventually come to your own answer.

My Purpose Is

_____

_____

_____

_____

_____

Time Management

Here are a few additional resouces for tips on time management.

I would highly recommend that you check out the *Wait But Why* website, particularly the article: "Why Procrastinators Procrastinate" (http://waitbutwhy.com/2013/10/why-procrastinators-procrastinate.html) by Tim Urban. In addition to being hilarious, this article and his procrastination matrix (http://waitbutwhy.com/2015/03/procrastination-matrix.html) will change the way you think about time management.

David Allen has an excellent book that gives you a system for getting things done. In fact, his book is called just that: *Getting Things Done*. It's available on Amazon and lots of other places, and it's brilliant.

What You Want Others to See

Your Appearance

List five things you want people to think about your professional appearance. Then list two actions you can take to reinforce each item on your list.

_____

_____

_____

_____

_____

_____

_____

_____

_____

_____

_____

_____

_____

_____

_____

Your Personality

List five things you want people to think about your personality. Then list two actions you can take to reinforce each item on your list.

_____

_____

_____

_____

_____

_____

_____

_____

_____

_____

_____

_____

_____

_____

Differentiation

List three things that make you different from other people. These
could be experiences, skills, ideas, etc.

_____

_____

_____

Skills

Choose three items from your list of skills that you created in
Exercise 2.4. These are the skills you want to emphasize, the
ones you want to make sure that your professors, classmates, and
potential employees will know that you have.

_____

_____

_____

Your Personal Brand

What Others Say

Ask your family, friends, acquaintances to tell you what characteristics they associate with you. List those attributes here.

» **Positive Qualities**

_____

_____

_____

_____

_____

_____

» **Negative Qualities**

_____

_____

_____

_____

_____

_____

Your Master List

After considering all the impressions you collected, and looking at those impressions in light of the values you listed in Exercise 2.2, create a master list here of five qualities you want people to recognize in you and five qualities you never want people to see in you. Then list two actions you can take to reinforce each positive item on your list and two items you can take to avoid each negative impression.

» Positive Qualities

_____

_____

_____

_____

_____

» Negative Qualities

_____

_____

_____

_____

_____

Researching a Potential Employer

So you're headed to a job fair next week. Or a networking event where you know there will be people from lots of companies you might like to work for. Maybe you're writing a cover letter for an internship that's been posted online or you've been called for an interview.

In all those situations, the first thing you should do is research. Luckily for you, we live in the age of the Internet, so you have a treasure trove of information at your fingertips. Start with Google; make your way through company websites, and check out social media posts. Learn what a company does, who works for it, and what its values are. The more you know, the more personalized your résumés, cover letters, and conversations can be.

To give you a better idea of how to research a company, let's pretend you're looking at mine. Say your career center just told you that I'm going to be at next month's job fair on your campus. You think what I'm doing sounds interesting and want to know more about me and what I do.

Go to my website, www.mymarchconsulting.com, and start with the "Who We Are" page. Read about my mission, how I'm different, and a little about me. (If you're looking at a large business or corporation, look at the names of the chief officers and board members and then read up on them.)

But back to the simple example. Go to the "Our Services" page and check out what I offer and what I do.

Next you could check out my blog; think about my writing style, what I'm writing about, and see if you have any connections to anything there. Maybe I wrote something about the state of higher education that is similar to your own ideas on the topic or to a paper that you wrote in one of your education classes.

Next, look at the media I have posted—get a feel for what I think is important and how I approach it. Finally, look at my "Resources" page and see what I'm offering my customers.

Jot down a few notes as you're looking at the website.

_____

_____

_____

_____

_____

_____

Your research doesn't end when you've looked at the last page of my website.

Pull up trusty Google and search for my name. Have I been in the news lately? For what? Did my company make any huge announcements? Does my company offer stock? Is it publicly traded? If it is, how has my stock been performing?

Look for social media accounts for me and for my company. LinkedIn can be especially helpful as you try to gather job-related information.

Next, you're going to step away from your computer and reach out through your network. Does anyone know someone who works for me? What have you heard about my company? When you checked out my LinkedIn account, did you see any mutual connections? If so, reach out to them.

Time for some more notes about what you've learned.

_____

_____

_____

_____

_____

_____

You're going to work like an investigative journalist. Yes, it's a lot of work, but truly, not more than a half hour or so with the help of the Internet. If you're really interested in a job opening at my company—and especially if you have an interview for an opening—you should do some more research, so go on to the steps below.

In my biography, look for what college I went to. Make a note of it and look it up if you're not familiar with it already.

Look for any organizations I might be a part of. Research those. You'll notice that I'm in Rotary and on a few boards. Look up those organizations.

Finally, you might type up a list of questions to ask me about my company. That way, even if you get nervous and tongue-tied, you have something to fall back on. Also, when I'm on the spot, I tend to forget a lot of things that I was dying to ask, so having notes certainly helps.

Write some questions based on your research.

_____

_____

_____

_____

_____

_____

Do you know why you're doing all this? So when you're talking to me or writing a letter or email to me, you can mention a fact or two that you've learned from your research. Do you know how many students have actually done that? None. Do you know who would instantly stick in my mind and impress me if they did? That's right.

Now go to my website: www.mymarchconsulting.com/ PutCollegeToWork and grab a worksheet that outlines this procedure exactly.

Résumés and Cover Letters

If you Google "résumé" or "cover letters," you're going to get overwhelmed by the advice out there. I rely on a number of good sources to keep up-to-date on changes in the job-hunting process that only supplement and add value to what I already know and what I've experienced as an employer who hires people myself. Here are my favorite sources where you can get more information when you're ready to draft your résumé and cover letter.

» Forbes Magazine

I would recommend checking out these articles and authors in particular:

Liz Ryan
> "Forget Cover Letters—Write a Pain Letter, Instead!" (http://www.forbes.com/sites/lizryan/2014/10/12/forget-cover-letters-write-a-pain-letter-instead/)
> "What's a Pain Letter And Can it Get Me A Job?" (http://www.forbes.com/sites/lizryan/2015/06/06/whats-a-pain-letter-and-can-it-get-me-a-job/)

» The Muse
(this independent site also gives excellent, up-to-date advice on all aspects of job searching)
> "The Cover Letters That Make Hiring Managers Smile (Then Call You)" (http://www.forbes.com/sites/dailymuse/2014/02/06/the-cover-letters-that-make-hiring-managers-smile-then-call-you/)

» Inc. Magazine

Tom Searcy
> "How to Write a Killer Resume" (http://www.inc.com/tom-searcy/how-to-write-a-winning-resume.html)

Peter Economy
> "20 Things You Should Leave Off Your Resume and LinkedIn
  Profile" (http://www.inc.com/peter-economy/20-things-you-
  should-leave-off-your-resume-and-your-linkedin-account.html)

Jason Fried
> "The One Trait That Guarantees a Good Hire"
  (http://www.inc.com/magazine/201405/jason-fried/
  hiring-based-on-effort-not-resumes.html)

As you'll notice, most of these articles say your results are tied to
the effort that you put not only into your previous jobs, but also
into applying for new ones. Jason Fried mentions how the worth
of a typical cover letter and résumé are dwarfed by a custom-made
website if you're looking to get a job as a web designer. Don't be
afraid to step out of the box and get creative. This entire process is
about THEM, not about you. There are thousands of other people
out there looking for jobs, just like you are.

Stand out from the crowd.

Index

About the Author

 **Kat Clowes figured out college** the hard way. A former "college student without a clue," Clowes spent ten years after graduation learning how she could have used her college resources and tuition dollars to build her career. After earning an M.B.A. and building a successful executive career, Clowes is now an independent educational consultant helping students maximize their money and time in college to gain meaningful employment after graduation. She has had unparalleled success with her students and loves teaching them how to market themselves and become the entrepreneurs in their own lives. Clowes also consults and mentors young professionals as they start up their own businesses.

Clowes has a BA in Communications from Santa Clara University, an M.B.A. from Mount Saint Mary's College with an emphasis in entrepreneurship, and a post-graduate certificate in independent educational consulting from UC Irvine. She lives in California with her husband and daughter.

"It's like the secret instruction manual to adulthood!"

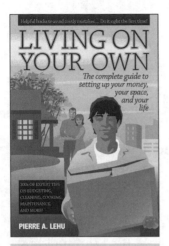

$18.95 ($19.95 Canada)

Did you know:

- **There are more germs in your kitchen sink than your toilet bowl?**

- **Dollar-store items like generic baking soda and bleach can save you hundreds in cleaning supplies?**

- **Reading on your front porch can prevent break-ins?**

"They" don't tell you these things, but *Living On Your Own* will, plus hundreds of additional tips that will save you time, trouble and money.

Living On Your Own

The complete guide to setting up your money, your space and your life

by Pierre A. Lehu

The perfect book for grads, young adults, and anyone who wants to take charge of their home and life, **Living On Your Own** is a completely practical guide to beginning (or perfecting) your life as an independent adult. Whether you're moving into a college dorm or into your first apartment — or if you want to make your life run more smoothly at any age — **Living On Your Own** will give you hundreds of useful tips on finances, household management, maintenance and life skills that will save any reader time, trouble and money.

This readable and comprehensive reference gives answers to all of the decisions, dilemmas, and questions that invariably arise when setting out on your own:

Looking for a place to live? Worried about your finances? Tired of sleeping on a mattress on the floor? Daunted by living on ramen? **Living On Your Own** will show you how to cope with landlords and roommates, master your budget and credit score, furnish an apartment fabulously and cheaply, and learn how to cook simple, healthful meals without spending a lot of money. Additional chapters cover home repairs, cleaning, health care, and more.

Covering everything from budgeting apps, cheap and healthy food, finding an eco-friendly detergent, to how not to catch an STD, **Living On Your Own** is an invaluable road map to early adulthood.

Available from bookstores, online bookstores, and QuillDriverBooks.com, or by calling toll-free 1-800-345-4447.